PANORAMA

An Introduction to Classical Mythology

CARRIE ZUBERBUHLER KENNEDY, M. ED.

Clew Publishing, LLC

Pittsburgh. Pennsylvania

2010

Published in Pittsburgh, Pennsylvania by Clew Publishing, LLC
2037 Lake Marshall Drive, Gibsonia, Pennsylvania, 15044
www.clewpublishing.com

Copyright © 2010 by Clew Publishing, LLC
Portions of this book were copyrighted in 1997 and 2005 by Carrie Z. Kennedy

Chapter notes and permissions information appear on pages 203-204.

Cover photo is of the ruins of a Greek temple in Selinunte on the island of Sicily.

ISBN-13: 978-0-9823338-0-8
Library of Congress Control Number: 2009907389
Library of Congress Cataloging-in-Publication data has been applied for.

First edition

Printed in the United States
Set in Adobe Jenson Pro
Design by Kevin E. Kennedy

This book is printed on paper approved by the Sustainable Forestry Initiative
(SFI) and the Programme for the Endorsement of Forest Certification (PEFCI).
The paper was produced in a mill that utilizes environmentally friendly
Elemental Chlorine Free (ECF) papermaking for enhanced permanence.

For Kevin and our girls,
Grace and Megan

TABLE *of* CONTENTS

· The Greek postage stamp, circa 1959, shows Athena, the goddess of war and wisdom, holding the reins of the winged horse, Pegasus.

◆ A 1942 United States
dime, featuring the head
of the Roman goddess
Liberty. So many people
thought the image was of
the Roman god Mercury
that the coins came to be
called "Mercury dimes."

PREFACE

The Greek hero Theseus stands next to the door of the Labyrinth, clutching his sword. He knows somewhere inside, prowling through the dark tunnels, is the Minotaur, a beastly man with the head of a bull. Theseus' father, King Aegeus of Athens, had been forced to choose fourteen youths every nine years as human sacrifices for the Minotaur, and Theseus is now determined to end this gruesome practice.

While Theseus is worried about slaying the beast, he is actually more concerned that he will become lost in the Labyrinth and not be able to find the door again. Just then, Ariadne, a princess who has fallen in love with Theseus, comes to his side. She offers him a ball of string and tells him to unwind it as he walks into the Labyrinth and then follow it back out. Ariadne's simple gift gives Theseus the assurance he needs, and he is able to slay the Minotaur and find the door to freedom.

This hero myth became so well known that Ariadne's ball of yarn—called a "clew" in Old English—became synonymous with anything that helped to solve a problem. Over time, the spelling of the word changed to "clue."

When journalist Bill Moyers interviewed the comparative mythologist Joseph Campbell for the 1988 PBS series *The Power of Myth*, they discussed Theseus' heroic journey:

Moyers: Sometimes we look for great wealth to save us, a great power to save us, for great ideas to save us, when all we need is that piece of string.

Campbell: That's not always easy to find. But it's nice to have someone who can give you a clue. That's the teacher's job, to help you find your Ariadne thread.

I wrote this book with the singular purpose of creating an Ariadne thread. Whether you are a student or a general reader, you are standing at the door of a complicated labyrinth: the rich, fascinating, but often overwhelming subject of mythology. And it is easy to get lost inside, with the intricate mix of history and story, the various versions of myths, the serious lessons of epics, and the long names that twist your tongue. I wrote *Panorama* as a guide that will allow you to enjoy the journey through the maze without losing your way. Here are a few features of the book:

+ Before presenting its collection of classical myths, *Panorama* sets the stories in a meaningful context with chapters on world mythology and the histories of ancient Greece, ancient Rome, and the European Renaissance. Another full chapter details the names and roles of all the important gods and goddesses, so the "cast of characters" will be familiar when you begin reading the myths.

+ Myths do not fall into a neat chronology, and grouping them by the main deity they feature does not help all that much. So the 25 myths in *Panorama* are divided into thematic units, making them easier to approach, easier to discuss, and easier to remember. The more challenging hero myths and epics follow this core collection.

Each myth in *Panorama* is accompanied by a picture of a common object—a feather, a match, or a butterfly like the ones on this page—that acts as a symbol for the story. When I teach mythology, I see how well an image can trigger a student's memory, and I want to make it as easy as possible for all readers to connect to a myth and remember its details and its lessons.

Panorama's sidebars contain helpful cross-curricular information, and the Teacher's Guide includes numerous suggestions that will allow for differentiated instruction. I learned early on in my teaching career about Howard Gardner's insightful theory of multiple intelligence, and I have seen how some students think through a subject logically, some need to connect to it personally, and others need hands-on experience for the information to make sense. *Panorama* and its accompanying material allow for all of this.

A panorama, by definition, is "a broad view of a subject" and comes from the Greek words *pan* (all) and *horan* (to see). I chose this for a title because my book gives readers a clear overview of mythology and all its delightful interconnections. *Panorama*, then, gives you all the clues you need to travel through the amazing labyrinth of mythology and still find the door.

Please note:

+ Any word highlighted in the main text or sidebars is vocabulary that students need to define in study material available for *Panorama*.

+ While the spelling of mythological names varies greatly, I use the Latinized versions of Greek names. The two exceptions are in the chapter on Virgil's *Aeneid*, and the quotes from Ovid's *Metamorphoses*, which both use Roman names for the characters.

+ While I toned down some myths, *Panorama* still contains violence, infidelity, and other mature issues. I strongly suggest that teachers and parents read ahead to select the most appropriate material.

+ In keeping with the style of modern texts, I delineate time using BCE (Before Common Era) and CE (Common Era).

"The door,
So difficult, which none of those before
Could find again, by Ariadne's aid
Was found, the thread that traced the way rewound."

OVID, *METAMORPHOSES*, BOOK VIII, LINES 175-178

INTRODUCTION

Three-headed dogs. Flying horses. A man so strong he can hold up the sky. Blazing chariots. Golden rivers. A woman with a head full of writhing snakes. This is the stuff of mythology.

Myths are the fantastic stories told around the world, from the icy plains of Norway to the steamy jungles of Africa to the dry deserts of Egypt. Unlike most modern books, ancient myths did not have one author. Instead, they were created by communities and then retold through generations, until they were written down as stories, songs, plays, and epic poems.

If not understood in context, these tales from the past may seem ridiculous. Most are exaggerated stories, defying logic and time, starring characters who perform impossible tasks. But myths are much more than just stories: They reveal the experiences of capable people working to make sense of the world's mysterious and often frightening ways. While modern science answers many of the questions ancient people had about the natural world—why there are seasons, for example, or how rainbows are formed—it is extraordinary to learn how these people worked to structure information and pass it on through generations. Donna Rosenberg, author of *World Mythology*, writes, "The analysis of myths proves that human beings, no matter how primitive their technology, are not mentally inferior. Their myths demonstrate that they possess the intellectual capacity to understand the world in which they live."

So how do these stories relate to the modern world? First, mythology provides a window into history. Because myths originated so long ago, their details often reveal the cultural features of civilizations which may no longer exist.

Second, a great deal of English vocabulary is based on the language of myth, especially the classic myths of Greece and Rome. A flake of cereal, for instance, harkens back to Ceres, the Roman goddess of grain. And an Achilles' heel is a person's weakness, because the only vulnerable spot on the Greek hero Achilles was the back of his foot.

Third, names in science—the planets, days, and months, for example, as well as many flowers, chemical elements, and constellations—are rooted in the vocabulary of mythology, so understanding myths enriches the understanding of the world.

Fourth, authors, artists, and playwrights frequently refer to characters from mythology, and thus much of the meaning of literature, art, and drama is lost without the core knowledge of myths. And that statue on the top of New York City's Grand Central Station? It is the Roman god Hermes, the protector of travelers. Mythological references are everywhere.

Finally, and perhaps most importantly, mythology offers timeless lessons on what it means to be human. The focus of many of the world's greatest myths is on universal emotions such as jealousy and love, grief and hope, fear and triumph, and so the characters in mythology are actually teachers. The choices these characters make, the challenges they face, and the way they handle adversity are lessons to apply to our own choices, challenges, and adversities. Each culture's mythology has its heroes and its villains, and we can gain insight into ourselves by recognizing the strengths and weaknesses of such characters.

Studying mythology provides connections to history, literature, art, drama, language, and science. And mythology allows for a better understanding of human beings and of being human. So grab a golden robe and strap on some wings—mythology awaits.

"These myths were born of hopes, and fears and tears, and smiles; and they were touched and colored by all there is of joy and grief between the rosy dawn of birth and death's sad night; they clothed even the stars with passion, and gave to gods the faults and frailties of the sons of men. In them the winds and waves were music, and all the lakes and streams, springs, mountains, woods, and perfumed dells, were haunted by a thousand fairy forms."

ROBERT G. INGERSOLL (1833-1899)

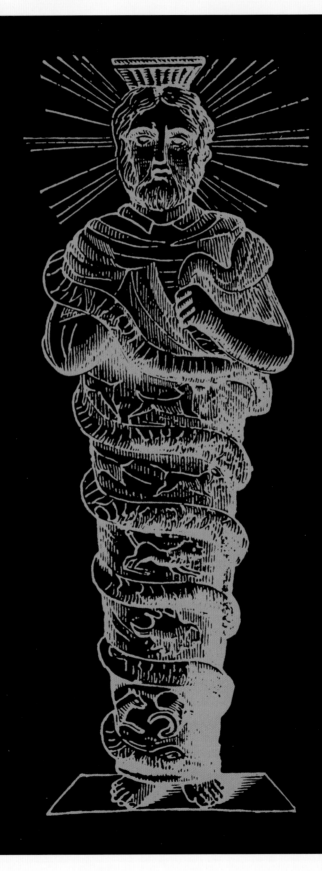

The World of Mythology

The word myth is often used to mean a lie or misconception, so mythological stories might be quickly dismissed as useless untruths. But although myths may be historically inaccurate and often feature unreal creatures, these stories should not be considered lies. In fact, underneath the exaggerations are timeless, profound truths about human beings. In addition, myths from around the world—told in societies that were geographically isolated from one another—are remarkably similar. Their stories feature different characters, but their underlying messages reveal how people throughout history have shared the same needs, the same fears, and the same fascinations.

Joseph Campbell, a scholar of comparative mythology, writes, "Whether I'm reading Polynesian or Iroquois or Egyptian myths, the images are the same, and they are talking about the same problems. ...It's as though the same play were taken from one place to another, and at each place the local players put on local costumes and enact the same old play."

At the root of it all, humans have always tried to understand the world around them. Using mythology as inspiration, they created wondrous artwork and exciting drama. By asking "how" and "why," they set the very foundation for philosophy and science. And by passing their stories along through generations, they built upon the system of human language and documented important factual and cultural history.

Indeed, the words story and history share the same Greek root: *historia*, which means "a learning by inquiry, a narrative." Traditionally, stories are thought to come from the imagination, while history is thought to consist of facts. But history is actually always developing as new information is uncovered and different perspectives are taken. Classicist David Sansone writes, "In fact stories and histories are written for very much the same purpose, namely in order to make sense of, or impose structure and coherence on, events."

+ A myth—a story of unknown origin, usually expressing a religious belief—comes from the Greek *muthos* (speech). The suffix *-logy* means "the science of," so mythology is the study of myths.

+ The etching on these pages shows Seriphis, a god with attributes from both Greek and Egyptian myths. Ptolemy I celebrated Seriphis, hoping to foster a common religious base between the Greeks and Egyptians after the death of Alexander the Great.

Story Genres

How do myths differ from other genres in literature? Myths, fairy tales, legends, tall tales, and fables are related—sort of like cousins—but each has a unique focus.

Myths are rooted in spiritual beliefs and involve gods and goddesses.

Fairy tales are make-believe stories with moral lessons involving fairies, magic, giants, witches, or dragons, and they often feature queens, kings, princes, and princesses. Fairy tales include "Sleeping Beauty," "Cinderella," "Rapunzel," and "Hansel and Gretel."

Legends are told as if they were based in history—such as "an old Irish legend says…" or Washington Irving's "The Legend of Sleepy Hollow"—but it is difficult to verify their accuracy. The main characters in legends are typically heroic figures who have overcome trouble or saved others from a tragedy.

Tall tales feature a person whose real-life story has been exaggerated, such as Johnny Appleseed, Paul Bunyan, or Pecos Bill. These were selfless characters who performed an admirable task, and the exaggerations make the stories more entertaining.

Fables include short fictional pieces told to teach a moral lesson. One of the most popular series of fables is credited to Aesop, an ancient Greek writer. His fables feature talking animals and always have some lesson—called a "moral"—to teach.

Although they are different, all five of these genres have become timeless ways to express common emotions and teach important lessons. Terri Windling, an editor of *Snow White, Blood Red*, writes about the value of fairy tales:

> The fairy tale journey may look like an outward trek across plains and mountains, through castles and forests, but the actual movement is inward, into the lands of the soul. The dark path of the fairy tale forest lies in the shadows of our imagination, the depths of our unconscious. To travel to the wood, to face its dangers, is to emerge transformed by this experience. Particularly for children…this ability to travel inward, to face fear and transform it, is a skill they will use all their lives.

Telling the Tales

Printed text is so common in modern cultures that it is difficult to imagine life without it. Books, magazines, newspapers, and billboards are everywhere, and modern technology—electronic mail, cell phones, fax machines—can send written information around the world in seconds. But for thousands of years, before computers and wireless communication and the printing press, humans relied on other ways to share their stories and ideas. The three most prominent methods were the oral tradition, art forms, and early written language.

Speech was the primary way to communicate for thousands of years, and the oral tradition kept information and stories alive from one generation to the next.

+ The German Grimm brothers, who collected and recorded European fairy tales in the early 1800s, wrote about an ugly frog who became a handsome prince. Such transformations are common in many story genres and act as metaphors for how people can change through their own actions or with the help of others.

+ The morals of Aesop's ancient fables— "Misfortune tests the sincerity of friends" or "Necessity is the mother of invention"—still hold true today.

+ **Oral** comes from the Latin *oris* (mouth). Both Greeks and Romans believed in **oracles**—priests or priestesses who spoke of the future—and an oral surgeon fixes a problem with someone's mouth.

Sometimes the oral tradition was as simple as a mother telling stories to her child, while other times groups would gather formally. In Greece, men called rhapsodes—literally "stitchers of songs"—retold myths in front of huge audiences, thus beginning the art of drama.

In addition to oral language, ancient civilizations used art to document stories and show important symbols. The Greeks, for example, decorated their vases with mythological scenes, and people in the Roman Empire often literally set myths in stone: Mosaics—scenes composed of small stone tiles—covered the floors of their villas. And long before villas, more primitive humans had used minerals and dyes to create images of prized animals on cave walls. The Lascaux Caves in France, for instance, are covered with herds of animals, and a life-sized bison adorns the ceiling in the Altamira Caves of Spain. And the oldest known piece of sculpture—a small stone figure of a woman—dates back to 22,000 BCE. Other sculpted images, made from antlers, ivory, or bone, have been found throughout the world and were likely sacred symbols.

Although early man may have used crude markings to communicate, the first known written language was created by the Sumerians in about 3000 BCE. Their cuneiform system consisted of wedge-shaped strokes pressed into wet clay tablets and was used primarily to keep records. At approximately the same time, Egyptians were using a system of about 700 visual symbols to represent words, syllables, and sounds. These elaborate hieroglyphics, or "sacred carvings," were only used and understood by elite members of Egyptian society. The Chinese written language began as small pictures and expanded over the centuries to include more than 40,000 symbols. The modern English alphabet can be traced back to the Phoenicians, who began using a letter system in about 1000 BCE. The Greeks added vowel sounds, which allowed writing to more closely imitate spoken sounds, and the Romans later adopted this alphabet for writing Latin.

Even with these developing languages, written documents could not be easily produced, and the vast majority of people were illiterate. In 1450 CE, however, with the invention of the printing press, texts could be produced en masse, and more people learned to read. Although other cultures had attempted various printing processes, it was a German named Johannes Gutenberg who perfected the first successful machine. The relatively simple alphabet shared by European languages eased Gutenberg's task, and printing quickly became affordable. Within 150 years, thousands of classical texts were available in a number of languages, and myths from many cultures were documented for the first time.

When these myths were finally recorded—after being told, retold, and acted out by countless people over thousands of years—it was not at all surprising that versions differed. Some bits were forgotten, an event was exaggerated, and places and names had changed along the way. Therefore, while a myth's basic message remains the same, versions will feature different details. This may seem odd to modern readers, who are more accustomed to stories with a single author, but it is precisely these differences that make mythology so fascinating.

- When people such as slaves were purposely not allowed to learn to read or write, the oral tradition became critical. Stories and songs were proudly handed down from one generation to the next.

- No one had been able to decipher hieroglyphics until a stone tablet was found near Rosetta, Egypt, in 1799 CE. The **Rosetta Stone** included the exact same passage written in hieroglyphics, in demotic (a simplified Egyptian language), and in Greek.

- The word alphabet comes from the first two letters of the Greek alphabet: *alpha* and *beta*. These, in turn, came from the Phoenician letters *aleph* and *beth*.

MAJOR WORLD MYTHOLOGIES

1. Inuit
2. Native American
3. Haitian
4. Aztec and Mayan
5. Amazonian
6. Incan

7. Celtic
8. Norse
9. Slavic
10. Roman
11. Greek

12. Egyptian
13. Mesopotamian
14. African
15. Indian
16. Siberian
17. Chinese

18. Korean
19. Japanese
20. Indonesian
21. Australian
22. Oceanic

Common Connections in World Myths

Swiss psychoanalyst Carl Gustav Jung suggested that myths—along with art, religion, and dreams—were actually part of a "collective unconscious," an experience all human beings share. Twentieth century French anthropologist Claude Lévi-Strauss set forth a similar idea when he wrote in *The Raw and the Cooked*, "I therefore claim to show, not how men think in myths, but how myths operate in men's minds without their being aware of the fact." Indeed, while countless myths have been told throughout the world, comparisons reveal they are surprisingly similar: They are told for the same purposes, and they share common themes.

First, as to purpose, myths were really a form of education relayed in an entertaining way. Some myths were shared for the sake of remembering a historic event, and most taught a moral lesson. And some of the most interesting myths were etiological, from the Greek word that means "cause." Throughout the ancient world, humans were trying to understand the mysteries of natural occurrences and explain how places or objects came into being.

Scientific advances have made these etiological myths seem somewhat childish. Modern people have reliable facts about the position of the planets, for instance, and know a great deal about weather patterns. Ancient people, however, lacked the technology to allow for such understanding; they simply did not know what they could not yet know. Yet they thought ingeniously and poetically in terms of the dawn embracing the night, and they saw images of their heroes in the starry night sky. So to learn from myths, readers need to see beyond rational thought.

In *Rethinking Adolescence*, author Jay D'Ambrosio writes that myths maintain their relevance "because they speak to us about the things that are true in life, the things that really matter, and the things that all people, regardless of time or culture, experience. The great stories that have moved us in a multitude of ways do so because they speak to us at the level of the heart."

Second, in terms of themes, most world myths fall into one or more of the following six broad categories: (1) creation, (2) nature and animals, (3) gods and goddesses, (4) heroes, (5) human relationships, and (6) death and the afterlife.

(1) Creation

Stories with a creation theme attempted to explain the big questions about how the world began and where humans came from. While each culture explored these issues from a unique perspective, a comparison of stories shows a predictable basic pattern. At first there is some void or chaos, and then a creator god brings order by dividing the world into elements such as ground, sea, and sky. Finally animals, plants, and people are formed.

The major factor that made the creation myths so different was geography. People surrounded by snow and ice, such as the Inuit people of North America, had origin myths with frozen ground and ice gods. In Egypt, however, the most powerful deity was Ra, a sun god. And in island cultures like Polynesia, which is surrounded by the Pacific Ocean, creation myths begin with a world covered in water.

✦ Egyptian carvings often show humans holding orbs that represent the sun.

Despite geographical differences, many cultures came to understand the world in terms of opposites such as sky and ground, hot and cold, dark and light, male and female, and youth and age. In the Taoist religion and in Confucianism, forces called yin and yang represent these opposites, and are believed to have existed inside a large egg. When the egg could no longer contain the conflicting powers, it cracked and the world began.

Following the myths that detail the formation of the world came those that described the origins of animals and humans. Aboriginals said humans were formed from nature, such as animals and plants. Ulgan, a Siberian god, was said to have formed mankind using rocks for bones and mud for flesh. Many cultures thought humans were made in the images of the gods and goddesses themselves.

(2) Nature and Animals

In modern societies, consumers can buy meat, milk, clothing, and other necessities without having to actually produce them. Such convenience is often taken for granted, and it is easy to forget that people in earlier civilizations spent enormous amounts of time and effort every single day to meet their basic survival needs. Nomads traveled from place to place, following animal herds and good weather. Even when people settled in one location, growing, cooking, and storing food, making clothing, and building shelter were huge responsibilities.

For these reasons, myths that attempted to explain nature—the weather, plants, animals, geographical features, the planets—were some of the most powerful and

+ The **yin yang symbol** contains both yin (black), which represents femininity, the soul, coldness, and night; and yang (white), which stands for masculinity, the spirit, warmth, and day. The two are held together in a unifying circle and each contains a small piece of its opposite, revealing how the forces are inseparable.

+ Korean myth features a Master of Rain, Master of Cloud, Earl of River, and Earl of Wind. These natural spirits are similar to those found in mythology from the Zhou dynasty in China.

+ Many ancient myths feature unicorns. While modern likenesses have horse bodies, traditional unicorns also have goat-like beards, lion tails, and cloven hooves. Unicorns were considered brave, selfless, and solitary and were extremely difficult to capture. To this day, they are associated with creativity.

meaningful stories. Early cultures that relied heavily on crops, for example, had to understand the change of seasons. Native Americans who lived in the plains region were utterly dependent on the buffalo for survival, so these animals feature prominently in their myths. Ancient people attempted to explain the passing of day into night and told stories about the stars. Some believed all of nature was animated and alive, including the mountains, rivers, and even the winds.

In addition to the desire to understand nature for survival, every culture—going back to the primitive people who created cave paintings—had a fascination with the mysterious and often dangerous animal kingdom. In Egypt, cats were considered sacred and were treated with the utmost respect. The bull, perhaps the most common animal in myths, was revered for its strength but feared for its vicious temper. In Aboriginal societies, the kangaroo features prominently in myths. And birds, from eagles to ravens to owls, were often considered sacred because they could fly and therefore represented a link to the heavens.

Many world mythologies also featured animals that were not real. Persian and Greek myths described the griffin, a creature with the head and keen eyes of an eagle and the strong body of a lion. The horselike unicorn had a single horn on its forehead and was considered magical by the Greeks, Romans, and Chinese. The colorful bird-like phoenix was thought to bring good luck in China, and both the Greeks and the Egyptians believed only one phoenix existed; each time it died, it was consumed by fire and reborn, rising up out of its own ashes.

Finally, many mythologies have characters that are part human and part animal. In India, the wise god Ganesha is sometimes pictured with the body of a human and the head of an elephant. Many gods, such as the Greek Zeus, took on animal forms to disguise themselves or to gain additional powers. And Romulus and Remus, the human twins associated with the founding of Rome, were reared as infants by a wolf. This idea of being raised in the wild is a common mythological theme and even extends to the modern story of Tarzan.

(3) Gods and Goddesses

While some mythologies had only one god, many were based on a group of gods, known as a pantheon. Each god and goddess in a pantheon represented a domain of life, and these domains were remarkably similar across the world's mythologies. It was common, for instance, to have a Mother Earth figure to symbolize life and to have another figure, often male, to symbolize death. Many gods and goddesses were associated with natural elements such as fire, water, the sky, the sun, and the moon. Likewise, particular gods and goddesses were associated with elements of human life such as love, marriage, revenge, wisdom, and war.

Although deities in a pantheon had specific roles, their personalities were often very complex, which made them even more fascinating to humans. In India, the goddess Devi has multiple functions, for she holds life in one hand and death in the other. Therefore, she can be loving and kind, or terrifying and merciless. Aphrodite, the Greek goddess of love, was often depicted walking among flowers

* Legends, fairy tales, and fables also have creatures with both human and animal traits. Fauns, mermaids, and fairies usually cause no harm, while goblins, werewolves, and vampires are dangerous.

* Egyptians would mummify cats and bury them with mummified mice so the cats could eat in the afterlife.

* The Indian god Ganesha rides on a rat, an animal that gets little respect in Western cultures but is considered intelligent and resourceful in India.

* **Monotheism** is a belief in one god, while **polytheism** is a belief in many gods. The root is the Greek *theos* (a god) plus the prefix *monos-* (one) or *poly-* (many). And an atheist does not believe in any god, because the prefix *a-* means "not."

* Baba Yaga was a powerful witch from Slavic myths. While many deities lived in splendor, she lived in a wooden hut that walked around on the feet of live hens.

and surrounded by doves, yet in many myths she represented the darker elements of love such as grief and jealousy. And it was not at all uncommon for gods and goddesses to change shape completely, disguising themselves as mortals or taking on the form and characteristics of an animal.

While deities in some religions are considered compassionate and ideal, others are more like humans and display jealousy and arrogance. A few deities are actually referred to as trickster gods. Conflicts among the deities in polytheistic religions are common, with sons overthrowing their fathers or siblings fighting for independence and dominance.

In order to keep these often temperamental gods and goddesses happy, many cultures made sacrifices. Some were simple prayers of thanks to acknowledge a good harvest or a healthy child. Others involved offering up meat to express gratitude to a deity after a successful hunt. The rituals were usually very elaborate, and some even involved human sacrifices.

While many mythological deities needed to be appeased, others required no sacrifices. In fact, most mythologies feature at least one figure who selflessly protected mankind. A Polynesian myth describes how Maui, the god of a thousand tricks, brought the beautiful islands of the South Seas up from the bottom of the oceans

> "Myths tell us how others have made the passage, and how I can make the passage... and also what are the beauties of the way."

JOSEPH CAMPBELL, *THE POWER OF MYTH*

◆ In some Polynesian cultures, tikis are carvings depicting humans and are used to mark sacred sites.

so people could live on them. He then used his wife's long hair to lasso the sun and slow it down, thus providing more daylight for the world. The Titan Prometheus was also said to be a champion for humans, going against the powerful Greek god Zeus to steal fire and teaching mankind how to feed and protect themselves.

(4) Heroes

Mythological heroes were considered larger than life because they set themselves apart from mere mortals. With fascinating strength, great wisdom, or powerful weapons, such heroes bridged the gap between gods and mankind.

Many mythological heroes were born semi-divine, which means one parent was mortal and the other immortal. Even though they possessed superhuman strengths, however, these characters usually had to prove themselves in some way before earning hero status. Many were made to pass tests or venture on long journeys to prove their devotion and endurance. The Greek semi-divine Heracles, for example, had to complete twelve difficult tasks before he was considered a hero and granted immortality, while the Babylonian hero Gilgamesh—whose story is considered the world's first work of literature—embarked on a journey to seek the truth about life and death.

Humans born without divine parentage could still become heroes. The mythological version of Yu the Great, the first monarch of China's Xia Dynasty, had saved his land from flood waters by becoming a dragon who used his tail to dig ditches, and then a bear who clawed paths through the mountains. In Norse mythology, warriors who gave their lives in battle were rewarded with eternity in Valhalla, the magnificent realm of the god Odin.

◆ In *The Hero with a Thousand Faces*, Joseph Campbell describes a universal formula for the mythological hero: "A hero ventures forth from the world of common day into a region of supernatural wonder; fabulous forces are there encountered and a decisive victory is won; the hero comes back from this mysterious adventure with the power to bestow boons on his fellow men."

While some heroes were best known for slaying monsters with brute strength, others proved their worth by using intelligence, strategy, and wit to trick their foes. Either way, they became role models, and their exciting stories were passed down through the generations. While it is difficult to find a hero without any faults, heroism in mythology was not about perfection. Instead, heroes bravely faced their fears and paid the consequences for their flaws.

(5) Human Relationships

While many myths focused on magical monsters, powerful gods, and larger-than-life heroes, others were simply about being human. These stories—exploring the complex relationships that existed between husband and wife, father and son, brother and brother, mother and daughter, or royalty and subject—were told to demonstrate the rules of behavior and to stress the importance of humility, trust, compassion, and love.

Some myths depicted humans behaving badly, and when someone showed arrogance or acted impulsively, the gods meted out divine punishment. The Greek god Apollo cursed King Midas with the ears of a donkey, for example, when Midas chose a lesser god rather than Apollo in a music contest. In a myth from China, two quarrelling brothers were turned into stars that never crossed one another's path.

When humans behaved admirably, myths commemorated their achievements and celebrated their rewards. The Anglo-Saxon myth of Beowulf tells of a mortal man who risked his life to slay the beastly Grendel and its equally beastly mother. For his bravery, Beowulf became a revered king. Inuit mythology tells about hunters who respected nature and were rewarded with visions of animals in their dreams.

The telling of myths was really teaching by example, and this is also true of other genres of literature such as legends, fairy tales, folk tales, and fables. Although these genres do not have the same spiritual basis as myths, they too were passed down through generations to teach and entertain. The famous fables of the Greek writer Aesop, who lived during the late 600s BCE, were simple stories with clear morals about how humans should and should not behave. Snow White, Cinderella, and Sleeping Beauty were fairy tale characters challenged by sinister women who wanted to get rid of them. In more modern times, classic novels—as well as quality movies, plays, and television programs—feature characters in dynamic relationships, which teach important life lessons to those who see or read them.

(6) Death and the Afterlife

Because no one has factual evidence of what happens after death, humans have always had both a fascination and a fear of this great unknown. In an attempt to extract some meaning from death, many mythologies describe burying the dead or returning their ashes to the ground. Because plants grew from this dirt, and many cultures believed humans were first born from Mother Earth, such rituals completed the notion of "a circle of life."

This relatively peaceful, natural view of death differs from other myths and legends that feature gruesome or eerie lords of the dead. Papa Ghede of Haitian myths wears a top hat and represents power and greed; the somber Hades of Greek mythology spends eternity in the dreary Underworld; and the skeletal Grim Reaper, a common symbol of death, carries both a scythe, which represents the cutting of the harvest, and an hourglass, a reminder of the passage of time.

While world mythologies hold different views about an afterlife, many share the concept of a judgment day at the end of the world. In Iran, stories describe how all

◆ *The Hare and the Tortoise* is one of Aesop's best-known fables. In it, an arrogant rabbit loses a race to a slow turtle because the rabbit, assuming he will win, decides to take a nap along the path. He wakes up in time to see the turtle cross the finish line. The moral? "Slow and steady wins the race."

◆ The Ibo tribe of West Africa has a myth explaining how death and burial came by accident: The kind god Chuku wanted humans to lay dead people on the ground so he could bring them back to life. His messenger got confused, however, and told humans to bury the dead.

the metal in the world will melt into a huge molten stream. Those who have lived a good life will pass through the stream unharmed, while those who have sinned will suffer as their imperfections are burned away. Norse myths predict a chaotic end to the world with two survivors who will then begin a new age.

This notion of new life is seen, too, in the concept of reincarnation. Some people believe death is not permanent and that spirits come back in different forms. Good spirits return as higher beings, while imperfect spirits take on lesser forms. The Egyptians performed extraordinary burial rituals, carefully mummifying the dead body and burying it along with food, treasures, and protective symbols, to ensure its passage into the next world. And Celtic legend says the famed King Arthur, who pulled the magic sword Excalibur from a stone, still lives on the Isle of Avalon and will return to rule Britain one day. The inscription on his tomb in Glastonbury reads, in Latin, "Here lies Arthur, the once and future king."

✦ Evergreen trees in mythology represent everlasting life because they do not shed their foliage. The pinecone is often considered a symbol of immortality.

"And many men say that there is written upon his tomb this verse: *Hic iacet Arthurus, rex quondam, rexque futurus.*"

SIR THOMAS MALORY,
LE MORT D'ARTHUR,
BOOK XXXI, CHAPTER 7

The History *behind* Classical Mythology

Before learning about the myths from ancient Greece and Rome, it is helpful to put them in historical context. The Greek civilization reached its peak in 500 BCE, at the time when the city of Rome was expanding. Over several centuries, the Romans took control of huge regions in what is now Africa, Europe, and the Middle East, including all the city-states of Greece. Because the Romans adopted much of the Greek culture, the myths of Greece and Rome blended together and are now collectively referred to as classical mythology.

When a large portion of what became known as the Roman Empire finally fell to German invaders in 476 CE, a period of confusion and chaos followed. Many of the traditions and accomplishments of the classical era were lost. Historians call this period the Dark Ages because there was a lack of recorded history or literature. The Dark Ages are now considered the start of the Middle Ages or the medieval period, based on the Latin for "middle" and "age." Best known as the time of knights, ladies, and castles, the Middle Ages were filled with conflicts over territory, over religion, and eventually over the feudal system in which peasants had been forced to work the land and serve their lords.

Historians refer to the period between 500 and 1400 CE as the Middle Ages because it came between the fall of the Roman Empire and the dawn of the European Renaissance. As explorers and scientists opened up the world, the great teachings of the classical era emerged again. This Renaissance, or rebirth, was the awakening of ancient ideas that actually marked the beginning of the modern world.

The time line on the following pages marks some of the major events of ancient Greece and Rome and the resurgence of interest in the classics during the European Renaissance.

• A Greek man named Herodotus, pictured in these etchings, lived during the fifth century BCE and was said to have "invented" history. He studied the causes and effects of human actions and recorded events of the Persian War in his work known as *The Histories*.

TIME LINE

2000 BCE

1200 BCE

336 BCE

BCE

6000	Farming communities appear in Greece
5000	Farming communities appear around Rome
2000	Minoan civilization flourishes on Crete
1400	Mycenaeans take control of Minoans after natural disasters strike Crete
1200	Legendary date when Mycenaeans defeat the city of Troy
1100-800	Greece's Dark Ages
800	Settlements reappear and city-states are established
	Beginning of the Archaic Period and the development of the Greek alphabet
776	First Olympic games are held to honor Zeus
753	Date the mythological Romulus is said to have founded Rome
700	Approximate date of Homer's epics, the *Iliad* and the *Odyssey*
594	Form of democracy is introduced in Athens
509	Rome declares itself a republic
500	Beginning of the Classical Period or Golden Age of Greece
490	Persian Wars begin; a united Greece wins at the Battle of Marathon
480	Greece again defeats Persia in the Battle of Salamis
479	Persian threat ends
469-399	Life of philosopher Socrates
460-377	Life of Hippocrates, the "father of modern medicine"
438	Completion of the Parthenon in Athens
431	Peloponnesian Wars between Sparta and Athens begin
427-347	Life of philosopher Plato
404	Athens surrenders to Sparta
384-322	Life of astronomer and philosopher Aristotle
338	Macedonian army defeats Greece
356	Birth of Alexander, son of Macedonian leader Philip II, who inherits his father's kingdom in 336 BCE and becomes known as Alexander the Great
331	The city of Alexandria is established in Egypt
330	Beginning of the Hellenistic Era, when Alexander the Great spreads Greek ideals throughout his empire
330-265	Life of mathematician Euclid
323	Death of Alexander the Great

Greece

'OOO BCE	6000 BCE	5000 BCE	4000 BCE	3000 BCE

Rome

27 BCE

1454 CE

1492 CE

287-212	Life of scientist Archimedes
250	Rome controls most of Italy
146	Macedonia and Greece fall to Romans
48	Julius Caesar is appointed dictator of Rome
44	Julius Caesar is assassinated by senators on March 15
29-19	Virgil composes the *Aeneid*
27	Caesar Augustus becomes Rome's first emperor; beginning of Pax Romana

CE

50	Rome is the largest city in the world with a population of one million
117	Roman Empire is at its largest
120	Completion of the Pantheon in Rome
391	Christianity is declared official religion of the Roman Empire
394	Olympic games are abolished by Christian emperors of Rome
476	Western portion of Roman Empire falls to German invaders

476-1400	Dark Ages and Middle Ages

Renaissance

1400	Approximate start of Renaissance in northern Italy
1436	Completion of the Duomo in Florence, Italy
1452-1519	Life of Leonardo da Vinci
1453	Eastern portion of Roman Empire falls to Ottoman Turks
1454	Johannes Gutenberg perfects printing press
1475-1564	Life of Michelangelo
1492	Christopher Columbus reaches what is to become the New World
1543	Nicholas Copernicus proposes that the sun is at the center of the universe
1564-1616	Life of William Shakespeare
1600	Approximate end of the Renaissance
1609	Galileo Galilei perfects telescopic lens and proves Copernicus' theory
1896	French baron Pierre de Coubertin organizes first modern Olympics, held in Athens

2000 BCE	1500 BCE	1000 BCE	500 BCE	I	500 CE	1000 CE	1500 CE	2000 CE

Dark Ages/Middle Ages

Renaissance

ANCIENT GREECE

Overview

While hunter-gatherers had populated mainland Greece and many of its islands for tens of thousands of years, the first farming communities appeared around 6000 BCE. By 2000 BCE, a settlement, which was later named the Minoan civilization to honor its legendary King Minos, was flourishing on the island of Crete.

Shortly after this time, the Mycenaean civilization was established in the southern region of mainland Greece. After a series of natural disasters struck the island of Crete in approximately 1400 BCE, the Mycenaeans took control of the remaining Minoans and became the most dominant force in Greece. Archaeological evidence proves the Mycenaeans had their own form of written language and that they were excellent builders and sailors.

The Mycenaean civilization did not last long, however. Historians believe a series of earthquakes and wars led to an economic recession, and within two hundred years people abandoned the great cities, and the civilization all but disappeared. Most of the skills and arts acquired by the Minoan and Mycenaean people were lost, including the ability to write; therefore, no written records exist of these lost years.

The region slowly redeveloped, however, and by 800 BCE, it emerged again as a powerful force. The years between 800 and 500 BCE are referred to as Greek's Archaic Period, as settlements were organized into city-states. By 500 BCE, Athens had emerged as a shining example of Greek's progress, and Greece began its Golden Age. Within two hundred years, however, internal conflict weakened Greece, and it was taken over by the invading Macedonians and eventually fell to the Romans.

Gods and Goddesses

The Greeks believed in a pantheon, or group of higher powers. Each one of the many gods and goddesses represented a specific aspect of life. Zeus, for example, was the leader of the gods, and he ruled the skies with his powerful thunderbolts. His brother Poseidon spent most of his time in the seas and could stir up storms with his staff, the trident. Their sister Demeter was in charge of the harvest, while Aphrodite was the goddess of love.

Greek city-states, most notably Athens, built phenomenal temples, statues, and monuments to honor their pantheon, and many are still standing today. Festivals and celebrations were also held to honor specific gods and goddesses, with activities such as music, sacrifices, dramatic productions, and sporting competitions. While people today may read from a sacred text and attend synagogues, churches, or temples as part of their religious practice, the ancient Greeks demonstrated their loyalty by telling and acting out myths and attending these celebrations.

Because of the geography of Greece, a mainland with approximately 1,400 islands surrounding it, the Greeks were excellent sailors, traveling frequently and conducting

> • Archaeologists have determined a lot about the history of the Minoan civilization by the murals—called **frescoes**—on the walls of the palace of Knossos. Because frescoes were painted directly on wet plaster, the images have lasted over time.

trade in surrounding regions. Their mythology, therefore, along with their arts and culture, were heavily influenced by civilizations such as Egypt, Mesopotamia, and Phoenicia, and it also spread into these other cultures.

The Olympics

Fitness was critical in ancient Greece because of the need for strong warriors. Athletic events, however, were also seen as a way to honor the gods and to provide entertainment. In 776 BCE, the first official Olympic Games were held in Olympia, Greece, to pay respect to the most powerful god, Zeus. During these ancient games, conducted every four years for nearly 1,200 years, all battles were suspended. As the tradition continued, men from all regions of Greece came to participate.

The contests in the Olympics included individual sports like wrestling, chariot races, foot races, and javelin and discus throws. Competition was fierce and frequently turned bloody, and winners brought great honor to the cities they represented. The victorious athletes were crowned with laurel wreaths, which they would display on the doors of their homes, likely originating the practice of ornamental wreaths.

The Olympics were officially abolished in 394 CE by the Christian emperors of Rome. In 1896 CE, however, a French baron named Pierre de Coubertin began the tradition again, inspired by the Greek idea that the games could be a unifying force in an often-warring world. The 1896 games were held in Athens, and the Winter Games came more than a quarter century later in 1924. Although some games were cancelled during the two World Wars, the Olympics have been held steadily since then.

Greece's Golden Age

Greece's Golden Age began in about 500 BCE. During this period actors performed in front of vast audiences, scientists began to organize their studies into disciplines, and philosophers celebrated the power and importance of the human mind. The brief Golden Age, lasting only two centuries, is a dot on the world's time line, but it stands out as a truly shining era: Western civilization was born in Greece.

Theater and the Arts

Modern theater originated in the once-religious rituals to honor Dionysus, the Greek god of wine. Although these celebrations were originally wild and unstructured, a group of men called the chorus soon began to dance, sing, and recite poetry during the festivals. The art of drama was born, and Dionysus became associated with drama as well as wine.

Theater, which derives from the Greek *theatron*, "a place for watching," became a focal point of Greek life. Male actors performed comedies and tragedies while wearing masks to represent different characters. Very few Greek comedies have survived in their entirety, but historians do know from existing fragments that they contained crude humor and ludicrous plots. Many of the respected Greek tragedies still exist, however, and the majority of those have roots in myth. Numerous versions of the myths told today are based on the stories of the ancient Greek playwrights.

+ Although women were not allowed to compete in the ancient Olympics, they held their own athletic competitions to honor Hera, the Olympian queen.

+ Pierre de Coubertin designed a symbol for the Olympics in 1912. The five intertwined rings represent the continents of Asia, Africa, Europe, Oceania, and the Americas, and every nation's flag contains at least one of the colors used in the design.

+ *Tragos* means "goat" in Greek, and the word **tragedy**—a play or literary work with a serious theme—means "song of the goat." Poets often received goats as prizes in contests, but the word likely comes from the fact that actors wore goatskin dresses while performing.

In addition to the theater, Greeks placed high importance on crafts like jewelry, pottery, and sculpture. Artisans had workshops around a town's marketplace, or *agora*, and sold practical and luxury items. Because Greeks traveled and traded so frequently, they saw a great deal of art from other cultures. Greek art, therefore, was influenced by African, Egyptian, and Middle Eastern cultures.

Lastly, music and dance were extremely important parts of Greek life. In *Sailing the Wine-Dark Sea*, Thomas Cahill writes that although Greece had trained performers, "there is evidence that every Greek, whether king or serf, looked forward to the many opportunities for singing and dancing. Even our tattered and incomplete records yield at least two hundred terms for different kinds of dancing." Performers sang poetry, often accompanied by a lyre, a U-shaped stringed instrument played like a small harp. Paintings on Greek vases depicted men and women playing such instruments surrounded by dancing figures.

Science and Medicine

Though Greeks first attempted to make sense of their world through myths—creating stories to explain the existence of phenomena such as rainbows, eclipses, and the change of seasons—they later developed a more scientific approach to their thinking. In fact, the Greeks made fundamental and far-reaching contributions to medicine, astronomy, mathematics, and physics.

Hippocrates (460-377 BCE) is considered the father of modern medicine. He approached the treatment of the human body in scientific terms and understood how the body works together as one organism. He researched, developed, and prescribed medical treatments for various illnesses and authored numerous medical books.

The astronomer Aristotle (384-322 BCE) found evidence to prove Earth was round and created a model of the universe. Although he incorrectly placed Earth at the center, his attempt to structure the heavenly bodies paved the way for other astronomers. Years later, the Greek Aristarchus proposed a sun-centered model, but it would be thousands of years before his radical idea was accepted.

The mathematician Euclid (330-265 BCE) is recognized as the father of geometry, the study of the properties of lines, surfaces, and solids. His most famous piece of writing was called *Elements*, and many of its theories are still applied today.

Archimedes (287-212 BCE) is considered the most brilliant mathematician from ancient Greece. He reportedly made his most important discovery when he stepped into his bath and realized that his own weight altered the water level. He used this principle to measure the volume of an object and subsequently its density. Archimedes also invented a screw-shaped device to raise water from one level to another, and this design is still used today for irrigation and other purposes.

These men made important individual contributions, to be sure, but it was the Greeks' collective new approach to thinking that transformed the world. Never before had humans searched in such a fundamental, organized way to find the answers to big questions, and their work became the foundation for modern science.

- **Agoraphobia** is the fear of open or public spaces, and comes from *agora*, the name for a Greek gathering place, and *phobos*, "fear." Phobos was one of the sons of Ares, the Greek god of war.

- **Lyrical** means "like a rhythmic poem or song," and **lyrics** are the words of a song. Both terms come from the practice of singing along with a lyre (which, by the way, is pronounced to rhyme with "tire.")

Hippocrates

- Students of medicine traditionally take some form of the **Hippocratic oath**, a promise to care for their patients following the same ethical code first put forth by Hippocrates.

- When he realized how his body had displaced the bath water, Archimedes supposedly shouted "Heureka!", the Greek word for "I've found it!" Today, the interjection is spelled **Eureka!**

"...the most influential of all Greek intellectual innovations is undoubtedly the development over the course of two centuries of philosophy as a systematic study." THOMAS CAHILL

Philosophy

The modern definition of philosophy refers to the analysis of different elements of the universe, and the term itself comes from the Greek words *philos* ("loving") and *sophos* ("wise"). In ancient Greece, philosophers such as Socrates, Plato, and Aristotle were great thinkers who actively explored ideas about government, ethics, and the physical universe.

Socrates (469-399 BCE) was a teacher who proclaimed himself the wisest of men because he knew he did not know everything. Instead of lecturing, he would ask a series of questions to encourage his students to use logic and reasoning. Many citizens of Athens were inspired by Socrates, but others felt he denied the gods because he focused so much on human thoughts and abilities. Socrates was eventually executed by being forced to drink poison.

One of Socrates' finest students was Plato (427-347 BCE), who recorded the final days of his teacher's life. He went on to write a book called *Republic*, which details what Socrates described as the ideal ways in which to live. Plato himself was best remembered for his studies of what he called "ideal forms," including Truth, Goodness, and Beauty.

Just as Plato was a student of Socrates, Aristotle (384-322 BCE) was a student of Plato. In addition to contributing a great deal to science, Aristotle studied logic, ethics, philosophy, psychology, and politics. Because he used a rational approach in all of these fields, he is often considered the founder of Western science.

Socrates

Plato

Aristotle

- **Spartan** has come to mean "harsh" or "austere" and is based on the strict lifestyle of the Spartans.

- Each year, an assembly of Athenians could expel someone in their city-state for ten years for being a menace. Citizens voted by scratching a name on a small piece of pottery called an *ostrakon*. To **ostracize** someone now means to exclude him from a group.

- Athens was not a true democracy because women and slaves had no say in political life.

- Pericles (c. 495 - 429 BCE) was the elected "strategos" (general) of Athens during the peak of its Golden Age, between the Persian and Peloponnesian Wars. He developed Athens' politics, promoted education, and oversaw ambitious projects. Too ambitious perhaps? His opponents accused him of spending too much to glorify Athens.

- The Lincoln Memorial in Washington, D.C., was modeled after the Parthenon. A huge statue of Abraham Lincoln sits inside his memorial, just as an enormous statue of Athena was built inside the Parthenon.

The Cities of Sparta and Athens

Located in the southern region of Greece's mainland, the powerful city of Sparta controlled most of the land known as the Peloponnesus. After its massive slave population rebelled, Sparta required all male citizens to be trained as soldiers. In keeping with this strict lifestyle, boys and girls were taken from their parents at an early age and housed in barracks. Boys were treated harshly to make them fearless warriors, and girls were trained physically so they would bear strong children.

While archaeologists have found fine statues, bronze vessels, and other forms of artwork from ancient Sparta, the Spartans did not keep historical records and did not celebrate art, science, and philosophy in the same way the Athenians did. After the slave rebellions, the Spartans focused their attention and resources on building a superior army and became the dominant military force in Greece.

Athens, located in the eastern region of Greece's mainland, was very different from Sparta. First, in 594 BCE, Athens established an early version of democracy (from Greek for "the people"), and allowed its male citizens to vote and hold office. Second, Athenians placed great importance on trade and expansion, and developed their minds as well as their bodies. Music, dance, philosophy, drama, fine art, and science were highly respected, and what ancient Athenians contributed to these fields is remarkable. Third, while Sparta built strong walls for defense, the architects of Athens often built simply to celebrate, and they constructed countless temples and monuments to honor their pantheon of gods and goddesses. The Parthenon, masterminded by Athens' powerful politician Pericles, was built with 20,000 tons of marble at a cost that would equal billions of today's dollars. Completed in 438 BCE to honor the patron goddess, Athena, its remains still stand on the Acropolis.

Greece in Battle

Although Athens, Sparta, and Greece's other city-states shared the same language and myths, they were so geographically isolated from one another that they remained quite independent. When the Persian army attacked Greece, however, the Greek city-states banded together under the leadership of Athens to defend their nation.

The Greeks' first major victory in the Persian Wars was in 490 BCE at the Battle of Marathon, when the Athenian army, although vastly outnumbered, used daring strategy to turn back the Persian army. Ten years later, the Persians attacked Athens, but the Greeks rallied at the Battle of Salamis, one of the first sea battles in history. The Greeks trapped Persian ships in a strait and were able to destroy half the fleet. By 479 BCE, the threat of a Persian invasion had ended.

After battling the Persians, Greece became embroiled in a civil war between Sparta and Athens, beginning in 431 BCE. Known as the Peloponnesian Wars, these battles flared when Sparta feared Athens was becoming too powerful. Athens stayed behind its walls and tried to hold off the approaching Spartans, but a devastating plague spread through overcrowded Athens and weakened it considerably. Attempts to attack the Spartan coastline failed, and by 404 BCE, Athens was so economically weak that it surrendered.

Sparta entered into battle with the city-state of Thebes just a few decades later, and in 338 BCE, a powerful army from Macedonia swept down from the north and defeated Greece. The Macedonian ruler Philip II took all of the Greek city-states and had major plans for his new territory, but he was assassinated shortly after the victory. Philip's son Alexander inherited the kingdom at the young age of twenty.

Alexander the Great

Alexander, better known as Alexander the Great, went on to conquer Egypt and Persia and expanded his empire through the Middle East and into parts of India. Rather than trying to abolish Greek culture and ideas, however, Alexander did just the opposite. Because he had been tutored by the Greek philosopher Aristotle, and because he claimed to be a descendent of the Greek heroes Achilles and Heracles, Alexander was determined to spread Greek ideas throughout his new empire.

New cities in Asia and northern Africa were developed based on Greek culture, and Alexander himself founded the city of Alexandria in Egypt, which flourished as a center of the Hellenistic Era for more than three hundred years. The forty-story Lighthouse of Alexandria—the tallest building in the world at the time—served as a beacon of light both physically and figuratively and is now one of the Seven Wonders of the Ancient World.

Scientists, mathematicians, and astronomers in Alexandria built upon the ideas set forth by great Greek thinkers, and vast numbers of Greek manuscripts were collected and organized in the famed Library of Alexandria. Although Alexandria would later fall to the Romans, the city was, as described by classics translator R.C. Seaton, "a useful bridge between Athens and Rome."

+ A Greek man, likely Pheidippides, was said to have run from Marathon back to Athens to announce Greece's victory in the Battle of Marathon. The distance he ran was 26 miles, and a **marathon**—run in the first modern Olympics—is just over 26 miles long.

+ Pheidippides was so exhausted from his run that when he reached Athens, he gasped **"Nike!"** ("victory") and died. Nike (NIE kee), pictured below, was the winged goddess of victory, and the Nike athletic company uses a stylized version of her wing as its logo.

- The Greeks had traditionally called themselves Hellenes, literally "of Hellen," a man they considered the father of their race. Historical time lines place the Hellenistic Period between the death of Alexander and the beginning of Roman rule.

- A Greek legend features King Gordius, who predicted that the man who loosened his complex Gordian knot would become a great ruler of Asia. While others attempted to untie the knot, Alexander the Great sliced through it with his massive sword. To cut a **Gordian knot** means to solve a problem boldly and decisively.

The Fall of Greece

Alexander the Great crossed deserts and mountains, and in just over a dozen years, had acquired the largest empire in the ancient world. When he died of a fever in 323 BCE, however, his generals struggled for power. Many of the Greek city-states tried to use this period of political instability to free themselves from Macedonian rule, and some city-states eventually asked the Romans for help. The Roman army was able to defeat the Macedonians, but they did not stop there. By 146 BCE, the weakened regions of Macedonia and Greece had both fallen under Roman rule.

The glory of the independent Hellenic civilization had ended, but the stories of mythology and the brilliant advances made by the Greeks would live on.

> "There was nothing the ancient Greeks did not poke their noses into, no experience they shunned, no problem they did not attempt to solve. ...Whatever we experience in our day, whatever we hope to learn, whatever we most desire, whatever we set out to find, we see that the Greeks have been there before us, and we meet them on their way back."

THOMAS CAHILL, *SAILING THE WINE-DARK SEA*

ANCIENT ROME

Overview

Archaeological evidence shows that the fertile region around Rome had already been settled by farming communities as far back as 5000 BCE. Once the city of Rome was established, these small cities became stronger and more organized. By 250 BCE, Rome had control over most of Italy; by 146 BCE, the Roman army had conquered the vast territories of Macedonia and Greece; and by 50 CE, Rome had a population of one million people, making it the largest city in the world.

The Roman Empire was at its largest and strongest in 117 CE, stretching almost 2,500 miles from east to west and reaching from northern Africa to northern England. While the Empire enveloped numerous cultures, it was Greek myths, Greek drama and arts, and Greek literature that most inspired the Romans.

Roman innovations in architecture, irrigation, and road building can still be seen today, and a lasting period of prosperity known as the Pax Romana stands out in Rome's history. But leaders had a difficult time keeping pace with the enormous expansions, and many emperors were corrupt. Civil wars broke out in the third century CE and the Empire never recovered. Roman influence lives on, however, and the Romans joined the ancient Greeks as founders of the Western world.

◆ Roman myths tell of the twins Romulus and Remus, who were abandoned as infants and raised by a wolf. The twins later wanted to thank the wolf by building a city in her honor, but Romulus killed Remus in a quarrel. It was Romulus, then, who established the city of Rome in 753 BCE.

Gods and Goddesses

Because the Roman Empire encompassed a wide variety of cultures, its citizens believed in numerous gods and goddesses. The majority of its deities, however, came from the pantheon of ancient Greece. After renaming most of these deities—the Olympian ruler Zeus, for instance, became Jupiter, and the goddess Athena became Minerva—the Romans retold the Greek myths and added some of their own.

As with many other cultures, Romans believed individual gods and goddesses were responsible for distinct areas of human life. And the deities the Romans chose to honor reflected a great deal about their culture. The violent Ares, for example, had not been highly respected by the Greeks, but the more war-oriented Romans called him Mars and considered him to be one of the most powerful gods.

Just like the Greeks, the Romans held festivals and designed statues and buildings to honor their pantheon. While the Parthenon was the most spectacular Greek temple, the Pantheon was the most honored Roman temple. Completed in 27 BCE and rebuilt in 125 CE after a fire, this structure is still used in Rome.

In 313 CE, Christianity was first recognized within the Roman world, and it was declared the official religion in 391 CE. With this decree, the deities from classical mythology were deemed false gods. References to these ancient gods and goddesses are still plentiful, however, and are found in the names of the planets and some of the months and days, titles and logos for major companies, references in books and plays, and common vocabulary.

The Roman Way

The Roman people built upon the cultural traditions and progress of the lands they had conquered, and engineering, architecture, and the arts continued to thrive. And Latin, which started as a local language in a small farming town, grew to become the official language of the vast Roman Empire and eventually became the foundation for numerous languages in the Western world.

Music, Theater, and the Arts

Music, theater, and the arts had been highly celebrated in many parts of Greece, and the Romans capitalized on their successes. The oldest known Latin plays, for instance, date to 200 BCE and are attributed to Plautus, a writer who had been inspired by Greek plays. Plautus was especially fond of the Greek's comedies and crafted entertaining tales that often featured upper class families and their slaves. He managed to offer sophisticated moral messages through the antics of his characters, and his plays later became the foundation for the works of William Shakespeare and other playwrights during the European Renaissance.

Romans also continued to celebrate the decorative mosaic, which the Greeks had used in floor designs. While earlier Greek mosaicists had primarily used bumpy natural pebbles to create scenes and borders on their floors, craftsmen had become more ambitious during the Hellenistic period. As a result, the mosaics created throughout the expanding Roman Empire were created with tiny tesserae, small cubes of stone and colored glass. The smaller material allowed for more detailed pictures, and gorgeous, well-constructed mosaics have been found in numerous excavated ruins. Just as archaeologists learned a great deal about the Minoans from their frescoes, mosaics reveal much about Roman history because they depict everything from famous rulers to domestic themes to scenes from mythology.

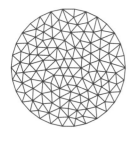

+ The term **tessellation** refers to a repetitive, grid-like pattern. Tessellations are studied in geometry and sometimes appear in modern art.

+ The Colosseum is an ancient **amphitheater** that still stands in Rome. The Greek *amphi-* is a prefix meaning "on both sides": classical Greek theaters had been semicircular, and so the Roman's new design was essentially two classical theaters facing one another. (In science, an amphibious animal lives both on land and in the water.)

Engineering and Architecture

The Romans were masters of architecture and engineering. One example of their skills was road building, a necessity for the Roman army. Because they needed an easier way to transport supplies and weapons across the vast territory, Romans designed an incredibly complex system of well-built roads. First, they dug all the way down to solid bedrock and filled these trenches with stones, pebbles, and sand. For main roads, the soldiers then placed interlocking paving blocks on top of this solid foundation. Roads were built with a slight mound in the middle so rain would roll off into drainage ditches on either side. By the second century CE, the Roman Empire had over 250,000 miles of roads, allowing both its army and its merchants to travel easily. The roads were constructed so well that many are still in use today.

Aqueducts were another Roman feat of engineering and solved the problem of how to carry water across long distances. Aqueducts were essentially troughs of water held up by a series of archways, and they transported millions of gallons of water to cities and villages to ensure clean drinking water and an irrigation system for crops. Huge sections of these elegant aqueducts still stand in Italy and France, attracting tourists from around the world.

In addition to their other functions, aqueducts allowed the Romans to create public bath houses. Using either aqueducts or springs, as well as elaborate systems of underground air ducts to circulate warm air, the heated baths were used to cleanse, relax, and heal. The more lavish public baths also featured exercise rooms and saunas, with slaves to clean and oil the bathers. Men had separate facilities from women and children, and people often met at the baths for social purposes.

The Latin Language

The Romans had a written language, but they had used it for practical purposes only—creating legal contracts, for example, or inscribing gravestones. Therefore, while the Romans were heavily influenced by the Greeks' mythology, art, architecture, and science, they were perhaps most inspired by Greek literature and by how Greek writers had celebrated the use of written language. The 200 years between 100 BCE and 100 CE are referred to as Rome's Classical Period and mark the height of ancient Roman literature.

It was during this time that the Roman poet Ovid wrote *Metamorphoses*, an invaluable collection of stories that wove together Greek and Roman mythology. In 30 BCE, Virgil began researching and writing his famous epic called the *Aeneid*. While Virgil's work borrowed a great deal from the style and themes of the Greek Homer's poems, the *Iliad* and the *Odyssey*, the *Aeneid* gave Romans their own national epic written in their own language: Latin.

An increased interest in literature and poetry led the Romans to become more vested in both written and spoken Latin. But because it was so difficult to mass-produce written texts, even those Romans who learned to read did not have much available material. It was the spoken word, therefore, that became a revered art form in Roman times. Poets constantly read their works aloud, theaters provided a place

+ **Via** is the Roman word meaning "by way of," and roads were therefore called *viae*. A **viaduct** is a bridge that leads a road over a valley, and if a letter is sent by plane, it is said to be sent "via airmail." Aqueducts carried water, and the term came from *aqua* (water) and *ductus* (a leading).

+ The city of Bath in England was founded by the Romans, who used the region's natural hot springs to create a famous public bath house. The bath house has been modernized and opened as the Thermae Spa in 2006.

+ A classical form of Latin was used for writing, while a less structured form called Vulgar Latin was used in common speech. In 382 CE, Pope Damasus I commissioned a writer to translate the Old Testament directly from Hebrew, not Greek. This version of the Bible became known as the Vulgate Bible, or the "common translation." Although it was not a derisive term at the time, vulgar has come to mean common or crude, as in **vulgar** language.

- Rhetoric is persuasive speech, and a **rhetorical question** — "How many times must I tell you?"—is asked for effect; the person asking it does not expect an answer.

- Latin America is made up of roughly 20 countries where Romance languages are spoken, although the name most commonly refers to regions where people speak Spanish or Portuguese.

- A **romance** was originally a tale written in a Romance language about heroic, chivalrous knights. Modern romance novels and movies feature love, excitement, and adventure, and the verb "to romance" means to flatter or woo.

for audiences to hear stories, and politicians and court representatives perfected their speaking skills—their rhetoric—until they could address masses of people about the important issues of the times.

Although Greek was still spoken in the eastern regions, Latin became the main language throughout the Roman Empire. When the Empire began to crumble during the third century CE, however, Latin began a very slow and somewhat confusing decline. Latin was still spoken in many regions taken over by Germanic tribes, the majority of Christian literature was created in Latin, and written Latin continues to be recognized as a language of scholars to this day. But a variety of spoken languages, including Spanish, Portuguese, French, Italian, and Romanian, slowly emerged in Europe, followed by written versions of these languages, eventually pushing Latin aside. These Romance languages—those based on the Latin or "Roman" language—are considered "sister languages" and share many similarities.

English, although it uses the same alphabet as Latin and these sister languages, is not considered a Romance language because it arose from a combination of Germanic dialects. But because Latin influenced German, over half of the words in the English language have Latin derivatives. Furthermore, the Latin and Greek languages, along with the body of classical myths, provide the roots for countless terms in the fields of science and medicine.

> "Latin is more of an immortal language than a dead one. It lives on with the modern Western languages, for many words have Latin derivatives. The study of Latin…gives one a sense that language can be much more than mere communication; it teaches one the beauty of just the right word used in just the right manner."
>
> W. WILLARD WIRTZ,
> FORMER
> U.S. SECRETARY
> OF LABOR

COMMON LATIN WORDS *and* PHRASES

ad nauseam	to the point of disgust
agenda	things to be done
alibi	literally "elsewhere," used as a legal defense
alumni	pupils, now used to refer to graduates
bona fide	adjective meaning in good faith, used to describe something real or authentic
circa	around, used when providing an approximate date for a historical event
et cetera (etc.)	and others
ipso facto	by the very fact
mea culpa	my fault
pro bono publico	for the public good, often just *pro bono*
semper fidelis	always faithful, the motto of the United States Marine Corps

- 34 -

Sport, Weapons, and Warfare

Rome's survival depended heavily on the strength of its army, so great importance was placed on sport and combat. One form of entertainment, for instance, was watching gladiators fight one another, often until one died. These men—some condemned criminals, some volunteers seeking fame—also raced on chariots at breakneck speeds, fought lions, executed prisoners, or wore blindfolds to battle their opponents. Historical evidence also reveals how the floor of the Colosseum could have been flooded so men could entertain thousands of Romans with elaborate mock sea battles. Fighting was even common at funerals, where the competitor who was killed would accompany the soul of the dead person into the Underworld.

The Roman army, which was originally made up of volunteers who protected the city of Rome, developed into an immense force of paid men. Soldiers used advanced weapons and innovative strategies to defeat their enemies. The army was divided into groups of 3,000 to 6,000 men called legions led by senior officers. Legions would often form a "tortoise" when entering a battle: Marching close together, the men would hold their shields over their heads to create a shell-like cover to protect them from enemy weapons.

The Rulers of Rome

At first Rome was a monarchy, meaning it was ruled by a series of powerful kings. But in 509 BCE, a dishonorable monarch was deposed and Rome declared itself a Republic. This new system of government was led by an assembly of citizens known as the Senate, and the Romans set up a strict system of controls so Rome would never again be ruled by one man.

But just as democracy in Athens had favored wealthy males, the Roman Republic was also led by rich men, and power was centered in Rome. However, a series of revolts by the plebeians, the name given to the working class, gave a stronger voice to common people and provided them with representatives known as tribunes.

After defeating many enemies, including the Gauls, the Samnites, and the Greeks, the city of Rome gained considerable power. By 250 BCE, it controlled Italy. Then, after finally defeating the Carthaginians of Northern Africa in a series of battles known as the Punic Wars, Rome became the largest power in the Mediterranean.

The Republic was indeed large, but it was not strong. The government was unable to keep pace with the expansions and was losing control. In an effort to restore order, an immensely successful military leader named Julius Caesar was appointed dictator in 48 BCE. While many in the middle and lower classes considered him a hero, a group of senators feared he was gaining too much power. On March 15, 44 BCE, Julius Caesar was stabbed to death by these conspirators, including his closest friend, Brutus, who had helped organize the assassination.

The senators had hoped to restore the Republic to what it had been years earlier, but their actions actually prompted bitter civil wars and led to the end of the Republic. Before his death, Julius Caesar had adopted his great-nephew Caesar Augustus (born Gaius Octavius) as his son. Augustus was named Rome's first

+ The Romans created the measurement of a **foot**, based on the distance from the average man's heel to his toes. They also originated the **mile** based on the Latin *mille*, thousand. If the Roman army marched a thousand paces, it would equal a mile, or 5,280 feet.

+ Monarchy comes from the Greek *monos*, "one" and *archein*, "to rule."

+ Senate derives from the Latin *senex*, which means "elder." It is the root of words like senior, the Spanish *señor*, seniority, and senility.

+ Tribune is from the Latin "chief" and refers to a person who speaks fairly for all. Newspapers often use "tribune" in their titles, indicating their goal of representing the people.

+ Tribunes and other representatives voiced their disapproval of an idea by shouting **"Veto!"** ("I forbid!"). The term is still used when a leader rejects a plan or proposal.

- The etching below shows Caesar on a horse, and the one above is the scene of his murder. Caesar reportedly recognized his good friend Brutus among his attackers and uttered **"Et tu, Brute?"** which means, "And you [too] Brutus?" The phrase is now used by someone who is saddened by the betrayal of a close friend.

- The ides (a Latin word meaning "half division") marked the middle of a month. March 15, **the ides of March**, was especially important, however, because Romans held a military parade to honor Mars, their revered god of war.

Brutus.	A soothsayer bids you beware the ides of March.
Caesar.	Set him before me; let me see his face.
Cassius.	Fellow, come from the throng; look upon Caesar.
Caesar.	What say'st thou to me now? Speak once again.
Soothsayer.	Beware the ides of March.
Caesar.	He is a dreamer, let us leave him. Pass.

WILLIAM SHAKESPEARE, *JULIUS CAESAR.* ACT I, SCENE II, LINES 19-24

emperor in 27 BCE, and he proved to be a fair and wise ruler. With his leadership, the new Roman Empire experienced what is now known as Pax Romana, "the Roman peace." Temples, roads, and theaters were built, the arts flourished, and for the next two centuries, the Empire experienced much less violence and upheaval.

The Fall of the Roman Empire

While Caesar Augustus had made great strides in building the Roman Empire, successive leaders—including Tiberius, Caligula, Claudius, and Nero—became increasingly corrupt. The Roman Empire was now incredibly diverse, made up of Africans, Germans, Celts, Egyptians, and Greeks who struggled to stay united. As the central government weakened, a series of civil wars broke out in the third century CE. The vast region was divided into eastern and western empires. Because its army could not defend itself against German invaders, the western half fell in 476 CE. The eastern portion, which came to be called the Byzantine Empire, remained intact until its capital, Constantinople, fell to the Ottoman Turks in 1453 CE.

The fall of the western portion of the Empire is commonly seen as the start of the Dark Ages, which were the earliest years of the medieval period. But just like ancient Greece, the Roman Empire had a lasting impact on Europe and on the whole Western world. Roman engineering and architecture had profound influence on later builders, Rome's fine art still inspires, and many aspects of the Roman governing system became the foundation for the American political system. Finally, the Latin language is at the root of countless common English words, as well as terminology in fields such as science, medicine, religion, and the law.

• This etching is of Nero Claudius Caesar Augustus Germanicus, the fourth emperor after Augustus. He began his rule at age sixteen and was responsble for increased trade and massive construction projects. Many historians paint him as a tyrant, however: He ordered the death of his own mother and was thought to have "fiddled while Rome burned," meaning Nero simply stood by during Rome's devastating fire of 64 CE. In fact, some historians believe he may have caused the fire to clear a space for a bigger palace for himself.

ROMAN NUMERALS: AS EASY AS I, II, III

The Romans had a number system based on letters. Roman numerals are still sometimes used, although the system was slightly modified during the Middle Ages. The current system is based on the following:

1 = I   5 = V   10 = X   50 = L   100 = C   500 = D   1,000 = M

So the number 23 is written XXIII, and 75 is LXXV. Since it is difficult to read four I's in a row, 4 is written as IV (one before 5) and 9 is written as IX (one before ten). Therefore, 19 would be XIX, and 124 would be CXXIV.

Roman numerals may appear on clock faces; they are used when preparing a formal written outline; they identify sons who have been named after their fathers (Andrew II); and they number major sporting events (Super Bowls or the Olympics) and historic events (World War I).

A C-note is a slang term for the American $100 bill.

The European Renaissance

Overview

+ Renaissance comes from the Latin prefix *re-*, meaning "again," and *nasci*, "to be born."

In the late 1300s CE, civilizations on different continents that had developed in relative isolation began to merge. Portuguese, Spanish, French, English, and Dutch explorers set sail to open up new trade routes, and for the first time in history, an international economy was formed. In 1492 CE, Christopher Columbus became the first European since the Vikings to reach the Americas, and in the early 1500s, the Portuguese reached China and Japan.

In addition to this physical expansion, there was a mental shift in Europe as well. Scholars, inspired by the mythology, philosophy, science, mathematics, art, and architecture of the ancient Greeks and Romans, tried to blend Greek and Roman ideas with their own beliefs. This Renaissance—"rebirth" or "reawakening"— originated in northern Italy in roughly 1400 and spread northward through Europe into the 1600s. Historically, the Renaissance brought an end to the difficult Middle Ages and marked the beginning of the modern world.

The Expansion of Ideas

While Greek and Latin manuscripts had been found and studied during the Middle Ages, it was the scholars of the Renaissance who began the widespread celebration of classical ideas about politics, science, philosophy, and literature. They recognized how the ancient Greeks and Romans had celebrated the human intellect and human life and began to look more closely at their own cultural values. This way of thinking, later termed humanism, led to an emphasis on learning and the arts.

Just as Athens had been at the center of the Golden Age in ancient Greece, the Italian city of Florence, located along the Arno River, was the heart of the Italian Renaissance. It proudly proclaimed itself the "new Athens," and with a thriving economy and wealthy families who supported artists and philosophers, Florence succeeded in becoming the center of the thrilling Renaissance era.

+ In the collection of essays called *The Greatest Inventions of the Past 2,000 Years*, Randolph Nesse says the most significant invention is the printing press. Printing, he says, "transformed writing into the first mass medium, and the world has never been the same since."

Science and Technology

The expansion of ideas during the Renaissance affected technology as well, and one particular invention allowed these new ideas to spread quickly: the printing press. Up until the mid-1400s, speech was the primary source of communication because books had to be painstakingly copied by hand. By 1454 CE, however, the German metalworker Johannes Gutenberg perfected a system of printing using movable type. Tiny raised, reversed metal letters were placed right to left in trays. When secured together, these trays became a printing plate that could be inked and used to reproduce documents. For the first time, books were widely available in scholarly Latin as well as other European languages, and the resulting literacy ignited an educational revolution and unprecedented communication.

> "Facts which at first seem improbable will… drop the cloak which has hidden them and stand forth in naked and simple beauty." GALILEO GALILEI

GALILEO GALILEI

As inventors developed new technology, Renaissance scientists built upon the foundation of ancient Greek astronomers. Many Greeks had mapped out the celestial bodies and placed Earth at the center of the universe. Although this conclusion was incorrect, much of their research was accurate and proved helpful. In 1543 CE, Renaissance astronomer Nicholas Copernicus designed a model of the universe with the sun at the center. His theory, based on the ideas of the Greek Aristarchus, was still too radical to be accepted. But in 1609 CE, Galileo Galilei improved upon the telescopic lens and became the first human to see the craters of the Moon and stars that had been invisible to the naked eye. He also became the first scientist who could prove Copernicus' theories about the workings of the solar system. Although both Copernicus and Galileo faced severe ridicule for their radical ideas, their work was critical to the understanding of modern astronomy.

Literature and Drama

Authors of the European Renaissance wrote in very exciting times. First, many of the great classic works from the Greek and Roman eras became available in print and inspired writers such as Francis Bacon, who boldly proclaimed, "Knowledge is power." In turn, Renaissance writers had the unique opportunity to be published themselves, so their ideas could be received by a wide audience. Literacy surged as readers were exposed to almanacs, philosophical teachings, romance stories, poems, and travel books.

Drama, too, thrived during the Renaissance. Numerous public theaters were constructed and had many of the same features as the arenas built by the Greeks and Romans. Renaissance playwrights such as Christopher Marlowe and William Shakespeare produced tragedies and comedies, just as the classical writers had done. In fact, many Renaissance plays were based on myths or on the historical events that shaped ancient Greece and Rome. Because classical teachings were so respected during the Renaissance, audiences would have readily understood the playwrights' references to the ancient stories and events.

Shakespeare

+ A sun-centered model of the universe is a **heliocentric** one. Helios was the Greek god of the sun, and the Greek *kentron* (the root of "center") referred to a sharp point, like the one on a compass that is used to mark the center of a circle.

+ Celestial maps created during the Renaissance revealed a gorgeous combination of art and science. Maps of the stars were overlaid with intricate drawings of the constellations, which gave people a better sense of order when they looked up at the heavens.

+ It is commonly believed that William Shakespeare was born on April 23, 1564, and died exactly 52 years later on April 23, 1616.

- The Italian *chiaroscuro* (kee AR e SKYOOR oh) comes from the Latin *clarus* (clear) and *obscurus* (dark).

- Renaissance artists often created paintings that featured classical myths in a Renaissance setting. Gods and goddesses would be dressed in clothing of the period, for instance, or a prominent Renaissance woman would be painted as if she were the independent Artemis.

Art, Architecture, and Music

Humanism affected philosophers, scientists, and writers, and Renaissance artists embraced these ideas as well. While the paintings of the Middle Ages were flat and rigid, Renaissance painters learned how to render the human figure more realistically. Not only did they have a better understanding of human anatomy, but they also studied how light affected three-dimensional figures. This aspect of painting, called chiaroscuro, allowed them to create the illusion of depth and to depict curved objects. Renaissance painters also learned how to produce more accurate landscapes by using mathematical principals of perspective: closer objects appear larger than objects in the distance. Their depictions of buildings, landscapes, and human figures became powerfully life-like with the combination of chiaroscuro and perspective.

Art, therefore, became a more legitimate and honored skill. Renaissance artists such as Leonardo da Vinci, Raphael, Titian, and Michelangelo were valued as important contributors to society and were supported by wealthy citizens. In earlier times, paintings or sculptures had to be "finished" to be considered a work of art, but during the Renaissance, sketches and fragments of sculptures were appreciated because they gave insight into an artist's mind and revealed the genius of the creative process.

Raphael

LEONARDO DA VINCI

A Representative *of the* Renaissance

While many politicians, scientists, and artists had an impact on the Renaissance, Leonardo da Vinci was perhaps the best representative of the time. Born in 1452, da Vinci became a painter, sculptor, inventor, engineer, and architect and embodied the brilliance, energy, and broad thinking of the Renaissance. His drawings prove he understood the basic principles of flight more than 400 years before planes were built, and that he knew a great deal about the complexities of human anatomy.

Leonardo da Vinci also used advanced mathematical principles to create realistic landscape paintings, and his *Mona Lisa* portrait is one of the most recognized works of art ever made. Today, someone with diverse talents in the arts and sciences is called a **Renaissance man** or **woman**, and Leonardo da Vinci was the original "Renaissance man."

The Duomo in Florence, Italy, was the largest domed building of its time. The city is called *Firenze* in Italian.

The same mathematical principles that had opened up new understanding in art also affected Renaissance architecture. Perspective drawings allowed architects to render designs more accurately, and the concept of ratio became an important element in buildings. Renaissance architects traveled to Greece to study ancient structures and applied the classic notions of balance, proportion, beauty, and symmetry to their designs. Churches, which had traditionally been built to imitate the shape of a cross, now incorporated circles. And gigantic domes were constructed as roofs, requiring architects to have a thorough understanding of geometry and physics.

A ratio is a relationship between two things. A building that is 50 feet wide and 100 feet tall, for example, has a width/height ratio of 1 to 2.

Renaissance thinking affected developments in music as well. By studying the principals of the Greek mathematician Pythagoras and the theories of classic musicians, Renaissance musicians gained a better understanding of how sounds were produced, and they created instruments that could play more complex music. Composers of the Renaissance also studied how the Greeks had used music in their dramas to suggest joyful or sorrowful moods, and Renaissance performers, trying to recreate authentic Greek tragedies, developed the earliest form of opera.

Many of the earliest operas featured subjects from classical myths, including *Dafne* (composed in 1598 and based on the myth of Daphne), and *Euridice* and *Orfeo* (written in 1600 and 1607 respectively, and based on the myth of Eurydice and her husband, Orpheus).

The Lasting Impact of the Renaissance

The ancient cultures of Greece and Rome were the dominant sources of inspiration during the European Renaissance and had a profound impact on philosophy, science, technology, literature, drama, art, architecture, and music. In turn, the developments made by the people of the Renaissance became inspiration for modern life, as explorers discovered new lands, an international economy was established, and humanism influenced how men and women thought about their own lives.

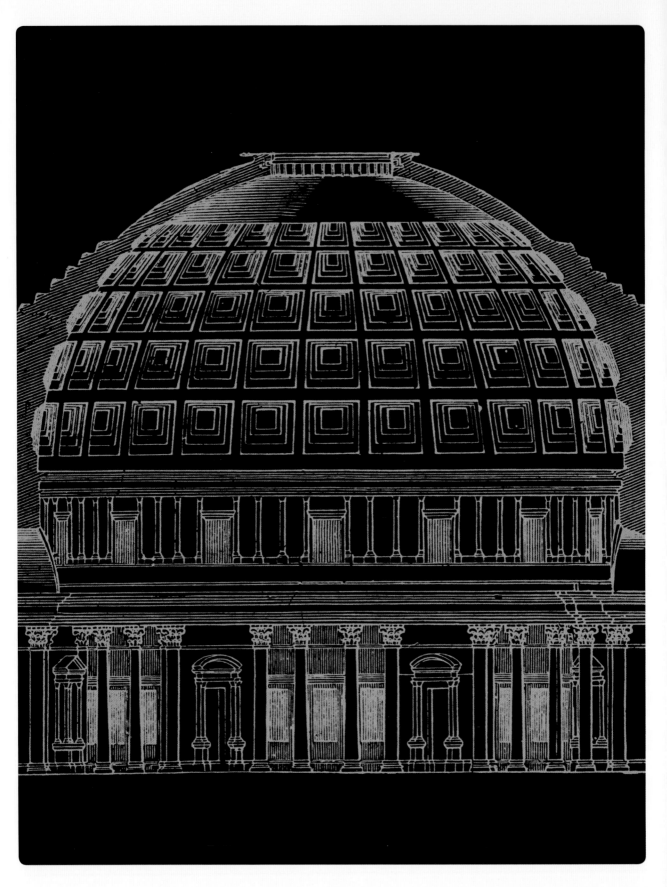

Origin Myths *and the* Classical Pantheon

"Where did I come from?" children often ask. The people of the ancient world were as baffled as any five-year-old because they, too, lacked the scientific understanding of conception and birth. But all people, from ancient times to modern, have struggled with the even bigger question: "Where did *everything* come from? The trees, the oceans, the stars in the sky? How did it all get here?"

This chapter shows that for the Greeks, order came from chaos because from the force they called Chaos all things were born: concrete elements such as earth, sky, and water, as well as the abstract concepts of love and fate. After the creation of several generations of gods and an epic battle for dominance, twelve Olympians ascended to power on Mount Olympus, and Greek life began.

Following the creation myths in this chapter is an introduction to the classical pantheon, the group of gods and goddesses recognized by the Greeks and later, with some changes, by the Romans. Learning this "cast of characters" will allow for an easier understanding of the myths, hero stories, and epics that follow.

◆ The etchings here show a cross section of Rome's Pantheon, which features a massive concrete dome 143 feet high and 143 feet wide. Thomas Jefferson used the Pantheon as a model when he designed the Rotunda, a building on the campus of the University of Virginia. Other examples of buildings inspired by the Pantheon are the Jefferson Memorial and the National Gallery of Art, both in Washington, D.C.

Earth *and* Sky

- In *Theogony*, Hesiod catalogues the origins of more than 300 gods and goddesses. Some were major deities (such as Zeus), some played minor roles (like nymphs), some were natural features (such as rivers and mountains), and the rest were personified abstract concepts (including strife and justice).

- Chaos shares an origin with **chasm**, which means "a deep gap or break." Chaos now describes extreme disorder or confusion.

- The plural form of Cyclops (SIE klopz) is Cyclopes (sie KLOPE eez).

The Greeks believed the force that began all life was Chaos, which had roots meaning "yawn" and "space." Hesiod, a Greek writer from the late eighth century BCE, described Chaos as a "dark void" in his piece *Theogony*, the first poem to document the Greeks' beliefs in the creation of the world. Later, the Roman writer Ovid, in his poem *Metamorphoses*, created an animated image of Chaos battling opposites such as light and darkness, heat and cold, weightlessness and mass all swirling together.

By all accounts, however, Chaos began to take shape. From Chaos came Gaea (Earth), Tartarus (the Underworld), Eros (Love), Erebus (Darkness of the Underground), and Nyx (Night). From the two darknesses came Aether (Light) and Hemera (Day). And Nyx also bore a host of creatures that personified the most mysterious and frightening forces in the world, such as dreams and death.

Gaea then bore the Mountains and Sea, as well as Uranus, a creature so big he covered Gaea and became Sky. When Gaea and Uranus first united, they created three monstrous creatures with 50 heads and 100 arms called the Hecatonchires, or "Hundred Handers." Three one-eyed Cyclopes soon followed. Disgusted by these offspring and concerned they might become too powerful, Uranus hurled them back inside Gaea to Tartarus, the darkest realm of the Underworld. When Uranus again united with Gaea, the Earth bore six daughters and six sons, known as the Titans.

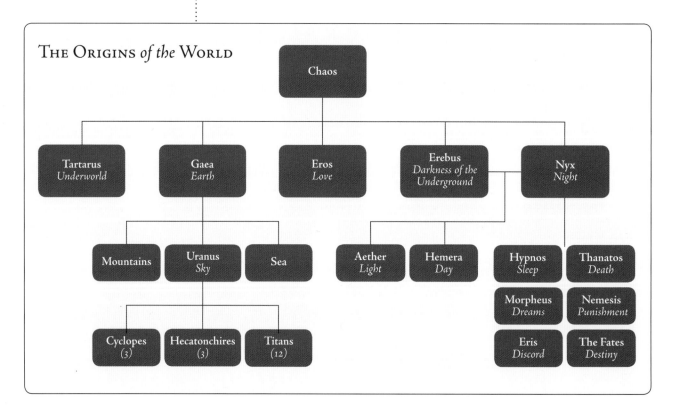

The Origins *of the* World

- Chaos
  - Tartarus *Underworld*
  - Gaea *Earth*
    - Mountains
    - Uranus *Sky*
    - Sea
      - Cyclopes (3)
      - Hecatonchires (3)
      - Titans (12)
  - Eros *Love*
  - Erebus *Darkness of the Underground*
  - Nyx *Night*
    - Aether *Light*
    - Hemera *Day*
    - Hypnos *Sleep*
    - Thanatos *Death*
    - Morpheus *Dreams*
    - Nemesis *Punishment*
    - Eris *Discord*
    - The Fates *Destiny*

THE BATTLE *for* POWER

The Separation of Earth and Sky

Uranus had despised the Hecatonchires and the Cyclopes, and he felt the same fear and contempt toward the twelve Titans. By banishing them to Tartarus, he thought he could remain in power forever. But the furious Gaea asked her children for help, and Cronus, her youngest son, came forward and offered to face his father. When Uranus lay down to sleep that night, Cronus castrated him with a sickle so he could produce no more children with Gaea. Thus the ties between Earth and Sky were permanently severed. Uranus fled from his wife and children in humiliation.

Like Father, Like Son

With Uranus dethroned, Cronus became the new ruler. Like his father, he feared the three Hecatonchires and the three Cyclopes and kept them locked up in Tartarus. The rest of his siblings, however—the other eleven Titans—were freed and began to multiply. Theia and Hyperion, for example, joined to create Helios, the sun; Selene, the moon; and Eos, the dawn. Oceanus and Tethys joined to form a staggering 6,000 children, including 3,000 rivers and 3,000 sea nymphs known as the Oceanids.

The most familiar offspring in all of Greek mythology, however, came from Cronus himself, who joined with his Titan sister Rhea. Cronus did not want any of their offspring to live, however, because he had been warned that he would lose his throne to one of his offspring, just like his own father had. Rather than imprisoning Rhea's children back inside Earth as his own father had, Cronus decided to keep the children himself. Each time Rhea bore a child—once each year for five years—he promptly swallowed it whole.

Distraught over her lost children, Rhea pleaded with her mother, Gaea, who had also suffered at the hands of a tyrannical husband. Gaea agreed to hide Rhea when it was time for her to give birth to her sixth child, a son she named Zeus. To fool her husband, Rhea returned from hiding and promptly handed Cronus a stone swaddled in a blanket. Without even looking, Cronus swallowed it and assumed he had tricked fate again by ingesting his child.

Meanwhile, Zeus was being raised by nymphs in a cave on the island of Crete. As a young god, he returned to free his siblings and help his mother overthrow Cronus. Zeus and Rhea concocted a potion that would make Cronus vomit, and the plan worked: Up came the swaddled rock, followed by Poseidon, Hades, Hera, Hestia, and Demeter, all fully grown. These five Olympians joined their youngest brother, Zeus, and declared war on the Titans. Cronus and the Titans positioned themselves for battle from the top of Mount Othrys, and the Olympians fought from Mount Olympus.

+ Myths from most cultures feature an Earth goddess because women were connected with giving life.

+ "Gaea" is the root for words that begin with **geo-** and relate to Earth or life. Examples include geology (the study of Earth's crust), geography (the study of Earth's surface and continents), and geometry (math dealing with how lines, surfaces, and solids relate to one another).

+ Hecatonchires comes from the Greek *hekaton*, one hundred, and *cheir*, hand. **Chirography** is a fancy name for handwriting (*graphein* means "to write"), and **chiropractors** use their hands to massage and realign a person's joints and spine.

+ Cronus (Roman name Saturn), acted as the god of agriculture. Another Greek god, Chronos, was associated with the passage of time. *Chronos* means "time," which explains **chronic** (long lasting), **chronology** (an arrangement of dates or events based on their occurrence), and **synchronous** (happening at the same time, because *syn-* means "together").

"Seizing it in his hands, he put it away in his belly, the brute, not realizing that thereafter not a stone but his son remained,...who before long was to defeat him by physical strength and drive him from his high station, himself to be king among the immortals."

THEOGONY, PAGE 17

• The word **titan** refers to a strong or powerful person; **titanium** is a strong chemical element; and the infamous ship *Titanic* was so named because, ironically, it was thought to be unsinkable. For more irony, consider that the *Titanic's* sister ship, which did not sink, was called the *Olympic*.

• Hesiod describes how Zeus sent Typhon to Tartarus, where he became the source for violent winds. This would explain a **typhoon**, a tropical storm with high winds.

• Mount Etna is on the island of Sicily—right off the toe in the "boot" of Italy—and is listed as the world's oldest active volcano.

An Epic Battle

Not all of the Titans took part in the mighty battle; some wisely chose to remain neutral as the colossal battle raged on. And one Titan, Prometheus, actually allied himself with the Olympians after getting impatient with his own family members. In fact, it was Prometheus who had the brilliant idea to free the three Hecatonchires and the three Cyclopes who were still imprisoned in Tartarus. Those six monsters, grateful to be released, pledged loyalty to the Olympians and offered invaluable gifts to Cronus' three sons: an invisible helmet for Hades, a powerful trident for Poseidon, and mighty lightning bolts for Zeus. With the strength of these new allies and the power of their gifts, the Olympians were finally able to end the ten-year struggle and defeat the Titans.

All the Titans who had remained neutral or who had allied themselves with the Olympians were free. Those who had fought against Zeus, however, were banished to Tartarus. And Atlas, one of the Olympians' enemies, was given the backbreaking task of holding up the sky so it would not fall and crush Earth.

The Olympians had won, but Gaea was not finished yet. Angry that so many of her children had been sent back to Tartarus, she released two terrifying beasts to attack the Olympians. Echidna, a monstrous snake, had an even more monstrous partner: Typhon. He had one hundred giant heads, venomous eyes, and a mouth that spewed lava. The Olympians took one look at this pair and scattered in fear. Brave Zeus, however, gathered his strength and turned to face Typhon.

Each tried to destroy the other in a mighty battle, and Typhon even tore up Mount Etna in an effort to crush Zeus. But the Olympian hurled one hundred lightning bolts toward the mountain, which fell back and buried Typhon. The gigantic beast was left there to spew fire and smoke from the mountain, while Echidna returned to her cave with her terrifying offspring: the Nemean Lion; the nine-headed Hydra; the two-headed dog, Orthos; the three-headed dog, Cerberus; the tricky Sphinx; and the dragon-like Chimaera. Zeus could have killed Echidna and her children, but he chose to let them live, recognizing that they could be used to challenge future heroes.

The war was over, and the triumphant Olympians took on their roles. Poseidon became ruler of the oceans, Hades descended into the Underworld to rule over the dead, Demeter became the goddess of the harvest, and Hestia became the goddess of hearth and home. The youngest of the Olympians, Zeus, married his sister Hera and became the ruler of the heavens.

+ Many ancients believed mountains had supernatural powers because they reached from the earth to what seemed like heaven, and some erupted with the heat of the Underworld. Temples were often built to imitate a mountain's shape, including the pyramids of the Aztecs, Egyptians, and Mayans.

+ Mount Olympus, located in the northeastern region of mainland Greece, is the highest mountain in the country with an altitude of 9,570 feet.

HESIOD DESCRIBES ZEUS' ATTACK ON THE MONSTROUS TYPHON

"When Zeus had accumulated his strength, then, and taken his weapons, the thunder, lightning, and smoking bolt, he leapt from Olympus and struck, and he scorched all the strange heads of the dreadful monster on every side."

THEOGONY, PAGE 28

Did you know?

Deities from classical mythology are so well known that their names are regularly used in fields as varied as art, geography, medicine, literature, botany, architecture, zoology, psychology, advertising, chemistry, entertainment, and business. In *The Dictionary of Cultural Literacy*, E.D. Hirsch and his colleagues write that mythology has a "vividness and memorableness" that makes it extremely useful. "For purposes of communication and solidarity in a culture, myths are just as important as history."

The images and descriptions here take just one figure —the Titan Atlas—and show how his name is used in a variety of fields.

1. Although Atlas was assigned the task of holding up the sky so it would not crush Earth, most sculptures and paintings show him holding the world on his back.

2. In architecture, an **atlas** (plural atlantes) is a sculpted, decorative figure on the exterior of a building. Such men usually have their heads bent forward and look as though they are straining to hold massive weight on their shoulders, arms, and backs.

3. The topmost vertebra on the spine forms a joint that connects the skull and the spine. It is called the **atlas vertebra** because it holds up the heavy round skull.

4. An **atlas** is a collection of maps and other facts about the world's geography.

5. The Atlas moth is one of the largest in the world, with a wingspan of 10-12 inches. It was given its name either because of its titanic size or for the map-like patterns on its wings.

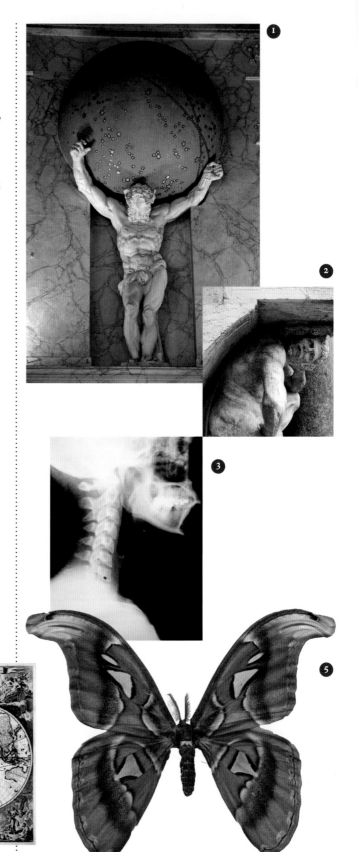

THE CLASSICAL PANTHEON

After they defeated the Titans, the six children of Rhea and Cronus began the new Olympian Age. Although Zeus was the youngest, his siblings owed their freedom to him and wisely named him their leader. Indeed, Zeus proved to be a better leader than his father, Cronus, or his grandfather, Uranus. Rather than insisting on complete power, Zeus set up laws and enforced any oaths sworn by mortals or immortals, but he often remained an impartial mediator.

Zeus was by no means perfect, however, and neither were the other Olympians. The pantheon shared the same emotions as humans did—anger, jealousy, compassion, joy, sorrow, regret—and this created unique relationships among them. Such connections were heightened because the ancients believed their deities looked like humans. And while the gods and goddesses were extremely powerful, they could be appeased with offerings and could also be persuaded to change their minds. All of these human traits meant the Greeks and Romans could relate to their pantheon of gods.

While humans and their gods may have looked alike, there remained one major difference: Humans were mortal, while the gods and goddesses were immortal. Members of the classical pantheon had ichor in their veins, not blood, and this potent liquid allowed them to live forever. And rather than common food and drink, the gods dined on ambrosia and sipped nectar, both of which were too rich for human consumption.

The following section looks at the six deities born to Rhea and Cronus, as well as the next generation of gods and goddesses and other major players in the pantheon. Twelve of these deities came to be known as the Olympians and included Zeus, Hera, Poseidon, Demeter, Apollo, Artemis, Hephaestus, Aphrodite, Ares, Athena, Hermes, and Dionysus. From the rooms of their golden palaces high atop Mount Olympus, these gods and goddesses looked down toward Earth, giving life to mortals, teasing them, forgiving them, punishing them, and even falling in love with them.

✦ A food that tastes or smells wonderful is sometimes called ambrosia, or "the food of the gods." And in science, nectar is the sweet liquid produced by flowering plants or a juice made from pureed fruit.

✦ The etching below shows Zeus wielding lightning bolts to defeat Titan giants.

Zeus (ZOOS)
Leader of the Olympians, god of hospitality
Roman names: Jupiter (JOO pi tur) or Jove (JOHV)
Symbol: thunderbolt, eagle, oak tree

After freeing his brothers and sisters from the tyrannical Cronus, Zeus was named leader of the Olympians. While he was not always benevolent, he generally remained fair. When his own family members argued, for instance, Zeus wisely tried to stay neutral, and he was known for helping immortals and mortals find compromises when disputes arose.

Unfortunately, Zeus may be best remembered for his infidelities. Before marrying his sister Hera, he had relationships with six women who had, in total, over 20 children. With Hera, he had three children, including Ares, the god of war. He then proceeded to father a huge number of illegitimate offspring—some accounts say as many as 80—with other mortal and immortal women.

Zeus was the god the Greeks honored with the ancient Olympic games, first held in 776 BCE. His symbol was a lightning bolt, the gift given to him by the monsters he released from Tartarus. He was also associated with the eagle and the oak tree.

The adjective jovial means playful or fun-loving because according to ancient astrology, people born under the sign of Jupiter—also known as "Jove"—were believed to have these traits. The planet Jupiter, the largest in the solar system, was given Zeus' Roman name.

"Zeus is the first, Zeus is the last, the god with the dazzling lightning. Zeus is the head, Zeus is the middle, of Zeus all things have their end. Zeus is the foundation of the earth and of the starry sky. Zeus is the breath of all things."

—AN ANCIENT ORPHIC HYMN TO ZEUS

Hera *(HEER uh)*
Queen of the Olympians, goddess of marriage
Roman name: Juno (JOO noh)
Symbol: crown, peacock, cow

The beautiful Hera married Zeus in a lavish wedding, and she even received a tree with golden apples from her grandmother, Gaea. But Hera had the most ironic role of all the Olympians. Because she was the goddess of marriage, mortals prayed to her in the hopes of finding a mate. Hera, however, spent most of her time keeping track of her husband and finding ways to get revenge on his often-innocent mistresses and illegitimate children.

Hera's name is the female version of "hero," and she was usually pictured with a peacock. Hera's messenger, Iris, traveled to and from Mount Olympus on a rainbow. And for centuries, it was believed that getting married in June—a month the Romans named to honor the goddess—brought blessings. June still remains a popular month for weddings in many parts of the world.

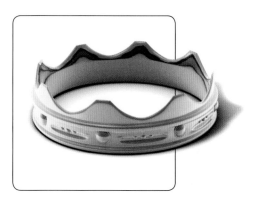

Poseidon *(poh SIE dun)*
God of the sea and of horses
Roman name: Neptune (NEP toon)
Symbol: trident, horses

After helping to defeat the Titans, Poseidon became the ruler of the seas. During the war, he had been given a three-pronged trident, and he used this weapon to stir up storms in the oceans. When angered, he could also strike the ground with it to cause damaging earthquakes.

Poseidon became the god of horses for two reasons. First, it was he who first presented the valuable horse to mankind, and second, the frothy foam on the ocean's waves was referred to as "white horses." Artists often show Poseidon riding over the ocean on the backs of galloping white stallions.

Although married to a sea nymph, Poseidon had many other relationships. And because he could transform into animals, his offspring took on strange characteristics. When he seduced Medusa, for example, he took on the shape of a bird, so one of their children was Pegasus, the winged horse. Other unions resulted in the golden-fleeced ram and the one-eyed Cyclops Polyphemus, who became Odysseus' rival. Poseidon had a palace on Mount Olympus, but he lived in a palace beneath the sea. Neptune, the most distant planet in the solar system, bears Poseidon's Roman name because of its blue color, and the planet is also the source for the name of the chemical element neptunium.

+ The weapon Poseidon carried comes from the Latin *tri-* (three) and *dent* (tooth). These are the same roots found in tricycle and dentist.

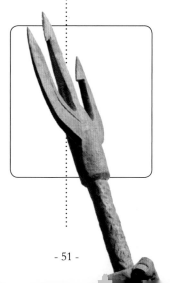

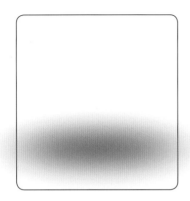

Hades *(HAY deez)*
God of the Underworld
Roman name: Pluto (PLOO toh)
Symbol: helmet of invisibility

Hades helped defeat the Titans by wearing his invisible helmet, shown—or rather *not* shown—above, and his name in Greek meant "unseen." He is not considered an Olympian, however, because he did not live on Olympus. In fact, he spent so much time underground, many referred to the Underworld simply as "Hades."

The Romans connected Pluto with wealth because he was surrounded by the gems buried deep underground. And the powerful chemical plutonium, also harnessed from underground, was given Hades' Roman name.

The god of the Underworld was not portrayed as bloodthirsty in myths; he just had the unpleasant task of lording over the dead. Humans did not like saying his name, however, for fear he might take notice of them.

Hades had two assistants: Charon was the ferryman who rowed the dead across the River Styx to the entrance of the Underworld, and Cerberus, a three-headed dog with the tail of a dragon, stood guard. Cerberus may have been friendly to those who came to Hades, but he turned vicious if anyone tried to leave.

Human souls, depending on their virtue, were sent to one of several places in the Underworld. Tartarus was where souls of the damned were sent for eternal punishments, while heroic mortals were delivered to the Elysian Fields and made immortal by the gods. The rest of the souls were sent to a neutral section of the Underworld where there was neither torture nor bliss.

Demeter *(de MEE tur)*
Goddess of the harvest
Roman name: Ceres (SEE reez)
Symbol: stalk of wheat

Demeter had the powerful role of determining the success of crops, and she could will fruits to ripen, grain to flourish, and flowers to bloom. She was portrayed carrying a sheaf of wheat, and mortals built numerous temples and held elaborate feasts to honor her.

Demeter had one daughter, Persephone, by Zeus. While Demeter is usually portrayed as a gentle and generous goddess, she became so enraged when Hades kidnapped Persephone that she refused to let anything grow on Earth. She punished mortals with famine for a full year until a compromise was reached, and then she celebrated her daughter's return with the seasons of spring and summer.

Demeter's Roman name, Ceres, is the root for the word **cereal**, a food that is made of grains such as rice, wheat, or corn.

Hestia *(HES tee uh)*
Goddess of the hearth and home
Roman name: Vesta (VEST uh)
Symbol: hearth

The goddess Hestia was rarely mentioned in mythology, but every household in ancient Greece built a temple to honor her: a hearth. In fact, the Greek word *hestia* means "hearth." Hestia protected the all-important flame within the home and watched over families. The oldest of the Olympians, Hestia was also the quietest and most reserved. While several immortals pursued her, she refused their advances and resolved to remain unmarried.

In fact, a Vestal Virgin—a term taken from Hestia's Roman name—was a high priestess in ancient Rome and took vows to remain chaste and unmarried. A Virgin, shown in the etching on the right, was responsible for tending the eternal sacred fire for Vesta and was highly respected. In fact, being a Vestal Virgin was the only privileged role for women in the Roman religious system.

Hestia never drew attention to herself and recoiled from competition and violence. In fact, she so disliked the unpredictable activity on Mount Olympus that she eventually left. Dionysus, one of Zeus' sons, took her place and is considered the twelfth Olympian.

The gods were "so close to human life and so involved with individual human beings, in affection or in anger, that they intervened in their lives and even appeared to them in person."

—BERNARD KNOX
IN HIS INTRODUCTION
TO ROBERT FAGLES'
TRANSLATION
OF HOMER'S *ODYSSEY*

Apollo (uh PAWL oh)
God of light, prophecy, and the arts
Roman name: Apollo or Phoebus Apollo
Symbol: lyre, sun, laurel tree, dolphins

Apollo was considered such an ideal god that the Romans, who changed all the other Olympians' names when they absorbed Greek mythology into their culture, left his name alone. They did often refer to him as Phoebus Apollo, however, which literally means "the radiant one."

Born to Zeus and the Titan Leto, Apollo was associated with the sun while his twin sister, Artemis, represented the moon. Apollo was known for his prophecies, and the oracle at Delphi, the city to which people traveled to hear their fates, came to be sacred to Apollo. He took the form of a dolphin (*delphis* in Greek) to lead Cretan sailors there to be priests in his temple. The Greeks considered this temple the center of the world, and it was said that inside the temple was the actual rock that Rhea had swaddled and given to Cronus to make him think she was handing over her son Zeus.

Apollo was often shown wearing a crown of laurel and holding a lyre, a hand-held harp. He was associated with the arts and rational thinking, and therefore represented moderation and embodied the Greek idea of a Golden Mean. In mathematical terms, a mean is an average, so Apollo represented a perfect balance.

Artemis (AR te miss)
Goddess of the hunt
Roman name: Diana (die AN uh)
Symbol: moon, silver bow and arrows

While Apollo was associated with many arts and sciences, his twin sister, Artemis, excelled in one thing: hunting. In fact, Artemis was so focused on her skills that she had little time for anything else. The only man she ever had feelings for was the hunter Orion, but Artemis' protective twin brother sent a scorpion to sting him. Artemis placed Orion's body in the sky to honor him (and Apollo placed the scorpion constellation on the opposite side so it would always chase Orion around the heavens).

Artemis remained fiercely independent, and women who wanted to remain unmarried prayed to Artemis for guidance. Because she often hunted at dusk, Artemis was associated with the moon. Portrayed as tall and athletic, she carried a powerful silver bow and arrow.

Hephaestus *(he FAY stus)*
Blacksmith to the gods
Roman name: Vulcan (VUL ken)
Symbol: hammer, anvil

The story of Hephaestus lacks heroic glory, and his early childhood was quite sad. In the most common version of his tale, Hera, upset by her husband's many infidelities, was determined to have a child by herself. Unfortunately, her son Hephaestus was born lame, so she threw him from Mount Olympus. When he grew up to be a master blacksmith, he presented his mother with an extraordinary golden throne. She assumed he was trying to win her over, but she underestimated his anger: The throne trapped Hera when she sat down.

After the other Olympians pleaded with Hephaestus, he freed his mother and was recognized for his incredible talent. Referred to by Homer as the "god of the dragging footsteps," Hephaestus overcame disabilities and built glorious palaces for each of the Olympians. He also crafted impressive shields, swords, and helmets for heroes, and hammered out Zeus' lightning bolts.

Hephaestus' Roman name, Vulcan, is related to fiery volcanoes, and vulcanizing is a scientific process in which a material like rubber is combined with additives and heated under great pressure to make it more durable. Hephaestus was married to Aphrodite, but their union was not a happy one.

Aphrodite *(af roh DIE tee)*
Goddess of love and beauty
Roman name: Venus (VEE nus)
Symbol: dove, roses

The goddess of love rode in a chariot drawn by doves and could make flowers bloom at will. She and Eros, her son and the god of love, were quite a team, making mortals and immortals fall passionately for one another.

Unfortunately, these two could also break hearts when they used their powers to play tricks. And because Aphrodite was so attractive and attracted to others, she was unfaithful and caused her husband, Hephaestus, terrible pain. She even had a long-standing relationship with Ares, the aggressive god of war.

The clever Hephaestus once fashioned a fine metallic net and suspended it over his and Aphrodite's bed. When the net trapped Aphrodite and Ares together, Hephaestus called to Zeus and the other Olympians, who all delighted in seeing the arrogant Ares caught in such an embarrassing situation.

While some myths say Aphrodite was the daughter of Zeus, others say she was created from the sea's foam. The planet Venus, which is the brightest in the solar system, was given Aphrodite's Roman name.

Ares *(AIR eez)*
God of war
Roman name: Mars (MARZ)
Symbol: helmet, spear

A son of Zeus and Hera, Ares was the god of war. Because the Greeks focused so much on philosophy, art, science, and other advancements, they did not revere the belligerent, bloodthirsty Ares. In fact, Ares was so argumentative and unpredictable that most of the Olympians did not care for him either, with one major exception: Aphrodite loved him, and they carried on a long romance.

Ares' sons were named Phobos (fear) and Deimos (dread), and Ares' bird was the gloomy and flesh-eating vulture. When the Romans adopted the Greek pantheon, they revered Ares because they were much more focused on the strength of their military than the Greeks had been. Ares' Roman name was Mars, and the name lends itself to the blood-red planet and to the month of March, which was originally the first month of the year.

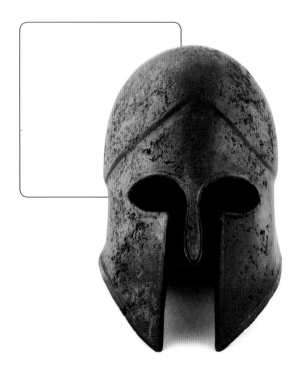

Athena *(uh THEE nuh)*
Goddess of wisdom and war
Roman name: Minerva (mi NUR vuh)
Symbol: owl, aegis, olive tree

While there were many unusual births in the Greek pantheon, Athena's was perhaps the most bizarre. Zeus' first wife was the wise and cunning Titan Metis. When Metis became pregnant, Zeus swallowed her whole, fearing that he, like his own father and grandfather, would be overthrown by a son. Zeus was struck by a horrible headache, however, and the pain became so unbearable that he begged for relief. Hephaestus came forward and split open Zeus' skull with his axe. To everyone's surprise, what emerged from his head was a daughter, Athena, fully grown and dressed in armor.

Instead of being a threat to Zeus, Athena became his favorite child, and Metis continued to give valuable guidance to Zeus from inside his head.

Images of Athena show her in full armor, and her shield, or aegis (EE jis), has an image of the snake-haired Medusa, a gift from the hero Perseus. But while Athena was a skilled warrior and strategist, she did not revel in war like her half-brother Ares. In fact, Athena was much more likely to search for a peaceful way to resolve conflict. She was associated with the olive tree, the symbol for peace, and was often shown with an owl, an animal that has come to represent wisdom.

The Classical Pantheon
The Second Generation of Olympians

Hermes (HUR meez)
Messenger to the gods; god of travelers and thieves
Roman name: Mercury (MUR kyur ee)
Symbol: caduceus, winged helmet and sandals

Hermes was primarily a messenger for the gods. Because he was so tricky and adventurous, however, he also became the patron of travelers and thieves. The adjective mercurial means "shrewd, changeable, or fickle"—all based on the quirky and dynamic Hermes, whose Roman name was Mercury.

One of the many sons of Zeus, Hermes was a precocious child. In fact, he invented sandals, the lyre, and the reed pipe mere hours after his birth. He even stole sacred cattle from his half-brother Apollo. It did not take long, though, for the brothers to become friends. Apollo allowed Hermes to keep the herd in return for the beautiful lyre, and Hermes offered the panpipes in exchange for Apollo's snake-entwined golden staff, the caduceus. This staff has since become a widely used symbol for healing because the two snakes represent immortality, and they face each other in peace.

Hermes wore a smooth, round helmet and winged sandals, which made him a speedy messenger. Such speed is associated with the element mercury, also known as quicksilver. In addition, Mercury is the name of the planet that revolves most quickly around the sun.

Did you know?

+ A mural inside the dome of the Capitol Building in Washington, D.C., features scenes from classical mythology. Called the *Apotheosis of Washington*, the painting shows a deified George Washington surrounded by thirteen maidens, one for each of the original colonies. Around the perimeter are figures who represent the nation's strengths, including Minerva (science), Neptune (maritime power), Mercury (commerce), Vulcan (mechanics), and Ceres (agriculture).

+ **Iris**, Hera's messenger who traveled on rainbows, is the name of a colorful flower and the colored part of the eye. **Iridium** is a chemical element named for Iris because it produces colored salts, and **iridescent** means "shimmering with color."

+ The word **martial**, Latin for "of Mars," means "warlike or aggressive," and **martial arts** are forms of combat, like karate, now practiced as sport or self-defense.

+ A statue of Mercury, shown at the left, stands on top of Grand Central Station in New York City. Unveiled in 1914, the piece was designed as a symbol to protect travelers who were entering or leaving the city by train. Mercury is flanked by statues of Hercules and Minerva.

+ The caduceus can be seen on ambulances, in hospitals, and in pharmacies. Sometimes just a single snake is entwined around the staff, a symbol associated with Asclepius, a famed ancient Greek healer.

+ The United States Mint produced a dime in 1916 just as America was entering World War I. The face side featured a profile of the Roman goddess Liberty wearing a winged helmet. So many people thought the image was of Mercury that the dimes were called "Mercury dimes."

Eros *(AIR os)*
God of love
Roman name: Cupid (KEW pid)
Symbol: arrows

The name Eros has appeared once already because Eros was one of the first things created from Chaos. The original Eros represented the idea of love, but the second Eros was recognized as the god of love.

Eros may have been born from Chaos and adopted by Aphrodite, or he could have been Aphrodite's child from Ares, Zeus, or Hephaestus. While many myths feature Eros as a handsome young man, his more universal image is as a chubby baby with wings, and he is known better by his Roman name, Cupid.

Eros featured prominently in many myths and represented the wide range of emotions associated with love, including lust, forgiveness, jealousy, compassion, and heartbreak. Eros carried with him a quiver full of arrows and shot people with them as he pleased or as he was commanded to do by other immortals. Many artists depict Eros with a cloth over his eyes to emphasize the fact that love is often blind.

Although the goddess Aphrodite was extremely jealous of the beautiful mortal Psyche, the girl showed so much devotion to Eros—and he loved her so deeply in return—that they were married with the blessings of all the Olympians.

Pan *(PAN)*
God of the forest
Roman name: Faunus (FAW nus)
Symbol: panpipes

A goat from the waist down and a man from the waist up, Pan was a god of the forest and fields. He is often pictured holding a musical instrument made of hollow reeds, commonly called the panpipes. He chased after woodland nymphs and loved to create trouble. In fact, the word panic in Greek means "of Pan" and refers to the fear and upheaval Pan caused when he frightened people in the woods.

Dionysus *(die oh NEE sus)*
God of wine and drama
Roman name: Bacchus (BAK us)
Symbol: grapes and vine leaves, wild animals

While Apollo represented moderation, Dionysus stood for excess and indulgence. From his bizarre birth to the mysterious rituals performed by his followers, Dionysus led an anything-but-moderate life.

Dionysus' mortal mother, Semele, became pregnant by Zeus. When Hera learned this, she persuaded Semele to ask to see Zeus in full armor. Zeus had sworn on the River Styx to fulfill any wish Semele made, but he knew his armor was too bright for mortals to withstand. Although Zeus begged her to reconsider, Semele insisted and was burned to ashes when Zeus appeared.

Before Semele died, Zeus pulled the unborn child from her womb and implanted it in his own thigh. Several months later, Dionysus was born from Zeus' leg, and Zeus asked water nymphs to raise Dionysus.

When Hestia eventually became weary of life on Mount Olympus, her nephew Dionysus took her place as an Olympian. Dionysus often sought the company of mortals, however, and taught them how to make wine and led them in wild celebrations. He and his companions, called the maenads ("mad women") or, in Roman times, Bacchae, would drive others to frantic actions. And while rituals to honor other gods involved the careful preparation of meat, Dionysus' followers ate flesh raw.

Over time, the wild celebrations to honor Dionysus became more cultured, evolving into presentations that were the earliest forms of theater. Thus, Dionysus was not only the god of wine but also the god of drama.

Persephone *(pur SEF uh nee)*
Daughter of Demeter
Roman name: Proserpine (pro SUR pi nuh)
Symbol: sheaf of wheat, flowers

Persephone, the daughter of Demeter and Zeus, adored her mother. She always helped Demeter in her role as goddess of the harvest and loved everything in nature. Unfortunately, Persephone was abducted by her uncle Hades and ate several seeds from a pomegranate while in the Underworld. Because she ate food from the land of the dead, she should have remained there. But under Zeus' ruling, Persephone spent part of each year as Hades' queen and the rest on the earth with Demeter. Persephone was sometimes called Kore.

Did you know?

+ Swearing on the River Styx—one of the rivers in Hades—was called a **Stygian oath** and was absolutely unbreakable.

+ Eros' sharp, gold-tipped arrows caused a person to fall madly in love, while his blunt, lead-tipped arrows made people flee from love.

+ Peter Pan, a character created by Scottish writer J.M. Barrie, shares his name and many of his qualities with the Greek Pan. They are both bold and mischievous and are often pictured playing panpipes.

The Muses (*MYOO zez*)
Nine women who represented the arts

Mnemosyne (nee *MOZ i nee*), the Titan goddess of memory, bore nine daughters to Zeus. The girls, known collectively as the Muses, each represented a field in the arts or sciences. As daughters of the goddess of memory, these women personified the revered oral tradition, and epic poets like Homer and Virgil began their works by invoking the blessings of the Muses. To this day, if writers or artists have no inspiration and are not producing good work, they complain they have "lost their muse."

Mnemosyne's name is associated with memory. A mnemonic device, for example—pronounced "nee MON ik"—is a tool used to aid one's memory. And amnesia is a medical condition that results in a loss of memory (the prefix *a-* means "not" and the base *mna-* means "to think or be alert").

◆ Erato, Muse of love and poetry, playing a lyre.

Calliope (kuh LIE oh pee)
Muse of eloquence and epic poetry. Her name means "beautifully voiced." Old-fashioned merry-go-rounds often feature a calliope, a type of organ that plays bright and pretty melodies.

Clio (KLEE oh)
Muse of history. Clio's name comes from Greek words meaning "celebration and glory."

Erato (AIR uh toh)
Muse of love poetry and marriage songs. Erato derives from Eros, the love that formed from Chaos.

Euterpe (yoo TUR pee)
Muse of music and lyric poetry. Her name means "to delight." Lyric poetry got its name because it was usually sung to music from a lyre.

Melpomene (mel POM i nee)
Muse of tragedy, often shown holding a tragedy mask. Her name derives from the Greek "to sing."

Polyhymnia (pol ee HIM nee uh)
Muse of sacred music, whose name comes from poly ("many") and hymnos ("song"). Songs that are sung in praise or glorification are called hymns.

Terpsichore (turp SIK ur ee)
Muse of dance. Her name comes from terpein ("to delight") and chorus ("dance"). The word chorus once referred to actors who narrated a story through song or dance. Now it commonly refers to a group of people singing together.

Thalia (THA lee uh)
Muse of comedy. Her name means "flourishing."

Urania (yoo RAY nee uh)
Muse of astronomy. This Muse's name comes from Uranus, the personification of the sky who joined with Gaea, the Earth.

Helios *(HEE lee ohs)*
The sun god
Roman name: Sol (SOL)

One of the best known of the lesser gods, Helios had the important task of wearing the sun as a crown and driving a chariot across the sky each day from east to west. Helios then sailed around the perimeter of the world at night so he could begin his journey again.

His Greek name is the basis for the lightweight gas helium, as well as a genus of plants known as *Helianthus*, commonly known as sunflowers. The buds of sunflowers exhibit "heliotropism," which means they move to face the sun as it crosses the sky from east to west. Helios' Roman name is the basis for solar, meaning "of the sun," and is used in words such as solar system, solar panel, and solar eclipse.

Selene *(se LEE nee)*
The moon goddess
Roman name: Luna (LOO nuh)

The sister of the sun god Helios, Selene was the goddess of the Moon, and her name is actually Greek for moon. Just after her brother touched down in his sun chariot, Selene would rise, carrying the light of the moon into the night sky. Her Roman name is the basis for lunar, which means "of the moon," and is used when referring to lunar phases, lunar modules, and lunar eclipses.

Did you know?

+ The word Muse is the origin of both **music** (the Muses were responsible for this art form) and **museum** (a place that teaches visitors about history, music, and astronomy).

+ The ancient Greek female poet Sappho said, "It is the Muses who have caused me to be honor'd: they taught me their craft."

+ If someone has heliophobia, she fears the sun. The term comes from Helios (the sun god) and Phobos (Ares' son, whose name means "fear").

+ It was once believed that the moon's phases affected people's moods, thus spurring the lore of humans turning into werewolves on the night of a full moon. And the term **lunatic**—used to refer to someone who acts crazy—originated because people believed the moon could drive a person insane.

+ A lunar eclipse occurs when Earth passes between the sun and the moon, casting a moving shadow against the moon. A solar eclipse occurs when the moon passes in front of the sun and darkens the daytime sky, a frightening phenomenon for ancient cultures. In China, people used to make great noise to scare away the sky dragon they thought was trying to eat the sun.

+ In addition to the chemical elements mentioned in this section, many others are named for mythological figures, including Cerium (Ceres), Prometheum (Prometheus), Uranium (Uranus), and Selenium (Selene).

The Offspring of Nyx (NIKS)

While Nyx, the goddess of night, and her daughter Hemera (HEE mur uh), the goddess of day, shared the same house, they were never there at the same time. In addition to Hemera, Nyx produced unpleasant offspring, including the Three Fates, Eris, Nemesis, Thanatos, Hypnos, and Morpheus.

The Three Fates (FAYTS)
Women who controlled life; also called Moirai (MOY rie)

The Fates were responsible for determining the length of a human life. Clotho spun the thread of life on a wheel, Lachesis measured its length, and Atropos cut the thread with her shears, thus ending a life. Even the most powerful god, Zeus, could not change the course of a person's life once the Fates had made their decision.

The saying "hanging on by a thread" may have originated because someone in a precarious situation was thought to be in the hands of the Fates. And the three witches who appear in the first scene of Shakespeare's *Macbeth* recall the Fates.

Eris (AIR iss), *goddess of discord*
Roman name: *Discordia (dis KOR dee uh)*

The vengeful Eris took pleasure in causing strife. It was Eris who inscribed a golden apple with the words "For the Fairest" and rolled it into the middle of an Olympian party. When three goddesses claimed it was meant for them, their feud set the stage for the bloody Trojan War. The word discord derives from Eris' Roman name and means "a lack of harmony or agreement."

Nemesis (NEM uh siss), *goddess of retribution*

Nemesis was responsible for doling out rewards and punishments. Her name derives from a Greek word meaning "to distribute," and the term nemesis has come to mean "a sworn enemy." The villain Lex Luthor, for example, is Superman's nemesis because he is jealous of the superhero and constantly tries to destroy him.

⬩ The Fates cutting the thread of life.

Thanatos (THAN uh tos), sometimes *Mors (MORZ)*
Personification of death

Thanatos was sent to claim the souls of the dead, similar to the fabled Grim Reaper. Thanatophobia is an unusually strong fear of death, and euthanasia is the controversial act of inducing death to end someone's suffering. It comes from the Greek *eu-* (well) and *thanatos* (death).

Hypnos (HIP noss), *god of sleep*
Roman name: *Somnus (SOM noos)*

Hypnos was the personification of sleep. His Greek name forms the basis of the sleep-like trance known as hypnosis, and his Roman name is the root for somnolent, which means "sleepy." In fact, several medicines that induce sleep have the word "som" in their names, and they are meant to cure insomnia (*-in* negates the root word).

Morpheus (MOR fee us), *god of dreams*

The brother of Hypnos, or sometimes his son, this god's name comes from the Greek *morphe* (form or shape). Morpheus could assume the shape of any human and appear in dreams. Metamorphosis is a complete change (*meta* means "over"), and morphine is a drug that can relieve pain and induce dreams.

THE CLASSICAL PANTHEON
Well-Known Mortals and Immortals

Adonis was a handsome youth loved by both Aphrodite and Persephone. He was killed by the jealous Ares, who took the form of a wild boar. As he died, each drop of his blood turned into a bright red anemone flower. People now use the name Adonis to refer to an extremely handsome man.

Aurora was the Roman goddess of the dawn. The Greeks called her Eos. The amazing bands of light that appear in the skies of the northern hemisphere are called the aurora borealis, a name that combines Aurora's lights and the movement of Boreas, the Greek god of the north winds.

Fortuna was the Roman goddess of fortune and chance. Her symbol was a wheel, which she spun at random and came to represent the unpredictable nature of life. The Wheel of Fortune has been used as an allegory ever since, and contestants on the modern game show *Wheel of Fortune* win or lose depending on the results of their spin. Fortuna, whose Greek name was Tyche, is also the likely origin of the concept of Lady Luck.

A *genius* in Roman mythology was a guiding spirit assigned to each man, while a *juno* was a woman's spiritual guide. A genius and a juno granted energy, joy, and intelligence, and Romans even offered their guides gifts on their birthdays. The word genius now refers to someone with extraordinary abilities and is associated with the Arabian mythological creature, the *jinn*, spelled "genie" in English.

The Furies were three sisters representing the conscience, and they punished sinners until the guilty person felt remorse. The Latin *furere* means "to rage" and is the root for furious (violently angry), furor (rage), and infuriate (to aggravate or make angry). The Furies, known as the Erinyes in Greece, were Allecto (Endless), Tisiphone (Punishment), and Megaera (Rage).

The Graces were three sisters who were daughters of Zeus. Aglaia (Brilliance), Euphrosyne (Joy), and Thalia (Bloom) were responsible for the pleasures and beauties of nature and life. Their name derives from the Latin *gratus* (pleasing), which is the root for words like gracious, graceful, grateful, gratifying, and congratulate. The Greeks called the sisters Charites (KAR i teez) from *charis* (kindness and beauty). Charis is the root of charisma, a word used to describe a joyful quality.

Centaurs were creatures with the body and legs of a horse and the torso, arms, and head of a man. Centaurs appear in other mythologies and are seen in modern stories and movies such as *The Lord of the Rings, The Lion, the Witch, and the Wardrobe,* and the *Harry Potter* series. Alpha Centauri is the brightest star in the Centaurus constellation and, after the sun, is the closest star to Earth.

Amazons were mythological women warriors, although there may have been some historical basis to their existence. The women mated only to produce offspring and then reared only the females. A strong or aggressive woman can be called an amazon, and Wonder Woman, a character from DC Comics, was named Diana (after the independent Roman goddess of the hunt) and was said to have been trained by the Amazons.

• It is said Amazon women fought valiantly in the Trojan War.

PLANETS, DAYS, *and* MONTHS

Archaeological evidence proves that every ancient culture showed some interest in understanding the heavens, a constant source of wonder. Tracking the movements of the stars and the phases of the moon, making connections between the position of the stars and the seasons, linking the movement of the sun with a time of day, coming to terms with the strange and often destructive forces of nature—these issues were fascinating, but they were also matters of life and death.

Ancient cultures put forth great effort to understand all of this complex information, especially using the apparent movement of the sun, moon, and planets to mark the passage of time. Developing a reliable calendar was an ongoing process of uncovering new data and trying new and improved approaches. While all cultures understood something about the heavenly bodies, it was the Greeks who established the most meaningful scientific foundation for our modern study of astronomy, and it was the Romans who put the finishing touches on the calendar system currently used in much of the world. And throughout the Western world, it is the classical pantheon, plus a handful of Norse deities and Roman leaders, that inspired the names for the planets, the months, and the days of the week.

Planets

The word planet comes from a Greek word meaning "wanderer," which refers to how these special heavenly bodies moved through the universe. In the case of Earth's solar system, eight known planets orbit around a central sun. Each of the planets has two different types of movement: Rotation refers to the way in which a planet spins like a top, while revolution refers to how a planet orbits around the sun. A planet's rotation equals one day on the planet, while its revolution corresponds to one of its years.

The four planets closest to the sun—Mercury, Venus, Earth, and Mars—are relatively small and rocky. They are therefore called the terrestrial planets, from the Latin *terra*, meaning "earth." The next four planets—Jupiter, Saturn, Uranus, and Neptune—are significantly larger than terrestrial planets and are comprised mostly of gas. They are called the Jovian planets because Jupiter, the most powerful god, was also known as "Jove."

Since the beginning of recorded history, humans have observed the planets now known as Mercury, Venus, Mars, Jupiter, and Saturn, along with the sun and moon. These seven heavenly bodies, which could be seen with the naked eye, inspired many myths and are the basis of the seven days of the week. The last two planets were discovered thousands of years later, only after the invention of the telescope. Uranus was first recognized in 1781 and Neptune in 1846. In keeping with the established solar system, these planets were given names from classical mythology.

FIRST MAN ON THE MOON · UNITED STATES

• NASA—the National Aeronautics and Space Administration—used the name *Apollo* for its ambitious moon program in the 1960s. *Apollo 11* was the spacecraft that landed on the moon on July 20, 1969 and allowed Neil Armstrong to walk on its surface. Historian William E. Burrows referred to the *Apollo* missions as the "greatest human adventure; the *Odyssey* of the millennium."

• A **terra cotta** pot is made from baked clay, an **extraterrestrial** is a creature from a planet other than Earth, and the **Mediterranean Sea** is a body of water in the middle (*medi-*) of the continents of Africa, Europe, and Asia.

> "In ancient societies, indeed in all pre-industrial societies, real darkness still filled much of men's lives, and the farmer, priest or seafarer was familiar with the star-patterns as the fundamental gauges of time and direction."

PETER WHITFIELD, *THE MAPPING OF THE HEAVENS*

The Sun

The sun has a prominent role in most of the world's mythologies because even ancient man knew of its importance to life. In classical myths, Apollo was associated with the sun and was the god of enlightenment. Louis XIV of France proclaimed himself the Sun King, and in several paintings, he is even portrayed as Apollo. The sun's astronomical symbol is likely derived from Egyptian hieroglyphics, but similar symbols have been found in other ancient civilizations.

The sun

Mercury

Mercury is the smallest planet and is closest to the sun, orbiting it in just 88 days. Because of its speed, it was named after Mercury, the swift Roman messenger god. Although no space probe has ever landed on Mercury, satellite pictures show it has a rocky surface much like Earth's moon. Mercury's astronomical symbol combines the god's winged helmet and his caduceus.

Mercury

Venus

The second planet from the sun, also called the Morning Star, shines very brightly and was named after Venus, the Roman goddess of love and beauty. Two of the continents on Venus also have female mythological names: Ishtar Terra ("land") was named for the Babylonian goddess of love, and Aphrodite Terra derives from Venus' Greek name.

Venus' surface was mapped in detail by the *Magellan* spacecraft. Although the planet may look beautiful from afar, it is covered with volcanoes and has a poisonous atmosphere. Venus' astronomical symbol represents a woman's hand mirror, and the symbol has come to indicate "female" in biology.

Venus

Earth

Earth is the only planet whose name is not connected to classical mythology. It does, however, derive from the Greek name for the planet: *era*. The astronomical symbol for Earth, a cross enclosed in a circle, represents the four points on a compass.

Earth

Mars

Jupiter

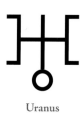

Saturn

Uranus

Mars

Because more than half of the planet Mars is covered with a reddish brown mineral, it appears red in the sky. Ancient humans associated this color with blood and war, and so the planet was named after the Roman god of war, Mars. The two moons that orbit Mars are named Phobos and Deimos, offspring of Mars and Venus who represented fear and dread. And a Martian is a fictional creature that supposedly comes from the planet Mars. The astronomical symbol for Mars represents the god of war's shield and spear. While Venus' symbol has come to represent "female" in biology, Mars' symbol means "male."

Jupiter

The largest planet is named for the greatest of the Roman gods. Jupiter is so large that 1,300 Earths could fit inside it. The planet has 16 moons, and the four largest are named for female companions of Jupiter: Io, Ganymede, Callisto, and Europa. The astronomical symbol for the largest planet is based on the Greek zeta, the first letter of Jupiter's Greek name, Zeus.

Saturn

Saturn was the Roman name for Cronus, who swallowed his first five children in an attempt to preserve his power. His youngest son, Zeus (Jupiter), was raised in secret and grew up to overthrow his father, so it is fitting for Jupiter to be larger than Saturn. A series of wide rings surrounds Saturn, and the planet has 18 moons named for characters from classical mythology, including Janus, Pan, Atlas, Prometheus, Epimetheus, Pandora, Rhea, and Titan.

Saturn, the god associated with the Greek Cronus, represented the harvest. The astronomical symbol for Saturn, therefore, is the sickle, or scythe, a tool used to cut stalks at harvest time.

Uranus

This planet was first seen by the German-born British astronomer Wilhelm Herschel in 1781. He wanted to name his discovery after King George III of England, but fellow astronomers thought it was inappropriate to name a planet to honor one country's ruler. Rather than calling it "George's Star," therefore, a name was chosen from among the classical pantheon in keeping with the other planets. The Greek sky god, Uranus, was eventually overthrown by Saturn, so it is fitting that Uranus is smaller than Saturn. Uranus is the only planet to use a Greek deity's name rather than a Roman deity's name.

Uranus' astronomical symbol, a modified "H," honors its British discoverer, Herschel, and the planet's moons are all named for characters created by the English playwright William Shakespeare and poet Alexander Pope. Some of the moons include Juliet, Puck, Ophelia, Ariel, Titania, Oberon, and Belinda.

Neptune

Neptune, discovered in 1846 by both French and British astronomers, is known as the "blue planet" and was named for the Roman god of the sea. Neptune was said to have used his trident to stir up storms at sea, and the winds on the planet are now believed to reach up to 1,500 miles an hour. The 13 known moons of Neptune are all named for classical mythological characters related to water or the sea, and this planet's astronomical symbol is a clear representation of the sea god's trident.

The Moon

Earth has a single moon that is approximately 240,000 miles away. The length of time from one new moon to the next is just over 29 days, and it is this period that inspired the use of a month to divide the year into parts; the words month and moon share the same etymology because their root means "to measure." Just like the symbol for the sun, the crescent-shaped moon symbol was seen in hieroglyphics and other ancient cultures.

Neptune

The moon

A Note *about* Pluto

Pluto, first discovered in 1930, was recognized as the ninth planet from the sun and was given the Roman name for the cold and distant Hades. In 2006, however, Pluto was renamed a "dwarf planet." How did a planet manage to get a demotion?

In April of 2006, the incredibly powerful Hubble Space Telescope measured the size of an object far beyond Pluto and showed it was actually larger than the ninth planet. Because improved telescopes would likely locate numerous other objects larger than Pluto, the International Astronomical Union (IAU) met to redefine the word "planet." The first two criteria were that a planet must have sufficient gravity to form a round shape and that it must orbit the sun. Pluto and three other objects that had been recently located met those two rules. So for several months, the IAU considered increasing the number of planets to twelve.

To limit years of potential change and confusion, however, the IAU chose to add a third condition: A planet must be large enough to be in charge of its own orbit. And because Pluto's small size allows it to be affected by Neptune's gravitational pull, it has been redefined in astronomical terms.

Pluto and its former moon, Charon (named for the ferryman pictured on the right), is obviously still considereed a significant find, but it is now referred to as a dwarf planet, along with two others called Ceres and Eris.

- Celestial maps, like this one from 1843, were first drawn during the Renaissance. While they were used by scientists, they were also celebrated as an art form, and many beautiful maps continued to be drawn into the 1900s.

- The International Astronomical Union recognizes 88 constellations. Leo the Lion, one of the zodiac constellations, is pictured here, and several other constellations are mentioned in *Panorama* in the myths of Phaethon, Perseus, Heracles, and the *Iliad*.

- Magnitude contains the Latin root *magnus* (great). Other words with this root include magnificent, magnify, and **magnanimous**, which means "noble-minded or generous," (*animus* means "mind or soul").

- The word constellation derives from the Latin *com-* (with) and *stella* (star).

- Claudius Ptolemaeus, known as Ptolemy (TALL uh mee), also explored and wrote about mathematics, geography, astrology, and the properties of light.

The Constellations

Modern people may think they see a dark sky at night. But because of artificial light "pollution," many never experience the rich blue-black of a truly dark sky, pricked by the white of a thousand stars. To the Greeks and other ancients, these deep night skies were a constant source of mystery and fascination.

The Mesopotamians were likely the first to chart the position of the stars, but ancient cultures all over the world studied the skies in an attempt to understand the world. Many ancient landmarks, including England's Stonehenge, Egypt's pyramids, and the statues of large heads found on Easter Island in the South Pacific, are thought to have been built to correspond with the movement of heavenly bodies.

Early civilizations actually had more precise maps of the sky than they had of the world. One rather obvious reason for this is because humans could study the stars simply by looking up, whereas no one had ever viewed Earth from above. Second, stars were thought to be an equal distance from Earth, so while star maps were flat, geographical maps were complicated by mountains, valleys, and bodies of water.

The Greek Hipparchus laid a foundation for the science of astronomy when he refined a tool called an astrolabe to measure the location of objects in the sky and then compiled an exhaustive star catalogue. He also developed a way to assign numbers to stars based on their brightness, or magnitude, a system astronomers have modified and still use today.

Astronomers from many ancient cultures also made sense out of the innumerable stars by grouping them—"connecting their dots"—into some recognizable image. Some of the best known of these constellations originated in ancient Babylonia, where astronomers noted a band of stars that appeared to pass around Earth. The Greeks later named these twelve star groups the zodiac ("circle of animals").

One of the most important ancient contributions to astronomy, however, was made by the Greek Ptolemy in the second century BCE, when he created his comprehensive *Almagest*. This treatise described the motion of the stars and planets, and included a detailed list of 48 constellations, all associated with Greek mythology. The International Astronomical Union still recognizes 47 of Ptolemy's original constellations, as well as 41 additional star groupings, many of which are only visible from the southern hemisphere.

Days

While the number of days in a month and the number of months in a year have varied greatly over thousands of years, the seven-day week has remained relatively consistent. Most historians believe the week was established by the Babylonians, who divided the lunar month into approximately four segments.

The Babylonians were thought to have named each day after one of the seven visible heavenly bodies. The Greeks and later the Romans adopted this system, but renamed the days to match their own names for the planets. European Romance languages, including French, Italian, Spanish, Portuguese, and Romanian, began to use Latin planetary names for five days of the week. For the other two days, they incorporated Judeo-Christian words: Sabbath (from the Hebrew for "to cease," referring to a day of rest) and *dominus* (Latin for "lord" or "master").

English is not a Romance language because it derives from German rather than Latin. The English names for the days of the week, therefore, reflect a unique blend of mythologies. When two Germanic tribes, the Angles and the Saxons, invaded England in the first century BCE, they renamed four days of the week to honor deities in the Norse pantheon that related to equivalent deities in the Roman pantheon. Thor, their god of thunder, for instance, was honored with the day that had been named for Jupiter. The Anglo-Saxons kept the association with the sun and the moon, and because they did not have a god who was the equivalent of the Roman god Saturn, they kept this reference for the seventh day of the week.

This chart provides specifics of these explanations: It shows how Spanish and French—two of the Romance languages—share classical origins, while English reflects an Anglo-Saxon influence.

+ **Fat Tuesday**—or *Mardi Gras* in French—is a celebration the day before the Christian Lent, which begins on a Wednesday. Butter, lard, and other fat perishables had to be consumed before fasting, so a feast was prepared to use up these ingredients.

+ Thor, the son of Odin, has many similarities to Jupiter: both are the sons of an Earth goddess, serve as sky gods, and are associated with thunder and oak trees.

English	Roman Deity or Entity	Latin	Spanish	French	Norse Deity	Anglo-Saxon
Sunday	the sun	dies Solis	domingo	dimanche	—	Sunnandaeg
Monday	the moon	dies Lunae	lunes	lundi	—	Monandaeg
Tuesday	Mars	dies Martis	martes	mardi	Tiw *God of war*	Tiwesdaeg
Wednesday	Mercury	dies Mercurii	miércoles	mercredi	Woden *Trickster god*	Wodnesdaeg
Thursday	Jupiter (Jove)	dies Jovis	jueves	jeudi	Thor *God of thunder*	Thuresdaeg
Friday	Venus	dies Veneris	viernes	vendredi	Freya *Goddess of beauty*	Frigedaeg
Saturday	Saturn	dies Saturni	sábado	samedi	—	Saeternesdaeg

Months

The Romans originally used a calendar with ten months, most likely one borrowed from the Greeks, which was based on the inconsistent phases of the moon and growth cycles of crops. It did not even account for approximately 60 days in the winter months. Over time, this calendar drifted significantly from the actual seasons, and Julius Caesar instituted the new Julian calendar in 45 BCE, replacing the lunar-based calendar with a solar-based one.

The Julian calendar also added the months of January and February to the beginning of the existing ten-month calendar; it extended February by one day every four years to account for extra hours that had accumulated; and it later renamed several months to honor Roman men. Then in 1582, Pope Gregory XIII adopted

+ Pope Gregory XIII, who held his position from 1572 to 1585, sought the advice of several Renaissance astronomers in order to improve the accuracy of the calendar. To adjust from the Julian model to the new calendar, he decreed that the day after October 4, 1582 would be October 15. This upset renters—who felt cheated out of almost two weeks' rent—but the new Gregorian calendar was eventually accepted.

+ In Gilbert and Sullivan's musical *The Pirates of Penzance*, a boy is told he must serve in the royal navy until his 21st birthday. Because he was born on February 29, however, no one is sure how to calculate the actual number of birthdays he has celebrated.

+ While the Greeks did not like Ares, the Romans considered Mars, their name for the god of war, one of the most important deities and named the month of March in his honor.

MARS.

a readjusted structure in which century years not exactly divisible by 400 were not altered with an extra day in February. This Gregorian calendar has since become the basis for modern time-telling in most parts of the world.

The following are brief histories of the twelve months in the calendar system.

January was named for Janus, a Roman god seen as a protector and as the guardian of doorways. Because January marks the end of one year and the beginning of the next, the month is a metaphorical doorway.

• The Roman god Janus had two heads, one that looked forward and the other that looked backward. He was perfectly suited to bid farewell to one year and welcome another.

February likely comes from the Latin word *februare*, meaning "to purify"; this is the month that can be lengthened by one day in order to realign the calendar to actual solar time. A year in which February has an extra day is called a leap year.

March had been the first month of a ten-month calendar and was named after Mars, the revered Roman god of war. During the reign of Julius Caesar, in an attempt to improve the accuracy of the calendar, the months of January and February were added, so Mars became the third month.

April likely stemmed from the word *aphrilis*, a reference to Aphrodite. The month was sacred to the goddess of beauty, and she was associated with flowers, which traditionally appear in this month.

May is thought to be named after Maia, a Roman goddess of the spring and a daughter of Faunus. Farmers associated her name with the time for sowing.

June was named in honor of Juno, the Roman goddess of marriage. To this day, June remains a popular month for weddings in much of the Western world.

• The prefix *oct-* can be seen in many words, including octopus (an eight-armed mollusk), octogenarian (someone in her eighties), octagon (an eight-sided shape), and octave (an interval of eight degrees in music, such as eight consecutive keys on a piano).

July was one of the two months renamed during the reign of Julius Caesar. It had been called Quintilis (*quint-* denotes five) because it was the fifth month, but the Romans renamed it "July" to honor Caesar.

August was another month renamed by the Romans. It was the original sixth month and was called Sextilis (*sex-* denotes six). The month was then renamed to honor Caesar Augustus, the grandnephew of Julius Caesar.

September, October, November, and December were the seventh, eighth, ninth, and tenth months in the original 10-month calendar (*septem-*, *octo-*, *novem-*, and *decem-* mean seven, eight, nine, and ten, respectively). When January and February were inserted at the front of the calendar, these last four months were pushed back and never renamed. They are now inaccurately the ninth, tenth, eleventh, and twelfth months of the year.

• The prefix *dec-* can be seen in words such as decade (a period of ten years), Decalog (the Ten Commandments), decathlon (a series of ten athletic events), and decimal (based on the number ten).

Classical Myths *by* Theme

After reading about the role of mythology in cultures around the world, after learning about ancient Greeks and Romans and how they inspired the revolutionary thinking of the European Renaissance, after being introduced to the classical pantheon and the other deities, it is time to begin reading classical myths.

The 25 stories included here are just a small sample taken from a large collection of retellings that have been passed down through generations. While there is certainly no "right" way to categorize these myths, *Panorama* groups them by theme. This approach will make remembering the myths a little easier and discussing them a lot more meaningful.

The first two sections look at the creation of humans and the power of the deities, and the myths that follow reveal the grace of compassion, the sorrow of unfulfilled love, the danger of arrogance, and the tragedy of human mistakes.

♦ Male actors wore helmet-like masks when they performed in ancient Greece. The large masks had exaggerated features that revealed the tragic or comedic nature of the play, and the same actor could put on a different mask in order to assume another character.

THE CREATION *of* HUMANS

According to the Greeks, mankind arrived after the natural elements of the world were established. The Greek poet Hesiod and the Roman poet Ovid both wrote about the fiercely determined Titan Prometheus, who created men and proved his devotion to them by stealing fire from the heavens to keep his precious creations alive.

Zeus, outraged that Prometheus had given fire to man, then orchestrated the creation of Pandora, the first mortal woman, who would introduce evils into the world. A final creation myth reveals how Zeus, who wanted to punish mortals even more, caused a terrible flood on Earth. But Prometheus was able to warn his son, Deucalion, and he and his wife survived. With help from the goddess of justice, these two mortals were able to repopulate the world with a strong race of humans.

＊ The etching below shows
   Prometheus creating a man and
   Athena bringing him to life.

SOURCES

The myth of Prometheus is based on Hesiod's *Theogony* and Ovid's *Metamorphoses*.

The myth of Pandora is based on Hesiod's *Theogony* and his *Works and Days*.

The source for the flood myth is *Metamorphoses*.

PROMETHEUS
and the Creation of Man

While most Titans were banished to Tartarus after being defeated by the Olympians, Prometheus and his brother Epimetheus were spared because of the assistance Prometheus had offered during the battle. He did not remain close with the Olympians for long, however. Without consulting Zeus, Prometheus formed humans—all men—in the image of the gods. Unlike other earthly creatures, Prometheus stood the men upright so they could look to the stars. Athena then breathed life into the creations, and Prometheus taught them skills such as sailing and farming. Despite these gifts, Prometheus knew men would perish without fire, and so he approached Zeus and asked that fire be allowed on the earth.

"Absolutely not," said Zeus, outraged that Prometheus had formed these creatures and clearly favored them over immortals. "Men do not revere their gods and make no sacrifices. They do not deserve fire."

The cunning Prometheus then offered a compromise: He would get man to sacrifice to the gods in exchange for the gift of fire. Zeus agreed and Prometheus left Olympus. After killing and skinning a bull, Prometheus stuffed one sack full with the bones of a bull but artfully arranged a slab of rich meat on top. In a smaller sack, he placed the best cuts of meat but covered them with the foul stomach and entrails.

Returning to Olympus, Prometheus asked Zeus which part of a bull men should sacrifice to the gods. Zeus greedily chose the larger sack that appeared to have good meat inside. When he realized he had been tricked, however, he was furious and refused to keep his part of the agreement. "Man will never have fire!" he roared. "They shall eat their meat bloody and raw!"

Prometheus could not stand to see his precious creations shiver and die, so he disobeyed Zeus. He stole fire for mankind—some say from the sun, some say from Hephaestus' forge, and some say from Zeus' very own hearth. Regardless, Zeus had had enough. He ordered Prometheus to be captured and chained to a mountainside, where he had to endure burning heat by day and freezing winds at night. To make matters worse, Zeus sent his eagle every morning to peck out Prometheus' liver, only to have it grow back each night. The immortal Prometheus suffered this punishment for 30,000 years until the Greek hero Heracles finally released him.

THE CREATION OF HUMANS

"And while other creatures on all fours
Look downwards, man was made to hold his head
Erect in majesty and see the sky,
And raise his eyes to the bright stars above."

OVID, *METAMORPHOSES*, BOOK 1, LINES 91-94

- In the Greek playwright Aeschylus' *Prometheus Bound*, Prometheus is an inspiration in the face of tyranny.

- Instead of an eagle, some versions of this myth have Prometheus being tortured by a vulture, the bird associated with Ares.

- A statue of Prometheus overlooks the skating rink in New York City's famous Rockefeller Plaza. Artist Paul Manship's figure holds a flame and is encircled by the symbols of the zodiac. The inscription on the wall behind the statue is from Aeschylus: "Prometheus, teacher in every art, brought the fire that hath proved to mortals a means to mighty ends."

Pandora

The First Woman

Although Zeus had taken his revenge on Prometheus for creating mankind, he still wanted to punish the men themselves, who now lived happily—and warmly—on earth. But how? Zeus knew Prometheus had carefully placed all sorrows and ills in a jar so that nothing would afflict mankind. Before being taken into the mountains for his punishment, Prometheus warned his brother Epimetheus to never open the jar and to never accept any offering from the gods because it might be a trick. The gullible Epimetheus, however, was no match for the wrath of the Olympian king.

With the help of the other Olympians, Zeus created a creature of his own: woman. Hephaestus sculpted her, Aphrodite gave her great beauty, Apollo gave her a ravishing voice, Athena taught her skills, the Graces adorned her with rare jewels, and Hermes gave her a clever and curious mind. After receiving all of these attributes, the woman was named Pandora, meaning "all gifts."

Hermes delivered Pandora to Epimetheus, who gladly accepted her for his wife. Although Epimetheus told her not to open Prometheus' jar, Pandora's curious mind got the best of her. Not long after she arrived, she pried off the lid and let loose all the evils that plague the world. Sorrow, madness, old age, violence, greed, hatred, toil, misfortune, argument, death, disease, jealousy, spite—all rushed out in a constant and terrifying stream. Pandora had been hurled to the ground but was finally able to slam the lid back on the jar and trap the last remaining element: hope, which had never been needed before. Now, the hope in man's heart allows him to cope in the imperfect world.

+ The prefixes *pro-* and *epi-* mean "before" and "after," respectively, and *mathein* means "to learn." Thus, Prometheus had forethought, while Epimetheus had only hindsight. In keeping, the **prologue** of a book is its introduction, while the **epilogue** serves to wrap up the ending (*logos* means "word").

+ The phrase **a Pandora's box** refers to a single, unwise action that will cause a whole series of problems.

+ There are clear similarities between Pandora and the biblical Eve, both of whom are tempted and introduce evil into paradise.

+ The young heroine in Lewis Carroll's story *Alice's Adventures in Wonderland* has a great deal of curiosity. Her dreamlike trip down a rabbit hole and through Wonderland reveals both the dangers and the rewards of a curious mind.

AFTER THE GODS CREATED PANDORA

"Both immortal gods and mortal men were seized with wonder when they saw that precipitous trap, more than mankind can manage."

HESIOD, *THEOGONY*, PAGE 20

THE FLOOD
Deucalion and Pyrrha

Even after punishing mortals with the evils in Pandora's box, Zeus still resented humans. While some were humble enough to respect the powers of the gods, many committed immoral acts. Outraged, Zeus reached for his lightning bolts and planned to destroy all people, but he feared Mount Olympus would catch fire. Instead, he decided to create a flood.

First he called upon Aeolus, the god of the winds, and instructed him to capture all of the winds except those that cause storms. Aeolus obliged and Notus, the south wind, poured violent rains on every mile of land. Then Zeus called upon his brother Poseidon to stir up the world's waters with his trident and cause devastating waves.

While some mortals managed to escape the rising waters, they soon perished without food. Only one man had received word about the impending destruction and had time to prepare. Prometheus had come to his son Deucalion in a dream and instructed him to build a boat, stocking it with animals and supplies. When the rains came, Deucalion and his wife, Pyrrha, drifted for nine days and nights and were the only two mortals to survive.

Zeus, upon seeing the tiny boat in the vast waters, felt compassion for the innocent couple. He commanded Aeolus to stop the winds and Poseidon to calm the waters. Deucalion and Pyrrha landed safely on the top of Mount Parnassus and offered thanks to the Olympians for sparing them. Then they went to the temple of the Titan Themis, who could instruct them on what they should do next. At the temple, they prayed, "We are too old to repopulate the world. Tell us, great Themis, how to renew our people."

Themis, the goddess of law and justice, smiled upon the couple and replied, "As you walk from this temple, cover your faces, and throw the bones of your great mother behind you."

The couple was stunned. Would any goddess actually ask them to dig up the bones of their mothers and strew them disrespectfully on the ground? They were unsure of how to proceed, until Deucalion suddenly understood. "Our great mother is the earth itself," he said, "and her bones are the stones we stand upon!" So, covering their heads, Deucalion and Pyrrha left the temple carrying dozens of stones. Those dropped by Pyrrha slowly transformed into women, and those that came from Deucalion's hand turned into men. Thus a new race was formed, and these new humans were as strong as the stones from which they descended.

- Between 3000 and 2000 BCE, a flood occurred in what is now the Middle East. The event was so devastating that similar flood myths can be found in all regions of that area. Typically, one mortal is told how to prepare and, after the rains subside, is left on a mountaintop. This myth is the classical version of the biblical story of Noah and the ark.

- After torrential rains, Noah released a raven and then a dove from his ark. The raven, which represents evil, did not return, while the dove came back with an olive branch in its beak. In practical terms, the branch meant the bird had found dry land; in spiritual terms, it symbolized the forgiveness of God.

- Themis was renamed Justitia by the Romans. Statues of her often stand in courthouses, where she is blindfolded and holds a scale to show that justice should be impartial.

- One of Deucalion's sons was Hellen, who became the legendary father of the Greek race and inspired the term *Hellenic* to describe things relating to Greece.

"The earthy part, damp with some trace of moisture,
Was turned to flesh; what was inflexible
And solid changed to bone; what in the stones
Had been the veins retained the name of veins.
In a brief while, by Heaven's mysterious power,
The stones the man had thrown were formed as men,
Those from the woman's hand reshaped as women.
Thence we are hard, we children of the earth,
And in our lives of toil we prove our birth."

OVID, *METAMORPHOSES*, BOOK 1, LINES 409-417

SECTION II

MYTHS SHOWING *the* POWER *of the* GODS

As seen in the descriptions in the last chapter, the classical gods certainly had their faults. They became jealous and vengeful, and they often made decisions without thinking about the long-term effects of their actions. Sound similar to human faults? Remember that unlike some other cultures, the Greeks and Romans viewed their gods as having human qualities, including both positive and negative traits.

This section contains three myths, each one illustrating how the gods fought among themselves for dominance and how their power struggles often had profound effects on mortals. The first myth shows the gods taking interest in the lives of mortals and illustrates how the wise, peace-loving Athena wins out in a contest against her uncle, the aggressive Poseidon, to name the city of Athens. In the second myth, the beautiful Persephone is abducted by Hades, and her mother's grief is so profound that it leads to the changing of the seasons. The last myth is about a maiden named Io who gets caught between the jealous Hera and her guilty husband, Zeus. Only after the two Olympians resolve their argument is the innocent mortal set free.

SOURCES

A source for the myth about the naming of Athens is *Nonnos: Dionysiaca, Volume II.*

The myth of Persephone is based on Ovid's *Metamorphoses* and a Homeric hymn to Demeter.

The myth of Io is based on *Metamorphoses.*

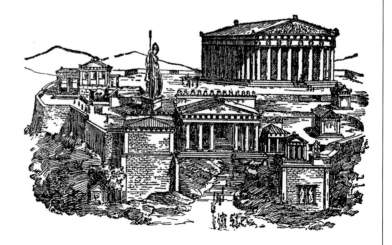

THE NAMING of ATHENS
A Desire for Peace

When Greece was first being settled, a noble king searched for a place to develop a new city. He was pleased to find a piece of land jutting from the plains into a sparkling sea. The land contained hills and a plateau and was surrounded by miles of fertile soil. The gods on Olympus, always interested in the activities of humans, blessed the spot and began to argue over who should be its patron. After a debate, it was decided the honor would belong to either Athena, the goddess of wisdom and war, or her uncle Poseidon, ruler of the seas.

When it came time for the two Olympians to present their offerings to a panel of judges, Poseidon went first. After a dramatic silence, he raised his trident high over his head and slammed it down with such force that it cracked the ground. From the chasm rose a huge, magnificent warhorse adorned with glittering armor. Poseidon described how his gift would create great fear in enemy lands and protect the city in times of war. The crowd was in awe of the great beast and agreed that Poseidon's gift was ideal.

But then the wise Athena stepped forward and knelt down, placing her spear and shield gently on the ground. She touched the soil with her palms, then rose and took several steps back. While the crowd looked on with puzzled expressions, a tiny shoot sprouted from the ground. Within minutes, a small tree with grayish leaves and small, odd-looking fruit had grown. After witnessing the astonishing emergence of the great warhorse, the crowd was unimpressed with Athena's small, plain gift. Athena smiled serenely, however, and explained.

"This," she said, "is an olive tree. Its fruit will feed the people of Greece and will become a principal export for merchants. The fragrant oil of the fruit can be used for cooking, for burning in lamps, and for cleansing and healing. This plant will flourish here in this fertile land and will serve the people well for all time."

The crowd, originally impressed with the fancy war horse, saw the broader benefits of Athena's simple gift and named the city after her. The city, named Athens, prospered as Greece's center for learning and the arts and went on to become a leading producer of olives.

- A patron acts as a protector or benefactor, so a patron of the arts might have season tickets to the symphony. The word comes from the Latin *pater* (father).

- Some versions of this myth say Poseidon's gift was a spring of water. The spring was saltwater, however, and the people knew they could not drink from it.

- The olive tree remains a symbol of longevity (it can live for centuries), fertility (it bears abundant fruit), knowledge (olive oil creates light when burned), and purification (the oil can soothe and heal).

- The etching on the opposite page shows an area in ancient Athens known as the Acropolis (*akros* means "at the top" and *polis* is "city"). The large building is the Parthenon, a temple to honor Athena, and near the center is the bronze Athena Promachos statue, which stood for over 1,000 years. Large-scale efforts continue in Athens to reinforce and maintain the remains of the Acropolis.

- The olive tree also symbolizes peace. The United Nations' flag shows a globe surrounded by olive branches. And the Great Seal of the United States (at left) shows an eagle clutching 13 arrows in one claw and an olive branch in the other; the country is ready for war but wants peace. Look on the back of a dollar bill to see this image.

PERSEPHONE
and the Origin of the Seasons

Persephone was the beloved only child of Demeter, goddess of the grain. Though Zeus fathered Persephone, it was Demeter who took care of her and taught her the responsibilities associated with being the goddess of grain. Indeed, Demeter was a devoted mother who cherished her daughter.

One day, from deep underground, Hades heard laughter above him and recognized it as Persephone's. When he traveled to earth, he saw his niece gathering wildflowers with her friends. Hades asked for Zeus' permission to make her the queen of the Underworld, and Zeus consented. Hades then swept Persephone up into his chariot and disappeared into a chasm. His movements were so swift that the maidens who had been in the field with Persephone did not know what had happened. The only thing they saw were Persephone's wildflowers strewn on the ground.

When Demeter learned of her daughter's mysterious disappearance, she begged for information, but no one could give her an answer. She frantically sought out Helios, the god who saw everything from his great sun chariot. When Helios told her what Zeus had agreed to, Demeter was furious with her brother but knew she could not override his decision. Refusing to return to Mount Olympus, Demeter roamed the land, mourning for her child.

Out of anger and sadness, Demeter neglected her duties. Within the year, plants had withered, fields lay barren, and mankind began to starve. Zeus, realizing the impact of his decision, sent Hermes to the Underworld with the message that Hades must return Persephone to her mother.

When Hermes arrived, he saw Persephone on her throne, pale and miserable. She had not had a happy moment since her arrival in the realm of the dead, and she had refused to eat or drink anything. When she heard Hermes' message, however, she leapt up with joy. Before she left, Hades bid her farewell and slyly offered her a gift of a pomegranate.

Demeter was ecstatic to be reunited with her daughter and held her for a long time before she could bring herself to ask, "Did you eat anything while you were in the Underworld?" The innocent Persephone replied, "Nothing until today, when I ate just a few seeds from a pomegranate."

Demeter, so happy just moments before, was distraught. She knew if Persephone had eaten food from the Underworld, the Fates would not allow her to return to earth. Crafty Zeus, however, intervened and struck a compromise with Hades: Persephone would only have to spend six months of the year as queen of the Underworld, one month for each seed she had eaten. The rest of the year she could spend with her adoring mother.

• This myth is etiological because it explains the seasons. In the fall, Demeter begins to mourn. During the winter months, Demeter is so sad that she does not allow anything to grow. When Persephone rejoins her mother, it is spring, a season of rebirth that leads to summer's glorious season of growth.

"Then Jove, to hold the balance fair between
His brother and his sister in her grief,
Portioned the rolling year in equal parts.
Now Proserpine, of two empires alike
Great deity, spends with her mother half
The year's twelve months and with her husband half.
Straightway her heart and features are transformed;
That face which even Pluto must have found
Unhappy beams with joy, as when the sun,
Long lost and hidden in the clouds and rain,
Rides forth in triumph from the clouds again."

OVID, *METAMORPHOSES*, BOOK V, LINES 566-576

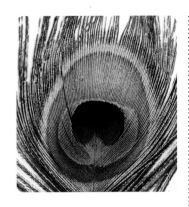

Io

Punishment of the Innocent

Io, the only daughter of a river god, spent as much time as she could in the woods near her father's river. When Zeus saw Io sitting by the water, he disguised himself as a mortal shepherd and approached her. They talked happily and Zeus asked Io if he could meet with her again. The following day, however, Hera became suspicious of Zeus and followed her husband.

Zeus indeed went back to see Io, transforming again into a shepherd. When Zeus felt Hera's presence, however, he turned himself back into his true form, and turned the lovely Io into a huge white cow. Hera saw Zeus sitting on a riverbank next to a cow and knew he was hiding something. Rather than immediately accusing Zeus, however, she commented on the beautiful cow and asked for it as a gift.

Zeus could not refuse this simple request and agreed to give the cow to his wife. Hera then delivered the cow to the beast Argus, her most trusted servant. Argus made an excellent watchman because he had one hundred keen eyes that never closed at the same time. The innocent Io was trapped.

The mighty Zeus had not forgotten Io, however, and he sent the wily Hermes to rescue her. Hermes also disguised himself as a shepherd and approached Argus, who was watching Io as she grazed in a field. Hermes began to tell the creature long stories and then played peaceful music for him on his reed pipes. Finally, every one of Argus' eyes closed, and Hermes swiftly cut off the beast's head. Before Zeus could transform Io back into a maiden, however, Hera came upon the scene.

Blaming Io for the death of her loyal servant, Hera sent a stinging fly to follow Io. Io roamed for hundreds of miles, trying to rid herself of the torturous insect. Meanwhile Hera, to honor the faithful Argus, took his one hundred eyes and placed them on the sweeping tail feathers of her favorite bird, the peacock.

Zeus looked down and saw that the lonely Io had wandered all the way to Egypt and was crying in pain along the banks of the Nile. He swore upon the River Styx never to see Io if only Hera would allow him to turn the mortal back into her true form. Hera took pity on Io, who was transformed back into a beautiful girl, with paler skin than ever before. Io was soon a queen in Egypt and was well loved by the people of her new land.

+ Another mortal woman whom Zeus seduced was Europa. He took the form of a bull and swam to Crete with Europa on his back. She bore him three sons, including Minos, who became Crete's king. Europe was named for Europa, and one of Greek's modern **euro** coins shows her on the back of a bull.

+ The etching on the right shows Hermes slaying Argus, who is covered in eyes. Io, as a cow, stands in the background while Zeus, on the right, witnesses the scene.

"She browsed on leaves of trees and bitter weeds,
And for her bed, poor thing, lay on the ground,
Not always grassy, and drank the muddy streams;
And when, to plead with Argus, she would try
To stretch her arms, she had no arms to stretch.
Would she complain, a moo came from her throat,
A startling sound—her own voice frightened her.
She reached her father's river and the banks
Where often she had played and, in the water,
Mirrored she saw her muzzle and her horns,
And fled in terror from the self she saw."

OVID, *METAMORPHOSES*, BOOK I, LINES 633-643

+ The name *Argus* was once commonly used in the names of newspapers to signify how reporters kept their eyes on important events. **Argus-eyed** is a term that means "alert."

+ This myth is etiological, explaining the circular markings on the end of peacocks' feathers.

+ Another etiological aspect of this myth is how it explains the name of the Ionian Sea, the body of water off the west coast of Greece. Io crossed this sea and ended up in Egypt, on the northeastern coast of Africa.

MYTHS *of* COMPASSION

Many myths, including those about Persephone and Io, were told to reveal the powers of the gods and goddesses and to show how their often self-serving actions affected mankind. Other myths, however, showed the compassionate side of the immortals and inspired ordinary men and women to treat one another with kindness and respect.

The following section contains four stories that illustrate compassion. In the first, Zeus puts humans to a hospitality test and rewards an aged couple, Philemon and Baucis, for their warmth and kindness. The second myth features a talented sculptor named Pygmalion who finally recognizes his own loneliness and receives help from the goddess of love. The third myth also features Aphrodite, but this time she is jealous and cruel. Only when she stops feeling sorry for herself does she see the true love between her son Eros and the worthy mortal Psyche. The final story—which does not feature deities and so is technically a legend rather than a myth—shows the powerful friendship between two young men, Damon and Pythias.

SOURCES

The myths of Philemon and Baucis and of Pygmalion are based on Ovid's *Metamorphoses*.

The myth of Eros and Psyche is based on the version told by Roman writer Lucius Apuleius in his novel *The Golden Ass*, translated by P.G. Walsh.

The legend of Damon and Pythias was first told by the Greek philosopher, writer, and musical theorist Aristoxenus during the fourth century BCE.

PHILEMON *and* BAUCIS
Just Rewards

The people in the town of Phrygia had become selfish and cold-hearted, refusing to help each other or provide shelter to strangers. Because hospitality was so important to Zeus, he decided to put the mortals in the town to a test.

Disguised as travelers, Zeus and his son Hermes came upon the town, knocking on doors and asking for food and a place to rest. Again and again they were refused, even as a storm blew in and night began to fall. Finally they approached a tiny cottage on the edge of the town and were welcomed inside by an old couple.

The husband, named Philemon, and his wife, Baucis, had married when they were young and had grown old in the cottage. They had always treated one another as equals and enjoyed being together, feeling rich in their love even though they had little money. Now both worked to welcome their guests, wiping down a table with fragrant mint, tending the fire, hurrying out to the garden. The weary travelers enjoyed olives, nuts, vegetables, and apples, along with a bowl of weak wine.

Philemon even set about trying to catch their only goose, willing to serve it to their guests. The goose kept ahead of the old man, however, and Zeus urged his host to leave the squawking bird alone, assuring the couple he was already sated.

Back at the small table, the shaky Philemon reached toward the bowl to give his guests the last of the wine. To his astonishment, he saw the bowl was full to the brim once again. He glanced quickly at his wife, and the two felt awe: They knew they were in the presence of gods.

Zeus and Hermes both offered gentle smiles and outstretched hands. They told the couple that many men and women of greater means had turned them away, and it was in this humble cottage that they had found warmth and comfort. The Olympians then led the couple up into the hills overlooking Phrygia. When they reached the top and turned to look into the town, Philemon and Baucis saw the selfish people's homes had been flooded, while their own cottage had become a beautiful temple with marble columns and a golden roof.

The mighty Zeus then offered to fulfill any wish the old couple desired. Philemon and Baucis whispered to one another before Philemon said, "We would be honored to become the guards of your temple and offer it as shelter to other travelers."

"And what about a wish for yourselves?" asked Zeus.

After more huddled whispers, the couple asked if they could die at the same moment so neither had to live without the other. Zeus smiled and assured the couple that they would spend many more happy years together and then be able to share their deaths as they had shared their lives.

So years later, as the couple stood beside their sacred home, they held hands and were transformed. Philemon became an oak and Baucis became a linden, their branches intertwined so they could hold one another and grow together for eternity.

♦ **Hospitality**—the act of being gracious to guests—derives from the Latin *hospes*, which means both "host" and "guest." Other English words that share this root include hospital, hostess, hotel, **hostel** (an inn for travelers), **hospice** (a home for the sick or poor), and **hostile** (unfriendly, because sometimes a guest can be a stranger or enemy).

PYGMALION
Learning to Love

Pygmalion was a dedicated sculptor who lived on the beautiful island of Cyprus. Although he was a young man surrounded by interesting, friendly people, Pygmalion chose to stay in his studio, sculpting day and night. In fact, he had grown to distrust others and insisted his own company and his own successes were enough.

Shortly after finishing a large statue for commission, Pygmalion was inspired to create a piece for himself. He began to hew a large chunk of marble and was amazed to watch his sculpture take form. As he crafted the figure and the face, he was struck by its beauty; he had never seen such a graceful woman, in art or in real life. He was amazed, too, because he felt as if he had little control over his creation and that perhaps some other power was working through his hands.

After finishing the statue, he polished the stone until the skin glistened, and he draped his masterpiece with a beautiful robe. He placed rings on her fingers and jewels around her neck. When he began to whisper words to her, he realized with shock that he had fallen in love with his own statue.

He ran to his window to breathe fresh air and caught sight of all the people below. He saw young couples, children playing, older men and women holding hands. He heard them all talking, laughing, and sharing ideas, and he saw how they gazed at one another. At that moment, Pygmalion was overwhelmed with the loneliness he had created in his own life.

The next morning, Pygmalion awoke when he heard a commotion in the street below his studio. From his window he saw the people of Cyprus in a parade, traveling to a festival in Aphrodite's honor. He quickly dressed and joined his fellow townspeople. Their journey ended at the temple built to honor the goddess, and Pygmalion, embarrassed and unsure of what to do, knelt to pray.

"Oh, great Aphrodite," he began quietly. "I once thought solitude was sufficient and saw those who depended on others as weak. But I realize now what I have lost. When I carved my marble girl, I fell in love. Please send me someone like her, for I finally understand the joy of companionship."

He left before he could see the flame in the altar flicker three times, a sign of Aphrodite's acceptance. When Pygmalion returned to his studio, he ran to his statue and kissed her, and with a pounding heart realized her lips were warm. Beneath his touch, her ivory skin turned soft, and she lifted her eyes to meet his. Pygmalion knew then that it was Aphrodite who had inspired him to create the statue to teach him the value of love, and he gave thanks to the goddess for her wisdom and guidance.

+ George Bernard Shaw's play *Pygmalion* features an arrogant, aristocratic man determined to improve the manners of a low-class woman. He then falls in love with—and learns a great deal from—his "creation." Shaw's play was later made into the musical *My Fair Lady* by Lerner and Lowe.

+ The novel *Frankenstein*, written by Mary Shelley and first published in 1818, shares similarities with this myth, but it ends in tragedy. When scientist Dr. Frankenstein creates life, he despises the imperfect specimen he produces and spends the rest of his life hunted and haunted by the creature.

+ Later authors gave Pygmalion's sculpture a name: Galatea.

"And then indeed in words that overflowed
He poured his thanks to Venus, and at last
His lips pressed real lips, and she, his girl,
Felt every kiss, and blushed, and shyly raised
Her eyes to his and saw the world and him."

OVID, *METAMORPHOSES*, BOOK X, LINES 292-296

EROS *and* PSYCHE
Love and Forgiveness

The Beautiful Psyche

Psyche was the youngest of three princesses and was so stunningly beautiful that people paid more attention to her than to the goddess of beauty herself, Aphrodite. Needless to say, the proud Olympian became furious that a mortal girl was getting such admiration while the temples in her honor were increasingly empty. Furthermore, Aphrodite assumed Psyche actually wanted the attention, while in fact the young girl longed to be loved rather than just adored.

The jealous Aphrodite sent her son Eros to punish the mortal, instructing him to shoot Psyche with a gold-tipped arrow and arrange for her to see an unworthy man when she awoke. Handsome Eros flew dutifully to the girl as she slept, but the moment he laid eyes on Psyche, he knew he could not carry out his mother's wishes. As he stared lovingly at her, she stirred and startled Eros, causing him to accidentally prick himself with the arrow meant for her. So the god of love himself fell hopelessly for the beautiful, innocent mortal. He slipped out of her bedchamber and did not tell his mother what had happened.

Weeks passed and Psyche was still being praised. This time Aphrodite took matters into her own hands and cast a spell on the townspeople to make them ignore Psyche. While Psyche welcomed the privacy and did not miss the empty flattery, her parents worried that their daughter would never marry. They sought the advice of an oracle and received a confusing prophecy: "Psyche will never marry a mortal man. She must travel into the mountains alone, and there she will be given to one whom neither man nor god can resist."

Psyche's parents were certain they had upset an Olympian and were terrified they would incur more wrath if they refused to cooperate. So they led a procession to the foot of the mountains and left their youngest daughter alone to await her fate. Although she had worn a brave face, Psyche began to cry until the gentle west wind, Zephyrus, lifted her across the mountains. He placed her in a secluded valley near the most beautiful palace she had ever seen. She was hesitant to approach it until she heard several female voices calling out, "Psyche, we are your invisible servants. Inside the palace, you will find all that you need: a warm bath, a delicious feast, and a bed where you can await your husband's arrival."

Psyche Meets her Husband

Psyche entered the quiet palace and was delighted to find her every need met by an invisible maiden. That evening, she fell asleep waiting for her mysterious husband. When he arrived in the darkness, she knew instantly that she loved him even though she could not see him. In a gentle voice, the kind man explained that while he loved her completely and could be trusted with her care, he could not, at least for now, reveal himself to her. Psyche found peace in this arrangement, for although it was

- Remember that Eros had two kinds of arrows: His sharp, gold-tipped arrows made people fall in love with the first person they saw, while one of his blunt, lead-tipped arrows would make them flee.

- *Psyche* is Greek for soul, and Psyche is often shown in paintings and sculpture with butterfly wings. Butterflies begin as caterpillars and emerge from cocoons, and their metamorphosis has come to symbolize the soul, transformation, and rebirth in many cultures.

- An African myth tells how the creator made butterflies using scissors to cut tiny bits of grass, flower petals, leaves, and sky.

unusual, she had never felt safer or more content. She loved her husband wholly, and for the first time, she felt truly loved by another.

As the weeks passed, however, Psyche often thought about her family; her parents had been so distraught when she last saw them, and she worried that her sisters were grieving, too. So that night, she asked her husband if her family could visit. Eros, concerned that any reunion would cause trouble, quickly said no. But Psyche was so sad that he eventually relented. When he warned her that her sisters would try to learn more about his identity, Psyche kissed him and promised she would never do anything that would result in their separation.

The next morning, Psyche's sisters were delivered to the castle by Zephyrus. Psyche embraced them and excitedly escorted them through her opulent palace and its lovely gardens. Rather than being happy for Psyche, however, the older sisters became horribly jealous. Psyche had always gotten the most attention, and now even her troubling prophecy had turned out to be a generous blessing.

The sisters put on happy faces, however, and subtly questioned her to find a blemish in the perfection. Although Psyche at first made up lies about her husband to cover her secret, she finally admitted that she had never actually seen him. The sisters pounced. Had she not heard the prophecy? Was she not terrified by the mysterious creature that claimed to be her husband? How could she trust him not to hurt her? Despite Psyche's attempts to explain her feelings, her sisters would not relent. By the end of their visit, they had planted doubt in her mind.

A Loss of Trust

That night, while her husband was sleeping, the curious Psyche lit an oil lamp and lifted it above their bed. Her eyes widened with amazement when she saw Eros himself, his angelic face in peaceful slumber, the white down of his wings glistening in the lamp light. More than satisfied, she tried to extinguish the lamp, but a drop of oil fell on Eros' shoulder and he awoke with a start.

He leapt up and backed away from Psyche. "You do not know what you have done!" he cried, his voice tinged with both sadness and anger. "I tried to protect you from my mother who wanted revenge on you, and I tried to warn you about your jealous sisters. I loved you so completely, and all I asked for in return was your trust. There cannot be love where there is no trust."

With these words, he flew out the window with tears in his eyes. Psyche ran down the stairs and into the gardens, calling out for his forgiveness, but he was nowhere to be found. When she turned back toward the palace, it too had disappeared, and she was left utterly alone.

She began to wander hopelessly, overcome with grief. In desperation, she visited one of Aphrodite's temples, but she was met with bitter words. "How dare you entice my son and then betray him," the goddess seethed. "Your arrogance once affected only me, but now you have brought pain to my child."

♦ In the etching above, Psyche holds up a lamp in order to see her husband and realizes he is actually Eros, the god of love.

♦ Apuleius writes that after learning about Psyche's troubles, her sisters were delighted and wanted to return to see Eros for themselves. They waited for Zephyrus to carry them into the valley, but instead he dashed them against the mountains as punishment for their jealousy.

Aphrodite Sets Forth the Tasks

Aphrodite was about to dismiss the girl, but Psyche vowed to do anything to win back Eros' love. The jealous goddess recognized Psyche's desperation and saw her chance for revenge. She led the determined Psyche to a barn containing a huge mound of beans, rice, barley, and corn. "Separate these into piles by nightfall," she said coldly. "If you succeed, perhaps I'll take your apology to Eros." Psyche was left alone, stunned by the assignment. She had been willing to do any task, but this was impossible. Her heart ached until she saw thousands of ants appear. With astonishing speed, the insects helped her separate the mound into neat piles.

When Aphrodite arrived at nightfall, she was furious; she had never expected the girl to succeed. "You clearly had help, but no one can help you with this next task, dear girl. You must bring me the fleece from the golden rams. But be careful," she said with a gleam in her eye. "They do not care much for mortals."

The next morning, Psyche found the pasture of the golden rams, and although she was fearful, her love made her brave. As she began to crawl under a fence, the reeds there whispered, "Do not go to the rams themselves; just collect the fleece caught in the briars along the river where they pass." Psyche gratefully took their advice and accomplished the task.

Aphrodite was again angered by Psyche's triumph and sent the mortal on another difficult mission: get water from a waterfall in the River Styx. Climbing among the slippery boulders that led to the river, Psyche lost her footing several times but never stopped. When she finally saw the waterfall, spilling violently over a cliff, she gasped in fear. But then an eagle snatched the vial Aphrodite had given to Psyche, collected water from the fall's spray, and returned the full vial to the girl.

Aphrodite was now livid and decided that the next mission would put an end to Psyche's luck and, in fact, her life. "Travel to Hades and collect some of Queen Persephone's beauty in this box," Aphrodite demanded, thrusting a velvet-covered container into the girl's trembling hands. "If she asks for an explanation, tell her that because of your betrayal, some of my beauty has diminished." Psyche thought the only way to enter the Underworld was by dying, so she climbed a mountain and was prepared to jump. As she stood on the precipice, the mountain beneath her spoke, revealing a secret passageway into the Underworld and advising her how to get past the ferryman, Charon, and the guard dog, Cerberus. Finally, the mountain warned her not to open the box of Persephone's beauty.

Psyche took the advice and finally reached Persephone, who kindly fulfilled her request. When the exhausted Psyche returned to the earth, she searched for some water to drink. Bending over a small pool, she caught sight of her reflection: Her clothes were torn and soiled, her hair was a tangled mess, and her skin was covered with scratches. She worried that even if Aphrodite forgave her, Eros would not love her because she was no longer beautiful. Despite the mountain's warning, Psyche was so curious to see what was in the box that she opened it, sure that taking just a bit of its beauty would cause no harm. The potent contents, however, were too strong for a mere mortal, and she fainted from the powerful scent.

+ The Grimm Brothers' fairy tale "Rumpelstiltskin" also features a scene where a young, innocent girl must separate grains into piles. Like Psyche, she is also assisted by ants. The drawing above is of the dwarf Rumpelstiltskin.

+ The Greek *psyche* (soul) is the root for words that have to do with the complexity of the mind, including **psychology** (the study of the human mind) and **psychiatry** (the branch of medicine dealing with the treatment of mental health). And **psyched** is a colloquialism that means "to be emotionally charged or happy."

The Happy Reunion

Meanwhile, the heartbroken Eros had been searching for his beloved Psyche and longed to be reunited with her. When he came upon her listless form, he was terrified she was dead. But after seeing the box, he realized what had happened and kissed her lightly on the cheek. She awoke and threw her arms around his neck.

"Foolish Psyche!" Eros said. "Your curiosity got the better of you once again, but you have proven your love for me with your courageous acts. I love your soul even more than your fair exterior and will never leave you again."

He collected the beauty that had escaped and carried the box and the beaming Psyche to Mount Olympus. When the couple arrived, Aphrodite listened as her son declared his love for Psyche, and the goddess' heart softened as she recognized their true devotion. Zeus himself offered Psyche ambrosia and nectar, the food and liquid that could make a mortal immortal.

When Psyche and Eros had a daughter, they named her Pleasure.

* A cherub, often confused with the baby-faced version of Eros (Cupid), is a winged guardian spirit in Christian theology. This famous stamp was released in 1995 and featured a cherub from the Renaissance painter Raphael's *Sistine Madonna*.

* The etching on the left shows Eros presenting Psyche to Zeus and Hera on Mount Olympus. Aphrodite sits on the cloud next to Ares in the foreground, with two doves behind her.

DAMON *and* PYTHIAS
The Best of Friends

Two young men, Damon and Pythias, were the best of friends. They had known each other since they were boys and grew ever closer with time. Each knew the other's strengths and fears, and they treated each other with trust and respect.

Someone who knew nothing about trust and respect was Dionysius, the tyrannical leader of Syracuse where Damon and Pythias lived. His sole intention was to guard his position, so he trusted no one. He treated those who served him harshly; as a result, they stayed loyal to him out of fear, not respect.

To prove his own power, Dionysius once sentenced a man to death because he dreamed the man had stolen from him. Unfortunately, Dionysius came to suspect that Pythias wanted to overthrow him, so he sentenced the innocent young man to death as well. Despite the fact that he had no proof, and despite the pleas from his subjects, who all loved the kind Pythias, Dionysius would not relent. He did not even allow Pythias to return home to make arrangements for his wife and family without a demand: Pythias must have someone imprisoned in his place as a kind of collateral. If Pythias did not return within three days, the one who stood in for him would be killed.

Pythias did not hesitate to ask Damon to take his place, and Damon did not hesitate to agree. When Damon arrived at the palace, the two friends embraced, and then, without a word, Pythias set out for his home. King Dionysius was shocked by this show of complete trust between friends and, as usual, became suspicious. He descended to the dungeon where Damon was being kept and stared coldly at the young man.

"Why would you agree to take his place, boy?" he demanded of Damon. "What scheme do the two of you have? What plan?"

"There is no plan, your majesty," replied Damon calmly. "I trust him completely. If tables were turned, I know he would do the same for me."

When three days passed and Pythias had not yet returned, Damon remained calm. As evening neared, Damon was marched out to a public square where throngs of people had gathered to sympathize with the innocent, selfless man. Just then, a man could be seen in the distance, running at full speed toward the square. It was Pythias, who pushed through the crowd to embrace his friend. He explained breathlessly that his horse had fallen lame; he had been forced to run the last few miles on foot.

The crowds cheered and even King Dionysius could not deny the purity he saw before him. He pardoned Pythias and set both friends free.

- Do not confuse King Dionysius with the Olympian Dionysus.

- Damon and Pythias have come to symbolize loyal friendship and have been referenced in literature, plays, and movies. Hamlet addresses his good friend Horatio as "Damon" in Shakespeare's play, and Louisa May Alcott's 1871 novel *Little Men* includes a chapter titled "Damon and Pythias."

- The plot of the 2003 DreamWorks animated movie *Sinbad: Legend of the Seven Seas* is based on this myth. In the movie, a prince offers to be imprisoned while Sinbad goes on a quest to prove his own innocence.

- Richard Bach, the author of the best-selling book *Jonathan Livingston Seagull*, once said, "If you love someone, set them free. If they come back, they're yours; if they don't, they never were."

• In Shakespeare's *Henry V*, the king refers to those who fight together as a "band of brothers." The phrase is still used to refer to units in the military whose members often heroically risk their lives to save others.

DAMON RESPONDS TO KING DIONYSIUS' SUSPICIONS

"There is no plan, your majesty,"
replied Damon calmly.
"I trust him completely. If tables were turned,
I know he would do the same for me."

MYTHS *about* UNFULFILLED LOVE

The characters in the previous section all learned the benefits of compassion and were content at the end of their stories. But another common theme in myths—as well as in plays, movies, and song lyrics—is a broken heart. One person may not return another's love, or two people who are desperately in love are kept apart despite their tremendous efforts. Whatever the situation, the result is pain, sadness, and a loss.

This section contains three myths, all titled with the name of a man and a woman who, for some reason, could not find happiness with each other. In the first, love plays tricks on the god Apollo and the nymph Daphne, resulting in a frantic chase and an unusual ending. The second is about two young lovers, Pyramus and Thisbe, who are kept apart by their feuding families. And the last myth features the love-struck nymph Echo, who falls for the vain mortal Narcissus. His arrogance destroys Echo's life and eventually his own.

SOURCES

All three of the myths in this section are based on Ovid's *Metamorphoses.*

DAPHNE *and* APOLLO
The Tricks of Love

Although the god Apollo represented the importance of moderation, he did not always practice what he preached. He was often arrogant, especially about his skill as a hunter. One day, while walking through the woods after killing a serpent, Apollo spotted the young Eros playing with a bow.

"You do know such weapons are intended for grown-ups, don't you?" Apollo asked haughtily. "I can kill beasts. I doubt you could kill a mouse."

Eros remained silent but quickly planned his revenge. First, he deftly shot Apollo with one of his golden-tipped arrows, the kind that would cause him to fall in love with the next person he saw. He then sped ahead to find his victim, and when he saw the nymph Daphne, he smiled devilishly. He knew that Daphne, the daughter of the river god Peneus, was a loyal follower of Artemis and wanted to remain unmarried. To heighten the chaos, he shot her with a lead-tipped arrow, the kind that would cause her to flee from love. He then settled back to watch.

When Apollo came upon Daphne, the nymph ran in terror toward the river. Despite Apollo's desperate pleas, Daphne did not stop. When she neared the river, she cried out to her father for help. Peneus transformed his daughter into a laurel tree. Her feet became roots that caught hold in the riverbank, her torso became a bark-covered trunk, and evergreen leaves sprouted from her fingers. From that moment on, Apollo wore a laurel wreath on his head as a way to remember his love for Daphne.

DAPHNE'S DRAMATIC TRANSFORMATION

"...her slender arms
Were changed to branches and her hair to leaves;
Her feet but now so swift were anchored fast
In numb stiff roots, her face and head became
The crown of a green tree; all that remained
Of Daphne was her shining loveliness."

OVID, *METAMORPHOSES*, BOOK I, LINES 552–557

- The laurel wreath has become a symbol of victory, and ancient Olympian athletes were crowned with such wreaths. Even today, winners of competitions might receive one to wear on their heads.

- "Resting on your laurels" is a phrase that means you have gotten lazy and complacent just because you were successful before.

- A laureate is the name given to a leader in a given field, such as a nation's poet laureate.

- What the Greeks called laurel is now actually known as the bay leaf, an herb used to flavor food. The plant known as mountain laurel, however, was named because it has a similar leaf.

Pyramus *and* Thisbe
A Classic Tragedy

In the ancient city of Babylon, a young man named Pyramus lived next door to a girl named Thisbe. They were devoted to one another and wanted desperately to marry, but their parents forbade it. Because of an ancient grudge, the families remained the bitterest of enemies and would not even consider the union.

Still, Pyramus and Thisbe communicated through a hole in the stone wall that divided their properties. One day, unable to accept the separation any longer, Pyramus suggested they go that night to a place where their parents could not find them. They planned to escape individually and then meet under a mulberry tree next to a well-known tomb in the town of Ninevah.

Pyramus and Thisbe left their homes in darkness, and Thisbe arrived first at the tree. Although she was nervous in this unfamiliar place, she would have gladly stayed to wait for Pyramus had it not been for an intruder: A lioness appeared from the dark woods and prowled toward the girl. Thisbe dropped her shawl and fled. The curious lioness tore the delicate shawl into shreds, and in the process, stained it with the blood of a recent kill.

Just at that moment, Pyramus arrived at the tomb and looked eagerly for his love. What he saw, however, was the lioness walking away from the bloodstained shawl, which he knew belonged to Thisbe. Assuming the worst, he pulled out his dagger and stabbed himself so he could join Thisbe in death. Thisbe returned to the horrifying scene, knelt beside Pyramus, and reached instinctively for the dagger. When she stabbed herself, the blood of the two lovers pooled at the base of a nearby mulberry tree. As the blood seeped into the soil, the mulberry's white berries darkened and remain a deep purple to this day.

The families of Pyramus and Thisbe found their beloved children and were stunned by the reality of their pointless feud. They ended their long-held grudge and mixed the ashes of Pyramus and Thisbe in the same urn so they could be together for eternity.

* The forbidden boy-girl relationship in "Pyramus and Thisbe" has been featured repeatedly in literature. Shakespeare wrote the famous play *Romeo and Juliet*, and updated versions of the story include the musical *West Side Story*.

* Shakespeare includes this myth in his comedy *A Midsummer Night's Dream*. One of the subplots is about a troupe of bad actors that performs this myth for entertainment at a royal wedding.

THE LOVERS COMMUNICATE THROUGH A HOLE IN THE WALL

"So, on their separate sides, they talked in vain
Till nightfall, then 'goodbye,' and on the wall
Each printed kisses that could never meet."

OVID, *METAMORPHOSES*, BOOK IV, LINES 77-79

ECHO *and* NARCISSUS
Selfless and Selfish Love

The goddesses on Mount Olympus had many attendants who cared for them, fed them, and entertained them. Echo, a friendly nymph known for being talkative, waited on Hera, queen of the Olympians. Hera's husband, Zeus, made good use of Echo's traits and would instruct her to distract Hera with chatter so he could spend time with other women.

Innocent Echo was simply following Zeus' orders, but when Hera found out what Echo had been doing, she was enraged. The goddess punished Echo by taking away her ability to speak on her own; she could only repeat the last few words someone else said. The once cheerful Echo was now forlorn, having lost the skill she most enjoyed.

Echo was walking alone in the forest one day when she spotted a handsome boy. Unbeknownst to her, he was Narcissus, a youth known equally for his good looks and his arrogance. Echo followed him, helplessly waiting for him to speak.

When Narcissus became separated from his hunting party, he sensed someone was near and called out, "Is anyone here?" to which Echo eagerly repeated, "Here!"

Narcissus frowned and said, "Who is there? Come to me!" And Echo happily replied, "Come to *me!*"

Now frustrated, Narcissus' voice became stern. "Make yourself known! I am here!" With that, Echo leaped out from behind a tree and said joyfully, "I am here!"

The rude boy looked at her with such disgust, however, that her smile disappeared. "Stay away, you ugly girl!" he said with a sneer. As he turned to walk away, he added, "I'd die before ever falling in love with you!"

To which Echo whispered, "Ever falling in love with you."

Embarrassed and ashamed for being so scorned, Echo ran to a nearby cave, retreating from all her friends. She neither ate nor slept; she merely repeated the words "ever falling in love with you" in a sweet, sad voice. Over time, her body withered, and her bones hardened to stones. All that remained was her soft voice.

Narcissus was indifferent to the pain he had caused Echo. However, Nemesis, the goddess of vengeance, had heard pleas from countless other maidens who had been rudely scorned by Narcissus. When Nemesis witnessed how Narcissus had treated Echo, she finally took action.

Nemesis struck Narcissus with thirst and invisibly led him to a tiny pool of clear water. Just as he leaned down to drink, Nemesis cast upon him another spell, one that made him fall hopelessly in love with his own reflection. Transfixed, he refused to be separated from himself, and he slowly withered away from hunger and a broken heart. His dying words to his own image were, "My impossible love, farewell!" And Echo's weak voice repeated, "impossible love, farewell."

• From the name Narcissus, the famous psychologist Sigmund Freud coined the term **narcissist**: someone who is so absorbed in himself that he ignores the feelings and needs of others and treats them rudely.

* The word **echo** comes from this myth. Ancient people often thought an actual voice repeated their words when they called out among the mountains, but echoes occur because sound waves bounce off solid surfaces and travel back to the ear.

* *Narcissus* is a genus of flower that includes all types of daffodils. These bulbs come up in the spring and blossom into white, yellow, or peach-colored flowers. Some lore says the Narcissus was given this name because its head bends down as if gazing at its own reflection.

NARCISSUS IS TRANSFORMED INTO A FLOWER

"On the green grass
He drooped his weary head, and those bright eyes
That loved their master's beauty closed in death.
...And then the brandished torches, bier and pyre
Were ready—but no body anywhere;
And in its stead they found a flower—behold,
White petals clustered round a cup of gold!"

OVID, *METAMORPHOSES*, BOOK III, LINES 502-513

MYTHS SHOWING *the* RESULTS *of* HUBRIS

SOURCES

The myth of Bellerophon is based on two original sources: Book VI of Homer's *Iliad* (translated by Robert Fagles) and Pindar's *Olympian Odes* (translated by William H. Race).

All of the other myths in this section are based on Ovid's *Metamorphoses*.

While the Greeks saw nothing wrong with being capable and confident, they would not tolerate excessive pride, a state they called hubris. The word means "to rush at impetuously," and those who acted with hubris were arrogant, self-serving, and likely overstepping their mortal bounds.

It is no surprise, then, that so many Greek myths focused on the dire consequences of hubris, and the following section contains eight such tales. The first is about the mortal girl Arachne who boldly challenges Athena to a weaving contest and is punished for her arrogance. The well-known myth of King Midas is about a man who makes a foolish and greedy wish and then is filled with regret.

The next three myths feature similar young men—Icarus, Phaethon, and Bellerophon—who long to experience the magic of flight but pay dearly when they attempt to reach unsafe heights. The myths of both Sisyphus and Tantalus deal with men who arrogantly test the gods and receive brutal eternal punishments. And the final myth about Niobe—the most violent story in this section—shows the horrifying results of a mother's hubris.

ARACHNE
and the Origin of Spiders

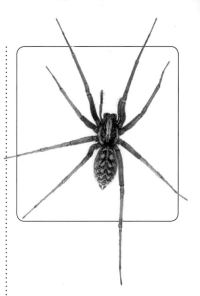

A mortal girl named Arachne had gained a reputation for her weaving. People from all over came to buy her tapestries and to see her work at her loom. Arachne, while indeed talented, had become so conceited that she bragged her skills were better than those of the goddess of weaving herself, Athena.

When word reached Olympus that a mortal girl was boastfully comparing herself to a goddess, Athena decided to give Arachne a chance to redeem herself. Disguised as an old woman, Athena went to see Arachne's tapestries. She complimented the young girl on her skills but warned her to stop likening herself to a powerful goddess. "If you admit your hubris and ask Athena for forgiveness, she will understand," the goddess advised.

She was shocked, however, by the girl's reply. "Who do you think you are, old woman? You are obviously jealous of me. I would gladly challenge Athena if she would dare to face me in a contest!"

With that, Athena rose up and transformed into her true appearance. With her eyes blazing, she stared directly at Arachne and declared, "Athena has come!"

Arachne blushed in spite of herself but then clenched her fists with resolve. She ordered two looms to be set up immediately.

When the contest began, Athena went about creating an orderly, symmetrical tapestry which showed the Olympians in all their glory. In the four corners, she carefully depicted scenes in which mortals had been punished by gods for their acts of hubris.

Arachne wove with equal skill and equal vengeance. Her tapestry teemed with detailed scenes of the gods deceiving mortal women, including tricks played by Zeus, Poseidon, and Dionysus. Her tapestry was so filled with these "crimes of heaven," as Ovid described them, that she only had room for a thin border of ivy.

After finishing her own work, Athena turned to see Arachne's tapestry. She was jealous because she could find no fault with Arachne's skill as a weaver. But she was also astonished by Arachne's gall at portraying the Olympians in such a negative way. When Arachne's eyes met Athena's, she finally realized the extent of her hubris and reached for a rope to hang herself. Athena, taking pity on the girl at the last moment, allowed her to live, but sprinkled her with a lotion that transformed Arachne—and all of her future children—into spiders.

- **Arachnids** are arthropods with four pairs of legs, including mites, ticks, spiders, and scorpions.

- Someone with a fear of spiders is said to have **arachnophobia**. The word alludes to two Greek characters: Arachne and Phobos, the god of fear and a son of Ares.

- To **"spin a yarn"** means to tell an entertaining story. The phrase likely began because women spent a great deal of time spinning yarn together and would share stories to pass the time. The process and the stories became synonymous.

- Some Native Americans have a tradition of making small webs from straps of sinew and hanging the "dream catchers" over their children's beds; bad dreams get caught in the web, but good thoughts will pass through.

MIDAS
and the Golden Touch

An old man named Silenus had lost his way and was found by Midas, king of Phrygia. Midas knew Silenus was a faithful companion to the god Dionysus, and so he took gentle care of him. Dionysus was so grateful for Midas' hospitality that he promised to grant Midas one wish. The foolish king did not think long before demanding, "Let everything I touch turn to gold!" Dionysus smiled and shook his head, knowing Midas would regret his greed. He kept his promise, however, and gave Midas the gift of the golden touch.

At first, anyone would have envied Midas. His path became gold as his feet struck the ground. One finger on his front door turned his home into a glittering palace. The marble statues inside all turned to solid gold. He was now wealthy beyond belief.

To celebrate, he ordered his staff to prepare a lavish banquet, but when he began to eat, he realized his folly. The bread he touched instantly turned solid, as did the fruit and sumptuous meat. When he tried to drink, not only did the glass transform, but the wine inside became a mass of gold. Midas realized that even with his immense wealth, he was doomed to starve.

Midas fell to his knees on his golden floor and prayed to Dionysus, begging him to reverse the power that had so quickly become a curse. Dionysus, feeling nothing but pity for the foolish old king, told him to go and bathe in the Pactolus River where magical waters would wash away his golden curse. Midas ran to the forest to rid himself of his greed. When he plunged into the water, his wish was washed away and turned the sand along the banks of the Pactolus River a beautiful golden color.

Now feeling an aversion to wealth, Midas spent less and less time in his palace. While walking in the woods one day, he happened upon Apollo, the god of music, and Pan, a lesser god of the forest. Pan, who played the panpipes, had challenged Apollo, the master of the lyre, to a music competition, and they asked Midas to be their judge. After they had finished, Midas once again blurted out a response he would later regret. "While Apollo's playing was beautiful, I prefer Pan's delightful pipes!" Midas had shown hubris by choosing a lesser god over an Olympian, and the offended Apollo replied that anyone who did not enjoy his music had the ears of an ass. He promptly punished Midas with gray, hairy, floppy donkey ears.

The embarrassed Midas covered his head with a turban. The only person who knew the truth was his barber, who nearly burst with the embarrassing secret. One day, unable to remain silent any longer, the barber dug a hole in a field and whispered the secret into the dirt. Later that year, reeds grew up from the hole, and when the south wind blows, the reeds still whisper, "King Midas has the ears of an ass!"

+ One version of this myth includes the tragic detail that Midas turned his own daughter into a gold statue when he embraced her. Luckily, she was restored to life after Midas washed in the Pactolus River.

+ It is a compliment to tell someone he has a "**Midas touch**" because it means whatever he does is successful.

"The sacred mountain's judgement and award
Pleased all who heard; yet one voice challenging,
Crass-witted Midas' voice, called it unjust.
Apollo could not suffer ears so dull
To keep their human shape. He stretched them long,
Filled them with coarse grey hairs, and hinged their base
To move and twitch and flop; all else was man;
In that one part his punishment; he wears
Henceforth a little ambling ass's ears."

OVID, *METAMORPHOSES*, BOOK XI, LINES 176-184

ICARUS *and* DAEDALUS
Flying and Falling

The Assignment

Daedalus was known throughout Greece as an artist, inventor, and architect. King Minos, the ruler of Crete, hired Daedalus to help him hide an embarrassing secret. Not long before, King Minos had tried to fool Poseidon by offering him an inferior bull rather than a sacred one. As punishment, Poseidon made the king's wife, Queen Pasiphae, fall in love with a bull, and she later gave birth to a hideous, wild creature which had the head and torso of a bull and the body of a man. Called the Minotaur, this unruly beast would eat anything and anyone in sight. King Minos needed Daedalus to design a structure to imprison it.

Daedalus accepted the challenge and began designing an elaborate, tunneling labyrinth with so many twists, turns, and dead ends that nothing could escape from it. After its construction, the Minotaur was placed in the center, and every nine years, seven boys and seven girls were put in the maze as a sacrifice to feed the bull. After Daedalus completed his assignment, he assumed he could leave Crete. However, King Minos saw Daedalus as a powerful ally who could design and build new weapons. Therefore, King Minos imprisoned both Daedalus and his son Icarus in a tower.

The Escape

While he was treated humanely and given a fine workshop, Daedalus could not stand to be locked up. He knew, however, that trying to escape on foot or by sea was impossible because the king's armies were guarding him carefully. The inventor knew he could not leave in a traditional way, so he would have to try something new: flying. He had feathers of all shapes and sizes delivered to his workshop and gave his son the task of categorizing them. After studying the wings of birds and experimenting with various constructions, Daedalus finally made two pairs of wings held together by wax.

The next morning, Daedalus carefully strapped one pair of wings on his son and another pair on himself. Gripping Icarus by the shoulders, Daedalus looked him straight in the eyes and warned him, "These wings are only tools and are not like the natural wings of the gods. If you fly too low, the spray from the sea will make the feathers too heavy. If you fly too high, the heat from the sun will melt the wax. Either way, you will drown. Our only goal is to get to land as soon as possible." Troubled with fear but desperate to escape, Daedalus then leapt out of the tower and called to his son to follow.

+ The word labyrinth comes from a Greek word meaning "labor into." Some labyrinths are like mazes, with many possible paths between an entrance and an exit, while others consist of a single winding path that leads to a center and back out again. The latter are often used for meditative purposes.

+ The Minotaur was eventually killed by the hero Theseus.

+ "Minos may own all else; he does not own / The air." Daedalus in Ovid's *Metamorphoses*, Book VIII, Lines 188-189.

+ This myth keenly illustrates the Greek concept of the **Golden Mean**, which teaches the importance of moderation. To fly safely, Icarus could not fly too high or too low. When he disobeyed, he was severely punished.

The Mistake

Both struggled at first to operate the wings, but they soon found their rhythm and were flying smoothly, looking down at the astonished faces of the people of Crete. While Daedalus led the way, scanning the horizon for land, Icarus, now confident with his skills, began swooping and banking around the sky. "This is what the gods must feel!" he yelled. "I could fly all the way to Mount Olympus!" Ignoring his father's distant cries and feeling strength surge through his arms, Icarus climbed higher and higher, relishing the warmth of the sun on his face. Icarus could have indeed climbed to the heights of the heavens, but he looked in horror to see wax dripping from his wings and the feathers peeling off and fluttering away. Daedalus, circling below, watched helplessly while his beloved son plummeted to the sea and disappeared.

Cursing his skill for invention, Daedalus flew on with aching arms and an aching heart. As soon as he reached land, he built a temple and hung his wings there as an offering to Apollo, the god who represented the Golden Mean. Daedalus recognized man's limitations and never flew again.

- This myth is etiological in that it explains the names of both the Icarian Sea and Icaria Island, both to the east of mainland Greece. The Icarian Sea is where Icarus drowned, and the island is where Daedalus landed and built the temple for Apollo.

- The main character in Irish writer's James Joyce's *A Portrait of the Artist as a Young Man* is named Stephen Dedalus. The name is an allusion to Daedalus because both men are frustrated artists. In Stephen Dedalus' case, he longs to fly away from the constricting politics and religion of Dublin in the early 1900s.

PHAETHON
The Son of the Sun

Clymene, one of the beautiful Oceanids, had fallen in love with Helios, the god of the sun. She bore his child, Phaethon, and raised him well. Although Clymene told him stories of his father and pointed each day to the sun as it rose high into the sky, Phaethon was ridiculed by others who thought he was lying about his famous father. The more he bragged to convince them, the less they believed him.

Finally, Clymene recognized Phaethon's anguish and allowed him to travel to the heavens to see Helios. When the young man stood before the mighty god, he himself doubted he was the son of the sun. His father, however, welcomed him gladly, even swearing on the River Styx to grant Phaethon any wish to prove his love. Without taking time to consider, Phaethon blurted out that he wanted to drive his father's chariot for one day.

Helios rose up in alarm, removed his radiant crown, and looked lovingly at his son. "Oh, young Phaethon!" he begged. "Ask me anything but that! Steering the sun chariot is truly difficult; even though I do it every day, the steeds are often stubborn, and the magnificent heights still frighten me. Even the mighty Zeus will not take the reins of my chariot, and so how will you, a child, handle the task?"

In desperation, Helios told Phaethon—here in Ovid's words—that "wild beasts lie in wait and shapes of fear," referring to the constellations in the zodiac, including the Bull, the Archer, the Lion, the Scorpion, and the Crab.

Tragically, Helios' grave concerns could not dissuade his son, who was foolishly determined to prove himself by taking on the task. So it was with a heavy heart that Helios led his son to the chariot. The team of steeds towered over young Phaethon. The massive sun crown nearly covered his eyes. The heavy reins were so thick, the youth could hardly grasp them. Helios attempted to instruct his son, warning him of the most dangerous passes. "If you fly too high, you'll burn the heavens; if you steer too low, you'll burn the earth. The best course is to stay in the middle."

Phaethon scarcely heard these last words because the horses had started to run, and they paid no mind to the feeble tugs on their reins. Phaethon changed quickly from proud to panicked when he realized he was alone in the sky. The horses moved wildly, heaving the chariot too high, careening from side to side, and then plummeting toward the earth. Phaethon regretted his wish desperately, but it was too late. With the heavens, sea, and land already damaged, Zeus had little choice but to intervene. He hurled one of his largest jagged thunderbolts, killing Phaethon and destroying the chariot. The team of horses was later reined in by Helios, who never let anyone else steer the sun again.

◆ Remember that an oath sworn on the River Styx, called a Stygian Oath, could never be broken.

◆ The Greeks believed Phaethon's fateful ride created the world's deserts and that the River Nile was so frightened by the burning flames that it hid its head. The source of the river actually remained a mystery for centuries.

◆ In Shakespeare's *Romeo and Juliet*, Juliet, desperate for night to come so she can see Romeo, wishes Phaethon were driving the sun's chariot. She says,

"Gallop apace, you fiery-footed steeds, / Towards Phoebus' lodging! Such a wagoner / As [Phaethon] would whip you to the West / And bring in cloudy night immediately." (Act III, Scene II, lines 1-4)

GAEA PLEADING WITH ZEUS TO SAVE THE WORLD

"...Even Atlas fails,
His shoulders scarce sustain the flaming sky.
If land and sea, if heaven's high palaces
Perish, prime chaos will us all confound!
Save from the flames whatever's still alive,
And prove you mean Creation to survive!"

OVID, *METAMORPHOSES*, BOOK II, LINES 284-299

BELLEROPHON
Great Expectations

Of all the creatures in classical mythology, the Chimaera was perhaps the most bizarre. A terrifying combination of lion, goat, and dragon, the Chimaera had been terrorizing the land of Lycia, and people were desperate for a hero. When the prince Bellerophon heard about the Chimaera, he pledged to kill the beast as a way of purifying himself after accidentally killing his own brother.

Poseidon allowed Bellerophon to use a winged horse named Pegasus, one of his own offspring that had been born to the Gorgon Medusa, but Bellerophon had great difficulty taming the magnificent beast. Athena then came to the mortal in a dream, and when he awoke, he found a golden bridle in his hand. Using this gift, he was able to calm Pegasus and quickly became a deft rider on the creature's wide back.

While other men had tried to kill the Chimaera while standing on the ground, Bellerophon was the first to attack the beast from the air. Bellerophon succeeded in slaying the monster and rode Pegasus on several other dangerous missions. Although the heroic Bellerophon deserved praise and respect, he became too hubristic.

Indeed, after performing his tasks, Bellerophon was convinced he could fly all the way to Mount Olympus and be welcomed by the gods and goddesses. When Zeus saw the mortal approaching, he sent a fly to sting Pegasus. The huge horse bucked violently, sending Bellerophon plummeting toward the ground. After landing in a briar patch, the brave, foolish Bellerophon was alive but humiliated and spent the remainder of his days wandering alone.

HOMER'S DESCRIPTION OF THE CHIMAERA

"grim monster sprung of the gods, nothing human,
all lion in front, all snake behind, all goat between,
terrible, blasting lethal fire at every breath!"

HOMER, THE *ILIAD*, BOOK 6, LINES 213-215

+ Pegasus, an offspring of Poseidon and the Gorgon Medusa, was a symbol of the imagination and was associated with the Muses. The Chimaera was one of the beastly offspring of Echidna and Typhon.

+ In modern zoology, the term **chimera** is used to describe an animal that has genetically different cells, such as some from a goat and some from a sheep.

+ While Bellerophon was not allowed on Mount Olympus, Pegasus was welcomed by Zeus, who gave the flying horse the job of fetching his lightning bolts.

SISYPHUS
and His Futile Labors

Sisyphus lived a life of frustration. He did not get along with his siblings, he was always seeking revenge on his enemies, and he fathered several unlucky children. It was not until he began methodically tricking immortals, however, that he received true punishment.

First, Sisyphus struck a deal with the river god Asopus: If Asopus provided an eternal spring of water for Sisyphus' kingdom of Corinth, Sispyhus would tell Asopus who had abducted his daughter. Asopus created the spring, and Sisyphus revealed the abductor: Zeus. While Zeus was indeed guilty, he was enraged that a mortal had gotten involved. He sent Thanatos, the personification of death, to claim Sisyphus. But Thanatos was tricked, too. Sisyphus conned him into trying on unbreakable handcuffs, and Death himself became a prisoner in Sisyphus' house.

After Ares released Thanatos, Sisyphus was to be sent to the realm of Hades. Before he was taken, however, he cunningly told his wife not to give him a proper burial. When Sisyphus reached the Underworld, he tricked a third immortal, Persephone. He told her he must return to the earth for three days so he could have an appropriate funeral and punish his wife for neglecting him. Persephone relented, but of course Sisyphus had no intention of voluntarily returning to the dreary land of the dead.

Zeus had seen enough. After learning how Sisyphus had tricked Thanatos and Persephone, he condemned the arrogant mortal to Tartarus, the most desolate region of the Underworld. Zeus then devised a grueling and futile task: Sisyphus spent every day pushing a gigantic boulder up a hill, and just when he neared the top, the boulder would roll once again to the bottom. Sisyphus could not stop and could never have the satisfaction of succeeding.

+ Sisyphus' son Sinon was the Greek who, near the end of the mythical Trojan War, convinced the Trojans to take a huge wooden horse inside their walled city. Greek warriors had hidden inside the horse and led a ransack on the city of Troy.

+ A **Sisyphean task** is long and futile.

+ Albert Camus wrote the essay "The Myth of Sisyphus" in 1940 during World War II. In it, he explored the concept of the absurd and expressed his desire for meaning and order in a frightening, random, and futile world. In the preface of a later edition, he wrote that although his essay "poses mortal problems, it sums itself up for me as a lucid invitation to live and to create, in the very midst of the desert."

ODYSSEUS SEES SISYPHUS IN THE UNDERWORLD

"…bound to his own torture,
grappling his monstrous boulder with both arms working,
heaving, hands struggling, legs driving, he kept on
thrusting the rock uphill toward the brink, but just
as it teetered, set to topple over—

                  time and again
the immense weight of the thing would wheel it back and
the ruthless boulder would bound and tumble down to the plain again—"

HOMER, THE *ODYSSEY*, BOOK 11, LINES 681-687

TANTALUS
Always Wanting More

Tantalus, one of Zeus' sons by an Oceanid, was only a demigod but became a favorite among the Olympians. He was often invited to dine on Mount Olympus, and the gods and goddesses held him in high regard. Tantalus, however, was hubristic and began to brag to mortals about his status. He threw elaborate parties and showed his friends trinkets he had stolen from Olympus, and he shared stories he had been told in confidence while dining with the gods.

These minor misbehaviors paled in comparison, however, to the time when Tantalus played host to the Olympians. Whether he was testing the gods or trying to humiliate them, Tantalus killed his own son, Pelops, and served him in the form of a stew. All the Olympians knew they had been tricked and refused to eat: all, that is, except Demeter. Still grieving for her daughter, Persephone, Demeter absentmindedly ate the stew and swallowed part of Pelops' shoulder.

The gods took action. First, Zeus restored Pelops to life and had Hephaestus fashion an ivory shoulder for him. Then the gods banished Tantalus to Tartarus, the most unpleasant domain in the Underworld. There he was made to stand in a pool of sparkling water that would recede whenever Tantalus bent to drink. Overhead, boughs of delicious fruit swayed just out of Tantalus' reach whenever he tried to eat. Tantalus would spend eternity hungry, thirsty, and frustrated because he had not appreciated the true bounty he had while he was alive.

- Tantalus' hubris started a curse on his family, and his unlucky descendants played major roles in the Trojan War.

- This myth is the origin of the word **tantalizing**, which means "tempting but out of reach."

ODYSSEUS SEES TANTALUS IN THE UNDERWORLD

"...time and again the old man stooped, craving a sip,
time and again the water vanished, swallowed down,
laying bare the caked black earth at his feet—
some spirit drank it dry. And over his head
leafy trees dangled their fruit from high aloft,
pomegranates and pears, and apples glowing red,
succulent figs and olives swelling sleek and dark,
but as soon as the old man would strain to clutch them fast
a gust would toss them up to the lowering dark clouds."

HOMER, THE *ODYSSEY*, BOOK 11, LINES 672-680

NIOBE
A Mother's Conceit

Tantalus' only daughter, the beautiful Niobe, unfortunately inherited her father's arrogance. While others recognized how Tantalus had taken advantage of the gods, Niobe exulted in her father's privileged position and made the same mistake he had by assuming she deserved special treatment. As the queen of Thebes, she even warned her people not to make sacrifices on the altars of the gods unless they wanted to fall from her favor.

Before long, however, a prophetess spread word to the women of Thebes. Leto, the mother by Zeus to Apollo and Artemis, was furious that her temples were bare and untended. Afraid of being stricken by the arrows of the revered twins, the women of Thebes planned a great festival for Leto and began a procession to her altar. As they passed Niobe's palace, they shrank in fear. Would the queen see them?

The bronze doors opened, and the regal Niobe appeared, surrounded by slaves and attendants. Her presence commanded silence. She stared down the leader of the procession and growled harsh words.

"Why would you worship Leto, the mother of only two children, when I, your queen, have borne seven sons and seven daughters, all more perfect than Leto's? I am a child of gods, too. My father, Tantalus, was a son of Zeus. My mother was a daughter of Atlas. I dare you to honor the mere Leto before you lay down your honors before me!" Her eyes still blazing, the queen turned on her heels and strode back through her doors.

Although the procession scattered in fear, many women returned in the secrecy of night to place their laurel wreaths in Leto's temple. Leto was pleased with the acts of the Thebans and furious with the arrogant Niobe. By dawn the very next day, Apollo sped to earth and found Niobe's sons in the meadowlands just beyond the city. One by one, he struck them down with his arrows.

Word spread quickly throughout Thebes and all were stricken with grief. Niobe's husband, King Amphion, even took his own life to end his pain. That evening, however, the queen stood with her sad daughters among the biers of her sons and her husband, and she raised her angry voice to the heavens. "You have taken my sons, Leto, but I still have my precious daughters! I am still greater than you!"

Just then, as the moon appeared in the misty sky, Niobe's daughters began to collapse around her. She tried to shield her youngest from the unseen arrows of Artemis and asked for one to be spared, but there was no mercy. The proud queen sat amidst the horrifying scene, absolutely frozen, determined not to hang her head. Despite her efforts, however, she could not stop the tears that fell from her eyes.

The gods eventually took pity on Niobe and carried her to a mountainside. There she sits, as hard and soulless as a rock except for a flowing stream of water. She is now considered a symbol of eternal grief.

+ When jealous Hera learned that Leto was expecting twins fathered by Zeus, she ordered all lands to refuse Leto shelter. The floating island of Delos finally welcomed the mortal. Zeus later anchored the island to the sea with pillars, and the land became sacred to Apollo.

+ On a cliff on Turkey's Mount Sipylus is a natural rock formation that resembles a woman's face. Homer actually refers to this natural statue in the *Iliad*, which dates to the eighth century BCE. Because the limestone in the mountain is porous, seeping water forms a continuous stream from the woman's face, believed to be Niobe's.

SECTION VI

MYTHS *about* COSTLY MISTAKES

The previous section showed what happened to mortals who acted with hubris, the word the Greeks used to describe arrogance. This final section relays four sad stories about mortals who make simple, innocent, or inadvertent mistakes.

In the first myth, the hunter Actaeon's life takes a fatal ironic turn after he happens upon a modest goddess. It shows the tragedy that can result from being in the wrong place at the wrong time. In the myth of Atalanta, a young woman tries to avoid her fate, but she and her new husband suffer mightily when he forgets to say two important words: "Thank you."

The third myth, Orpheus, contains one of the saddest moments in classical mythology when, in a split second, the musician Orpheus loses his beloved wife forever. And the myth of Oedipus is about a young man who, in an attempt to escape his fate, walks directly into it. After he realizes his mistake, he is overwhelmed with grief and shame.

SOURCES

The myth of Oedipus is based on Apollodorus' *The Library* and Sophocles' play *Oedipus the King*.

All of the other myths in this section are based on Ovid's *Metamorphoses*.

ACTAEON
Cruel Irony

The young mortal Actaeon was a fine hunter, and he spent many days in the woods with his friends and his pack of loyal dogs. After one successful morning hunt, Actaeon and his friends parted ways, and the youth walked with his dogs through the forest toward his home.

In these same woods, the Olympian goddess Artemis had also just completed her morning hunt. She and her attendants, a group of woodland nymphs, were getting ready to bathe in Artemis' sacred spring, which was nestled in a valley and sheltered by cypress trees and pines. When Actaeon happened to wander down into this beautiful valley, he caught sight of the unclothed goddess and her attendants.

As soon as the nymphs realized the mortal man's presence, they shrieked and tried to shield the goddess with their own bodies. But this was not enough for the fiercely independent and chaste Artemis, whose embarrassment had quickly turned to anger. She hurled water in Actaeon's face and cursed him, transforming him into a stag so he could never tell anyone that he had seen the proud goddess unclothed.

Artemis' curse then took an ironic turn. Actaeon—now a stag—panicked and ran, and his very own dogs chased after him in hot pursuit. The well-trained pack, dozens in all, caught the helpless stag, dragged him to the ground, and sunk their sharp teeth into his flesh. The transformed mortal tried desperately to call out, but he could not make a sound.

Actaeon's friends heard the howling dogs from across the forest and gathered around to watch the kill. "Why is Actaeon not here to cheer on his loyal dogs?" they asked. But of course these men did not know that poor Actaeon was indeed present at the scene.

When news of Actaeon's death spread to Mount Olympus, some of the pantheon thought Artemis had acted too harshly, while others praised the goddess for her fierce determination to protect her privacy.

◆ Modern writer Richard Connell's short story "The Most Dangerous Game" is about a wealthy, eccentric man named General Zaroff. This cruel man lures hunters to his private island and then, after treating them well, turns them loose into the forest and begins to hunt *them*. The innocent victims in Connell's haunting story echo the fear and confusion Actaeon felt when he suddenly found himself in the role of prey.

THE BRUTAL DEATH OF ACTAEON

"Now they are all around him, tearing deep
Their master's flesh, the stag that is no stag;
And not until so many countless wounds
Had drained away his lifeblood, was the wrath,
It's said, of chaste Diana satisfied."

OVID, *METAMORPHOSES*, BOOK III, LINES 252-256

ATALANTA
Running from Fate

The mortal princess Atalanta was known for her great athleticism and her great beauty. Unfortunately, when she consulted an oracle about marriage, she was given disturbing news: "Refuse any husband," the oracle told her. "But you won't refuse and yourself shall lose."

After hearing the confusing prophecy, Atalanta resolved never to marry. But throngs of men were in such awe of her strength and beauty that many sought her hand, and she was forced to come up with a plan. So she challenged any suitor to a foot race; the reward for winning was her hand, but the punishment for losing was death.

With her tremendous speed, Atalanta easily beat her opponents, and one by one her suitors were killed. A young man named Hippomenes was called to judge one of the races, and he questioned aloud why any man would risk death to marry Atalanta. The minute he saw her, however, he recognized her grace, spirit, and beauty. He, too, was willing to gamble his own life to be with her.

Just before his race, Hippomenes prayed to Aphrodite, imploring her to help him succeed. The goddess of love appeared and gave him three golden apples, instructing the young man how to use them to distract Atalanta during the race.

The next day, Atalanta stood next to Hippomenes at the starting line, and for the first time, she felt a stirring. She had raced the other suitors without passion and had no regrets when they were killed. But she saw in Hippomenes such eagerness that she felt pity for him. A moment later, however, the trumpet sounded, and she soon took the lead in their race. Hippomenes tossed the first of the golden apples Aphrodite had given to him onto the path, and the surprised Atalanta bent to retrieve it. She passed Hippomenes again, but then stopped to claim the second apple. Finally, with barely any strength left, Hippomenes hurled the last apple off to the side of the course. Atalanta paused, wanting to claim the apple and, perhaps even more, wanting Hippomenes to win. When she turned to retrieve the golden prize, Hippomenes overtook her and crossed the finish line.

Atalanta gladly married the handsome Hippomenes, but fate once again could not be escaped. Hippomenes forgot to thank Aphrodite properly for her help, so he and his new bride were punished. Aphrodite, a goddess known as much for her pride as for her beauty, turned the mortals into lions and made them pull a chariot for the Titan Rhea.

Of the two lions, Ovid wrote, "[I]n their eyes / Cruel anger blazed and growls they gave for speech." Atalanta had not refused marriage, so she did, indeed, lose herself.

+ This etching shows Rhea being pulled by two forlorn lions. One of Rhea's Roman names was Terra ("earth"), and the Phrygians called her Cybele.

"And now he flagged, his breath came fast and dry
And there was far to go; so then he threw
One of the three gold apples from the tree.
She was amazed and, eager to secure
The gleaming fruit, swerved sideways from the track
And seized the golden apple as it rolled.
He passed her and the benches roared applause."

OVID, *METAMORPHOSES*, BOOK X, LINES 666-672

ORPHEUS
A Song of Sadness

Calliope, the muse of epic poetry, had a son, Orpheus, who had inherited many of her talents. His strong, clear voice and his gift for poetry were legendary in Greece. And when he played his lyre, everyone who listened would fall into a peaceful trance. Even the trees and rocks responded, inching closer to hear the beautiful sounds.

The only thing Orpheus loved more than music was a nymph named Eurydice. Unfortunately, Orpheus and Eurydice were only married for a few days when she was bitten in the heel by a venomous snake and died. When Orpheus learned of his bride's death, he was inconsolable. For days, he remained almost paralyzed until he realized he must do the impossible by going to the Underworld and asking Hades to release Eurydice.

Armed only with his lyre, he traveled until he found a cave that led to Hades' realm. Orpheus first played beautiful music for Charon, convincing the ferryman to row him across the River Styx. Then, walking slowly toward the gates, he began to play again, this time soothing the beastly three-headed dog, Cerberus. At last, Orpheus approached the god Hades and sang of his deep love for Eurydice.

The habitually coldhearted Hades was so moved that he actually felt pity. When he finally spoke, he said, "I will release your wife on one condition: You must walk ahead of her and not look back until you reach the light. If you do not heed my demand, she will return to live with me forever."

Orpheus thanked Hades and began his journey. He could not sense Eurydice's presence when Charon rowed him back across the River Styx. He could not hear any footsteps behind him when he ascended toward the light. His heart pounded with fear, then sank with doubt. Had Hades tricked him? Only steps away from the opening of the cave, Orpheus impulsively turned his head to look for his love, and saw her ghost slip quietly into the darkness.

Panicked, Orpheus slid down the steep terrain and followed after her. He could no longer see Eurydice but called her name over and over until his throat was raw. Orpheus was now hopelessly lost. When he finally reached the River Styx, Charon turned his back on him. Hades had kept his word.

Orpheus returned to the world but was so overwhelmed with grief and guilt, he resented all others and refused all love. He was eventually attacked by a group of crazed women who were angered because he would no longer play his lyre. Orpheus' body was bathed and buried by the Muses, and some say nightingales sing constantly around his grave.

+ *Orfeo*, a musical work based on Orpheus' story, is considered one of the earliest operas. Composed by Italian Claudio Monteverdi, it was first performed in 1607. The piece was widely performed in 2007 in honor of its 400th anniversary.

+ Some versions of this myth say Dionysus was jealous of Orpheus, and he drove the women who killed Orpheus into a rage. The gods punished these women by turning them into oak trees.

"So to the music of his strings he sang,
And all the bloodless spirits wept to hear;
And Tantalus forgot the fleeing water,
...And Sisyphus sat rapt upon his stone.
Then first by that sad singing overwhelmed,
The Furies' cheeks, it's said, were wet with tears.
And Hades' queen and he whose sceptre rules
The Underworld could not deny the prayer,
And called Eurydice. She was among
The recent ghosts and, limping from her wound,
Came slowly forth..."

OVID, *METAMORPHOSES*, BOOK X, LINES 42-54

OEDIPUS
Mistaken Identities

A Cursed Birth

For years, King Laius and Queen Jocasta of Thebes could not bear a child. King Laius finally consulted an oracle, but rather than receiving encouraging advice, he heard a terrifying prophecy: If they had a son, he would grow up to kill his father and marry his own mother.

King Laius was too afraid to tell Jocasta about this prophecy, but after Jocasta became pregnant, the king relayed the oracle's warning. The couple agreed to get rid of the child, piercing his feet and instructing servants to hang their son.

The servants felt too much pity for the innocent boy and could not bring themselves to carry out the instructions. Instead, they presented the infant to a childless couple, King Polybus and Queen Merope of Corinth. They happily adopted the infant boy and named him Oedipus, a name meaning "swollen foot."

The Fate of Oedipus: Part I

Oedipus grew to become a strong, intelligent young man, but King Polybus and Queen Merope could never bring themselves to tell him they were not his real parents. When one of his peers teased Oedipus because he did not resemble his father, Oedipus was frightened. He consulted an oracle and received the same terrifying news King Laius had heard: Oedipus was destined to kill his father and then marry his mother. Out of love for the man and woman he had always believed to be his parents, Oedipus immediately fled Corinth for the nearby town of Thebes.

At this same time, King Laius was leaving Thebes and traveling to Delphi to consult the oracle once again. A beastly creature known as the Sphinx—with the head of a woman, the body of a lion, the wings of an eagle, and the tail of a dragon—had been killing the citizens of Thebes, and Laius wanted to ask the oracle for advice. The king's chariot came to a crossroads, where a young man was standing.

"Step aside!" shouted the charioteer rudely. "Lowly men must make room for their superiors!"

+ The psychologist Sigmund Freud used the story of Oedipus to illustrate his belief that young boys feel a need to take their fathers' place in order to receive love from their mothers. The theory remains highly debatable, but the **Oedipus complex** is still referenced in modern times, often as a joke.

Insulted by this remark, the young man—none other than Oedipus—refused to move. The charioteer ran the horses ahead and almost struck him, and then in a blind fury brought on by sadness, confusion, and youthful pride, Oedipus attacked the charioteer and the man inside, killing them both. One servant managed to survive by fleeing the scene unnoticed. Oedipus had unknowingly fulfilled the first part of the prophecy by killing King Laius.

The Riddle of the Sphinx

Shaken, Oedipus traveled toward Thebes. News of the king's death spread quickly, and the Sphinx continued to kill the helpless citizens. To try to calm the city, Jocasta's brother offered a generous reward: Anyone who could defeat the Sphinx could marry Jocasta and become the next king of Thebes.

Oedipus willingly volunteered and went in search of the beast. In addition to being oddly formed, the Sphinx had an unusual way of taunting its victims. It asked them, "What walks on four legs in the morning, two legs at noon, and three legs in the evening?" Because no one could answer the riddle, no one survived its questioning.

When the Sphinx asked Oedipus, however, the young man replied, "Man. He crawls as an infant, walks upright as a man, and uses a cane in old age." The Sphinx, mortified that someone had answered its riddle, leapt to its death.

The Fate of Oedipus: Part II

As promised, Oedipus was rewarded by marrying the queen of Thebes, none other than his own mother, Jocasta. For nearly twenty years, Oedipus, along with Jocasta and her brother, ruled peaceably, and Oedipus and Jocasta had two sons and two daughters. No one would have known the truth, perhaps, had it not been for a ruinous plague that swept through Thebes. In an attempt to learn of the city's fate, King Oedipus consulted a prophet named Tiresias.

Retribution

Tiresias concluded that the plague had been sent by the gods because the murderer of King Laius had never been found. Tiresias then gave the clue that the guilty man had killed his father and married his mother. Although Oedipus did not realize the situation at first, the evidence became clear. The servant whom Laius had instructed to hang his infant admitted he had not followed the orders; King Polybus and Queen Merope of Corinth confirmed they had adopted an infant boy; and the servant who fled from the chariot returned to Thebes and identified Oedipus as the killer.

Out of shock and shame, Jocasta hanged herself. And horrified by how blindly he had walked into his fate, Oedipus literally blinded himself, using a pin from one of Jocasta's brooches to gouge out his own eyes. When his sons, now recognized as his half-brothers, refused to stop his exile, Oedipus left Thebes and roamed from town to town. He finally died in Athens.

- Author J.K. Rowling devises several complicated riddles for her characters in her *Harry Potter* series, and in her fourth book, *Harry Potter and the Goblet of Fire*, the boy wizard solves a riddle asked of him by a sphinx.

- The Greek Sophocles wrote the play *Oidipous Tyrannos* circa 430 BCE. To the Greeks, a **tyrant** was someone who took power rather than inheriting a throne, and it has come to mean a ruthless or oppressive ruler.

- The Latin version of Sophocles' play is *Oedipus Rex* (*rex* is Latin for "king"). Fittingly, the name of one of the most ferocious dinosaurs that ever lived literally means "king of the tyrant lizards": **Tyrannosaurus rex**.

The Heroes of Classical Mythology

"In spite of their extraordinary abilities, no hero is perfect," writes Donna Rosenberg, the author of *World Mythology*. "Yet their human weaknesses are often as instructive as their heroic qualities. Their imperfections allow ordinary people to identify with them and to like them, for everyone has similar psychological needs and conflicts." Rosenberg makes a sound argument for reading about the triumphs and trials of the heroes. Indeed, no study of mythology is complete without a look at these larger-than-life characters, whose bodies were strong and whose actions were grand, but whose mistakes made them unmistakably human.

The first hero, Perseus, demonstrated bravery and devotion and is best known for killing the beastly Medusa. Jason, the second hero, is an adventurer who seeks glory and leads the Argonauts on a dangerous quest to capture the Golden Fleece. The next hero, Theseus, shows great physical heroism when he kills villains, and he also proves to be a wise leader. And the last is Heracles—Hercules to the Romans—who is perhaps the best known of the classical heroes. After committing a crime, he dedicates himself to completing twelve difficult tasks and is ultimately welcomed on Mount Olympus.

SOURCES

Sources for the myth of Perseus include *Pythian Odes* (Pindar), *Metamorphoses* (Ovid), and *The Library* (Apollodorus).

Sources for Jason include *Jason and the Golden Fleece* (Apollonius), and *Metamorphoses* (Ovid).

Sources for Theseus include *Odes* (Bacchylides), *Life of Theseus* (Plutarch), and *Metamorphoses* (Ovid).

Sources for Heracles include *The Library* (Apollodorus), the *Aeneid* (Virgil), and *Nemean Odes* (Pindar).

PERSEUS
and the Gorgon Medusa

The Birth

Perseus, one of the most respected heroes in classical mythology, was born against his grandfather's wishes. When an oracle told King Acrisius of Argos that any child born to his daughter, Danae, would eventually cause his death, the king locked his daughter in an underground prison so she could not become pregnant. Zeus, however, enchanted by the beautiful prisoner, took the form of gold dust and blew through a tiny window to seduce Danae.

King Acrisius was outraged when he heard a baby's cries coming from his daughter's prison. He knew, however, that killing his grandson outright would incur the wrath of the gods. So, trying once again to outwit fate, he forced Danae and her son into a large chest and floated them out to sea, assuming they would not survive. Zeus was watching over his baby, though, and he made sure the chest washed ashore on an island near the city of Seriphus. A humble fisherman named Dictys found the chest, and he and his wife helped Danae raise her son, Perseus, to become a strong young man.

The Sly Polydectes

Perseus and his mother lived happily in Seriphus until Dictys' sinister brother, the brutal King Polydectes, decided he wanted Danae for himself. Polydectes knew he first needed to get rid of Perseus, so he put a plan into action. First he falsely announced that he was engaged to be married, and then he demanded a horse from each man in his kingdom as a gift. Because Perseus was too poor to give a horse, he offered to complete a mission for the king. This, of course, was exactly what Polydectes had wanted all along.

King Polydectes had the perfect mission to get rid of Perseus forever: Find and kill the Gorgon Medusa.

The Mighty Medusa

The beastly Medusa and two of her Gorgon sisters lived in a remote cave and were so hideous that any person who saw them turned instantly to stone. While Medusa's sisters were immortal, Medusa had once been a lovely mortal maiden. Athena found her to be too vain, however, and turned her flowing hair into a mass of writhing, hissing snakes. Medusa was also cursed with sharp fangs, a serpent's tongue, and hard scales that covered her body.

Perseus would have surely died on this mission without divine help from his powerful father. Before Perseus departed, Zeus sent Athena and Hermes to assist him. Athena lent the youth her shining aegis, explaining how he could use it to see Medusa's reflection rather than looking at her directly. Hermes offered Perseus his winged sandals, a large sword, a bag for the Gorgon's head, and a magic cap to make him invisible. Finally, Athena instructed Perseus to find the Graeae, sisters and guardians of the Gorgons, because only they knew of Medusa's secret lair.

The Graeae, three old women who shared one eyeball and one tooth, were as hideous as the Gorgons. When Perseus came upon them, they were bickering over whose turn it was to use the eye. Perseus took advantage of their collective blindness and snatched the eye as one sister was tossing it to another. Angry but helpless, the Graeae agreed to tell Perseus where the Gorgons could be found in return for their precious eyeball.

Perseus followed their directions and waited until the three Gorgons were asleep. Perseus' movements were so swift and silent, he was able to kill Medusa and flee before the other Gorgons sensed his presence.

Another Heroic Deed

As he was flying back toward Seriphus, Perseus looked down to see a maiden chained to a rock near the ocean. It was Andromeda, the princess of Ethiopia. Her mother, Cassiopeia, had boldly boasted that Andromeda was more beautiful than the sea nymphs. Poseidon, ruler of the sea, was so offended by her hubris that he sent a sea serpent to terrorize the coast of Ethiopia until the couple sacrificed Andromeda to the monster. Distraught, Queen Cassiopeia and her husband, King Cepheus, finally relented and chained their daughter to the rock.

When Perseus offered to slay the serpent in return for Andromeda's hand in marriage, the royal couple quickly agreed. Using Hermes' sword once again, Perseus killed the monster and saved Andromeda. Perseus and Andromeda were married and stayed in Ethiopia where Andromeda bore a son, Perses. After a year, Perseus knew he had to return to Seriphus, so he and Andromeda left Perses to be raised by his grandparents.

- The eye remains a meaningful symbol in world cultures. The Eye of Horus (below) is an ancient Egyptian symbol of protection; the Eye of Providence can be seen floating above a pyramid on the reverse side of the Great Seal of the United States; and an old proverb states, "The eyes are the windows to the soul."

- Perses, the first son of Perseus and Andromeda, inherited Cepheus' kingdom. Myth says Perses' descendants moved east and founded Persia in his honor.

- Athena turned Andromeda, Perseus, Queen Cassiopeia, and King Cepheus into constellations after their deaths, along with the sea monster, Cetus (called "the whale"). Cassiopeia, seen at left, has five distinct stars that form a "W." As punishment, the queen, who is still trying to fix her hair, can often be seen tipped upside down (which is very undignified for royalty).

- 125 -

- Some versions of this myth say Medusa was pregnant with Poseidon's children when Perseus cut off her head. Several offspring sprang from her neck, including Pegasus, the famous winged horse.

- A jellyfish is sometimes called a **medusa**. These creatures can have bell-shaped tops, and many medusae can sting or kill prey using their snake-like tentacles.

"So he went into the palace, where Polydectes had assembled his friends, and turning his head aside, he displayed the Gorgon's head.
All who beheld it were turned to stone."

FROM APOLLODORUS, *THE LIBRARY*, BOOK II, SECTION 4

The Triumphant Return

Because King Polydectes assumed Perseus would be killed by Medusa, he had tried to seize Danae just after Perseus left. Luckily, Dictys had been able to protect Danae by hiding her in an altar. When Perseus returned and realized how Polydectes had manipulated him, he was bitterly angry, but he now possessed an ideal weapon. Perseus simply strode into the king's palace, apologized for his delay, and announced he had killed the Medusa. When Polydectes laughed in disbelief, Perseus closed his own eyes, thrust his hand into his bag, and pulled out the blood-stained head of Medusa. King Polydectes and his entire royal court turned instantly to stone.

To thank Dictys and his wife for all they had done, Perseus made sure they ascended the thrones of Seriphus. He also humbly returned the items that Hermes and Athena lent him. He even gave Athena the severed head of Medusa as a gift, and Athena placed it on her aegis.

The Power of Fate

Unfortunately, the story does not end here. Danae longed to return to her home in Argos, and Perseus wanted to make amends with his grandfather. But when Danae's father, Acrisius, learned his grandson was alive and returning to Argos with his wife and Danae, he fled to the nearby town of Larissa. Meanwhile, Perseus and the travelers stopped to rest—in Larissa—and while there attended an athletic competition. Perseus joined a contest, and when he threw a discus, it soared into the stands and killed a spectator: his own grandfather. The oracle had predicted the death of Acrisius, and fate, as usual, had won.

Perseus was horrified that he had caused Acrisius' death, and so he refused the throne of Argos. Instead, he traded kingdoms with a cousin and became the respected ruler of Tiryns. He and Andromeda remained faithful to each other for the rest of their lives and raised six more children together.

- As the goddess of war, Athena was always shown in full battle gear. The head of Medusa is either on her aegis or her breastplate, or she sometimes has a serpent around her neck.

- An **aegis** was an ancient shield or breastplate. Today, the word can also mean "protection," as in, "He acted under the aegis of the American Constitution."

Jason
and the Golden Fleece

A Rightful Heir

The story of the hero Jason begins with bitter sibling rivalry. Jason's father, Aeson, was fighting with his own half-brother Pelias about who would rule the kingdom of Iolcus. In the end, Aeson conceded the throne to Pelias on one condition: Jason would assume the throne when he came of age. Aeson then sent Jason away to be raised by the wise centaur Chiron so the vicious Pelias would not have him killed.

Years passed and Jason grew into a young man. With excellent training and an adventurous nature, he was eager to return to Iolcus and assume his rightful place on the throne. His uncle Pelias, however, was prepared to go to any length to preserve his power. Years earlier, Pelias had sought the advice of an oracle, who had responded, "Beware of a man wearing only one shoe; this man will lead to your death." So when Jason appeared at the palace of Iolcus with one sandal missing, —he had lost a shoe while helping an old woman cross a muddy river—Pelias knew Jason was his nemesis.

What Pelias did not know was that the woman Jason had helped across the river was the goddess Hera disguised as a mortal. Pelias had never shown respect to Hera, so the vengeful goddess orchestrated the events in Jason's life for the purpose of punishing Pelias.

Meeting Challenges

In an attempt to get rid of Jason, Pelias put a plan into action. He welcomed his nephew to his home and threw a grand party in his honor. Then, in front of all the guests, Pelias challenged Jason to lead a group of men on a mission to obtain the fleece from the famed golden ram in the town of Colchis. Once Jason completed the mission, he could return, heroically, and take his rightful throne. The evil Pelias knew the adventurous young Jason would not turn down this public challenge. He also knew his nephew would most likely be killed, for Colchis was located at the far end of the Black Sea, and the mission to capture the Golden Fleece would be fraught with danger.

Jason had a choice: refuse the challenge and lose the throne, or accept the challenge and risk his life. The adventurous young man accepted and began recruiting others to travel with him to Colchis. Seeking glory and fame, fifty volunteers came forward, including descendants of the gods themselves, such as Heracles and Orpheus. Indeed the sailors—known ever after as the Argonauts—were hailed as the bravest men in all of Greece.

◆ The story of Jason is one of the first in a long line of nautical adventures in Western literature. Different portions of the hero's myth were written by Homer, Euripedes, Aeschylus, and Appolonius.

◆ A man named Argus designed the *Argo* and was inspired by the goddess Athena, shown helping him in the etching below. Later, the Greek Ptolemy honored the ship with a constellation named Argo Navis.

The *Argo* was the largest ship ever built and was even equipped with a magical talking oar, which was hewn from an oak tree sacred to Zeus. The oar acted like an oracle and gave advice to the sailors along their journey. The advice was not always enough, though. At sea, the sailors were often blown off course, and when they landed on islands, they met up with giants, angry women, and vengeful kings. Luckily, the Argonauts survived the two most dangerous parts of their journey: the Harpies and the Clashing Rocks.

When they stopped for fresh supplies near the southern end of the Bosporus, the Argonauts found a starving, blind prophet named Phineus. Zeus was angry at the mortal prophet because he had revealed too much about people's futures, so he sent the Harpies to attack him. These horrible, vengeful, birdlike women stole food and left behind a sickening stench, and they had been terrorizing the poor Phineus for years. Two of the Argonauts baited the Harpies with food and were able to capture them. Iris, the Olympian messenger, appeared and said if the Argonauts spared the Harpies, Zeus would promise to leave Phineus alone.

The prophet was so thankful to be able to eat again that he offered to tell the Argonauts something about their future, and he advised them how to navigate through the mouth of the Black Sea. There they would encounter the famed Clashing Rocks, two floating islands at the mouth of the Black Sea that crashed together without warning. The Argonauts were to release a dove between the islands, and if it survived, their ship would survive. Heeding this advice, the Argonaut named Euphemus released one of the birds, which flew through the gap. The Argonauts rowed with all their might and made it through the obstacle.

• The Argonauts were one of the best-known group of heroes in classical mythology. The Greek *nautikos* relates to sailing, so the men were the "sailors of the *Argo*." Other words that derive from *nautikos* or *naus* ("ship"), or from the Latin *navis* ("ship"), are:

astronauts, "sailors of the stars" (*astron* means "star" in Greek)

nautical, referring to things having to do with the sea

nausea, the queasy feeling of seasickness

navy, the branch of the armed forces that fights at sea

navigate, to steer a ship or plane

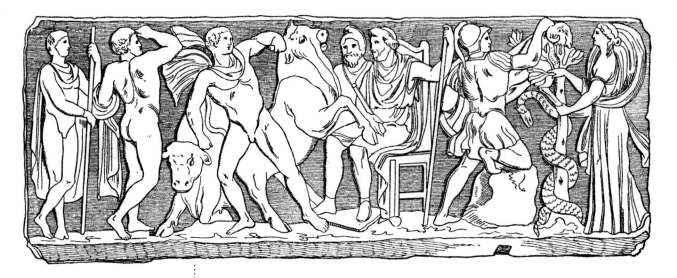

• In the center of the etching above, Jason tames the bulls while King Aeetes looks on from his throne. On the right, Jason takes the Golden Fleece while Medea distracts the serpentine beast who was supposed to guard it.

• Sailing on a quest for treasure is common in myths and legends. The medieval King Arthur, for instance, sailed in search of the Holy Grail. Although he found it, he lost many men in the process, just like Jason.

Help from Medea

After additional struggles, the weary sailors finally reached Colchis and the palace of King Aeetes, the proud owner of the Golden Fleece. Rather than attack Aeetes, Jason planned to arrive peacefully and make the king an ally. Jason even offered to fight the king's enemies in exchange for the prized fleece. Aeetes was suspicious, however, and devised a challenge for Jason that, like Pelias', was intended to kill him. If Jason could harness fire-breathing bulls and use them like oxen to sow the teeth of dragons, he would be rewarded with the Golden Fleece. What Aeetes did not mention to Jason was that the teeth were actually seeds from which savage warriors would sprout.

Jason would have surely died if the powerful sorceress Medea, Aeetes' daughter, had not fallen madly in love with the mortal hero. Using Medea's magic, Jason was able to tame the bulls and fend off the warriors, foiling Aeetes' plan. Aeetes was so furious that Jason survived, he refused to hand over the fleece. Once again, Medea helped Jason by distracting her father, and Jason was able to seize the ram and get back on board the *Argo*.

Jason, Medea, and the Argonauts immediately set sail but were pursued by several of Aeetes' ships, led by Medea's own brother, Apsyrtus. Medea took over. She let one ship catch up and allowed Apsyrtus to board the *Argo*, then she swiftly killed him and chopped him into pieces. As the *Argo* sailed away, she flung her brother's body parts into the sea, forcing the Colchian ships to stop and collect his remains so they could provide a proper burial.

Jason and Medea

Utterly astonished at Medea's loyalty and powers, Jason married her on the long and dangerous journey home. Back in Iolcus, the unstoppable sorceress once again worked her magic because during Jason's absence, Pelias had killed Jason's father, Aeson.

First Medea restored Aeson to life. Then she tricked Pelias' own daughters into boiling their father alive: She told the daughters she had a magical cauldron, and its boiling water could make their father young again. She proved her claim by tossing an old ram into the water and then lifting out a young lamb. The daughters eagerly threw their father into the cauldron, but the cool Medea simply let him boil to death and performed no magic.

While the whole point of Jason's mission was to come back and claim the throne of Iolcus, he and Medea had to flee the city because too many of Pelias' followers wanted revenge. Instead they traveled to Corinth, where they were welcomed by King Creon. Jason and Medea were happily married for over ten years and had two children together.

Jason, however, eventually fell in love with Creon's daughter, Glauce, and he saw a union with her as a chance to be the heir to Corinth. Jason told Medea he no longer loved her, and King Creon ruled that Medea and her children would be exiled from Corinth. All of the passionate love Medea had felt for Jason turned into an all-consuming and wicked hatred. She set fire to their home, killed Glauce, and then—horribly, inconceivably—murdered the children that she and Jason had together just to spite him. To complete the most dramatic exit in all of classical mythology, Medea flew off in a chariot pulled by fire-breathing dragons.

A Less-than-Heroic End

The astonished Jason was left alone, staggering in his grief. He had no bride, no children, and no welcoming home. While he had achieved brief glory when he attained the Golden Fleece, it provided him with no lasting happiness. It was sadly fitting that Jason died when a plank from the rotting *Argo* fell on his head.

THE FRIGHTENINGLY COMPLEX MEDEA

"Fear, admiration, envy, lust and hatred waltz hand-in-hand, for whatever else she is Medea is not a nobody: beautiful, high-ranking, reckless, intelligent and skilled, she cannot be simply dismissed."

CHRISTA WOLF, *MEDEA, A MODERN RETELLING*, PAGE XIV

⁃ While many of the women who fall in love with heroes are seen as secondary characters, Medea is as well known as Jason. In fact, several playwrights, from ancient times to modern, have written plays that focus on her character.

⁃ On the vase below, Medea shows Pelias' daughters how she can turn an old ram into a healthy lamb using her magic cauldron.

THESEUS
and the Minotaur

The Birth of a Hero

King Aegeus of Athens had been married twice, yet he still had no children to inherit his throne. While traveling through another town, however, he spent the night with a young princess, Aethra. The next morning Aegeus buried his own sandals and sword under a massive boulder and told Aethra that if she ended up bearing their son, she should wait until he was strong enough to move the boulder, and then she could send him on to Athens to assume the throne.

Aethra was indeed pregnant and bore a son whom she named Theseus. This boy was raised well and always sought out ways to combine his strength with his intelligence. In fact, Theseus was known in Greece for adding strategy and wit to the physical sport of wrestling. Although Aethra did not want to see her son leave, she knew that by his sixteenth birthday Theseus was strong enough to move the boulder. She told him the secret of his birth and watched with pride as Theseus pushed aside the rock to find the sandals and sword.

Welcoming Challenges

Instead of taking the safe and direct sea route to Athens, Theseus chose a dangerous land route. His intent was to make the road safer for travelers and to prove to himself and others that he was a worthy hero. Using his strength and wit, Theseus accomplished his goal, ridding the passage of numerous bandits, including the notorious Sinis and Procrustes.

Sinis, known as the "Pine Bender," would not only rob travelers, he would then kill them in an unusually gruesome way. After pulling the tops of two pine trees down to the ground, the bandit would strap victims' ankles to one tree and their wrists to the other. When Sinis let the trees go, the hapless travelers would be tossed up in the air and torn in half. Theseus wrestled Sinis to the ground and then allowed the bandit to experience this same torture.

Procrustes was another infamous bandit known for his vile method of killing. After luring weary travelers into his home and kindly offering them a place to sleep, he would show them to a room with a comfortable bed. That is where his hospitality ended, however. If his guests were too tall for the bed, he would chop off their heads to make them fit. If they were too short for the bed, he would put them on a stretcher and hammer them to just the right length. Again using strength and wit, Theseus tied Procrustes to the bed and hacked the tall criminal down to size.

+ Theseus lifting the stone to prove his strength is similar to the Celtic legend of King Arthur, who pulled a sword from a stone to become King of England, or the Greek story of how Alexander the Great sliced through the Gordian knot to become a great leader.

+ If someone tries to solve different problems using only one solution, he is said to be using a **Procrustean method**. Not all problems can be shaped to fit one answer, just as not all guests will fit the same bed.

Theseus Arrives in Athens

After ridding the route of its monsters, Theseus arrived in Athens. Although King Aegeus did not yet know Theseus was his son, the young man had become famous for his heroic acts, and the city held a banquet to welcome the stranger to Athens.

One person, however, knew Theseus' identity: King Aegeus' new wife, Medea. After punishing Jason and making her dramatic exit, Medea had traveled to Athens, married Aegeus, and borne a son. With her magical powers, she recognized Theseus and knew he was a threat to her own son's rise to power. She lied to King Aegeus, saying the stranger intended to kill him, so Aegeus agreed to let Medea mix a poisonous drink for Theseus. At the banquet, however, when the king saw the young man reach for the poison, he also caught sight of the sword beneath his cape and recognized the sandals on his feet. The king knocked the cup from Theseus' hand and embraced him. Medea and her son were banished from Athens, and Theseus was welcomed as the rightful heir.

The Monstrous Minotaur

Theseus spent several months enjoying a relationship with his father and quickly became an important part of the Athenian community. However, Athens was approaching a tragic time. Years earlier, Crete had attacked the city, and to spare the lives of thousands, the ruler of Athens had agreed to sacrifice seven men and seven maidens every nine years to feed the beastly Minotaur that lived on Crete. The Minotaur, half bull and half man, was actually the product of a relationship between Queen Pasiphae of Crete and a wild bull. Even though she had been tricked into mating with the bull, Pasiphae's husband, King Minos, was so mortified by his wife's child that he hired the inventor Daedalus to create a huge labyrinth to hide the Minotaur. The young men and women would be locked inside and would eventually be devoured by the beast.

◆ According to Ovid, the Maeander River in Anatolia (modern Turkey), with more than 600 turns, inspired Daedalus to create the complex Labyrinth to house the Minotaur. By the nineteenth century, **meander** came to mean "to wander aimlessly."

◆ Below is a 1989 photo of the meandering waterways of Indonesia's Mahakam Delta.

THE BRILLIANT DESIGN OF THE LABYRINTH

"The structure was designed by Daedalus,
That famous architect. Appearances
Were all confused; he led the eye astray
By a mazy multitude of winding ways,
Just as Maeander plays among the meads
Of Phrygia and in its puzzling flow
Glides back and forth..."

OVID, *METAMORPHOSES*, BOOK VIII, LINES 160-166

Although Aegeus did not want his son to go, Theseus insisted on being one of the sacrificed youths. He assured his father he could slay the Minotaur and end the sacrifices once and for all. He promised to raise a white sail on their return voyage so all of Athens could celebrate.

When the ship landed on Crete, King Minos' daughter Ariadne fell instantly in love with Theseus. He vowed to return her love if she could help him with his mission. Ariadne told Theseus everything she knew about the Labyrinth and gave him a ball of thread so he could mark his path while in the maze. Following her advice, Theseus was able to locate the beast, slay him, and follow the thread back to the opening of the Labyrinth. Ariadne, Theseus, and the other youths hurried back to the ship and escaped their Cretan pursuers.

An Unhappy Return
The ship stopped on the island of Naxos, and Ariadne was left behind. One source says Theseus' ship was unexpectedly blown out to sea without Ariadne on board, another says Theseus abandoned her because he did not truly love her, and others say the god Dionysus had fallen in love with Ariadne and made Theseus leave. Regardless, Ariadne happily married Dionysus. But Theseus was so distracted on his return voyage to Athens that he forgot to raise the white sail as he had promised. Aegeus, who had been waiting for his son to return, saw the black mast on the horizon and assumed the worst. The distraught king threw himself off a cliff and drowned in the sea that has since been called the Aegean Sea.

Wise Leadership but an Unfortunate End
Although distraught over the death of his father, Theseus married a woman named Antiope, had a son, and ascended the throne of Athens. He became a fair and wise leader and is credited with establishing the basis of modern democratic rule when he allowed the citizens of Athens to vote.

After his first wife died, Theseus married a youthful woman named Phaedra. In a tragic turn of events, the young Phaedra became infatuated with Hippolytus, Theseus' son from his marriage to Antiope. When Hippolytus refused Phaedra's love, she killed herself but got revenge in her suicide note. In it she accused Hippolytus of attacking her. Although Hippolytus denied the wrongdoing, Theseus did not believe his son and banished him from Athens. Only after Hippolytus was killed on a chariot did Theseus learn his son had been telling the truth.

Sadly, Theseus never recovered from this horrible misunderstanding and died a lonely old man. It was not until many years later that Theseus was recognized as a hero in Athens for his brave acts and wise rule. His body was properly buried along with Aegeus' sword.

- Some sources say Ariadne received the ball of thread from the Labyrinth's designer, Daedalus, who wanted Theseus to slay the Minotaur.

- Ariadne's thread is the basis for a common word. The Middle English word *clew* referred to a ball of thread. The story of Theseus was so well known that over time, clew came to mean "a hint that helps solve a problem." The spelling of the word has changed to **clue**.

- The original meaning of *clew* is still used in sailing terminology: clew lines are the ropes used to raise and lower the sails.

A TOAST TO HONOR THESEUS

"'Your years, your glories, should we wish to count—
Your feats surpass your years. For you, our prince,
Our valiant prince, we bring a nation's prayers,
To you we drink, we drain our draughts of wine.'
With cheering crowds and cries of well-wishers
From end to end the royal halls resound;
No place of grief in all the city's found."

OVID, *METAMORPHOSES*, BOOK VII, LINES 448-454

◆ The etching above shows Theseus slaying the Minotaur while Ariadne holds up a length from her clew.

◆ It was the royal marriage between Theseus and Antiope that is celebrated in William Shakespeare's *A Midsummer Night's Dream*.

HERACLES
and His Twelve Labors

A Birth and a Curse

The fair mortal Alcmene was a loyal wife, so Zeus knew the only way to seduce her was to disguise himself as Alcmene's husband. Thus, the unsuspecting Alcmene became pregnant with twin sons—Iphicles, fathered by her husband, and Heracles, fathered by Zeus.

When Hera learned her husband had committed adultery yet again, she sent two large serpents to kill the babies just after they were born. The demigod strength of Heracles was already obvious, however, for he easily strangled the vicious snakes.

Years later, Hera tried again to ruin Heracles by cursing him with temporary insanity. Tragically, he killed his wife, Megara, and their children. When his sanity was restored, he was so distraught and overcome with guilt that he exiled himself from his home in Thebes and sought the advice of an oracle.

The prophecy was clear: Heracles was to report to his cousin Eurystheus, the king of Tiryns, and perform a series of tasks. By dedicating himself and completing these difficult missions, not only would Heracles receive penance, he would gain immortality as well.

The First Six Tasks

I. Eurystheus wanted to find out Heracles' true strength. His first assignment, then, was to kill the Nemean Lion, a beast whose hide was so thick that no arrow could pierce it. The mighty Heracles simply strangled it with his bare hands and used the beast's own claws to remove its hide. From then on, Heracles wore this impenetrable pelt on his back.

2. Convinced now that Heracles could slay any creature, Eurystheus sent him to kill the Lernaean Hydra, a nine-headed water snake that was terrorizing the people of Lerna. One of its heads was immortal, and Heracles knew that if he cut off any one of the other eight, two would grow back in its place. Heracles sliced off the immortal head and buried it. He then cut off the other eight and asked his nephew to help him burn the stumps to stop them from multiplying. Heracles also dipped the tips of his own arrows into the Hydra's poisonous blood to make them more lethal.

3. Eurystheus now wanted to possess something of beauty, so he commanded Heracles to capture a golden stag that was sacred to Artemis. The stag stayed hidden for an entire year, but finally Heracles was able to seize it while it slept. Heracles took great care not to harm the magnificent creature because he did not want to incur the wrath of Artemis.

- Hercules was the Roman name for this hero. His Greek name, Heracles, meant "the glory of Hera." Indeed, Hera took glory in creating problems for him.

- The adjective **herculean** refers to something that requires a huge amount of strength and stamina.

- The constellation Leo is associated with the Nemean Lion, and the constellation Hydra is linked to the Lernaean beast. The cruel Hera had sent a crab to nip at Heracles' feet while he was trying to subdue the Hydra, and it was immortalized as one of the zodiac constellations.

4. Heracles' fourth task was to capture the wild Erymanthian boar, which was wreaking havoc on the town of Arcadia. Heracles chased the beast into the mountains where it became trapped in the deep snow. He then put it in chains and carried it, alive and kicking, all the way back to his master.

5. Eurystheus may have assigned the next task simply to shame Heracles, for it was a truly degrading request: clean the stables of King Augeas, which housed thousands of cattle and had not been cleaned in 30 years. Heracles used both his brains and brawn for this task, diverting two rivers so their waters would flow through the stables, washing them out and even fertilizing the surrounding pastures.

6. Heracles' sixth task was to get rid of a flock of man-eating birds that haunted Lake Stymphalus. These massive carnivorous birds preyed on men, scooping them up with their claws. To get the birds out of the trees, Heracles borrowed two huge bronze rattles from the god Hephaestus, and shook them with all his might. The startled birds took to the air, and the few creatures that escaped Heracles' arrows fled the region, never to return.

⁂ Sources say Heracles took time away after his fourth labor and joined the Argonauts. He was left behind accidentally, however, and did not complete the journey.

⁂ Cleaning the Augean stables was the only humiliating task. The others involved killing or capturing dangerous animals, or obtaining prized possessions.

⁂ Eurystheus was supposed to assign only ten tasks, but because Heracles had help on the second and sixth labors, Eurystheus gave him two more tasks. In the Hellenic postage stamp below, Heracles (on the left) is assisted by his nephew as they attack the Hydra.

+ The Hellenic postage stamp on the right shows Heracles wearing the hide of the Nemean Lion and hoisting the Erymanthian boar over his head to show it to Eurystheus, who cowers from inside a vase.

+ In the mid-1540s, Spanish explorer Francisco Orellana, shown below, claimed he was attacked by women warriors when he and his crew were sailing a massive river in South America. He referred to the body of water as Rio Amazonas because he likened the women to the Amazons of Greek mythology. And that is how the Amazon River got its name.

Francisco Orellana

The Second Six Tasks

7. Heracles' first six tasks had been located in and around Tiryns, and he accomplished each with relative ease. Eurystheus, therefore, began to ask for more elaborate feats. The seventh assignment was to capture a fire-breathing bull that was burning all of the crops on the island of Crete. After traveling across vast waters to Crete, Heracles caught the creature and transported it back to Eurystheus.

8. The eighth task required Heracles to go to Thrace to capture the four man-eating mares of King Diomedes. As the son of Ares, Diomedes had a savage soul and fed his prized mares the flesh of innocent people. Heracles stole the horses, but Diomedes pursued him. Heracles then gave Diomedes a taste of his own awful medicine: He captured the king and fed him to his own mares. Heracles was able to tame the beasts, harness them to a chariot, and drive them back to Tiryns.

9. Wanting another possession, Eurystheus next sent Heracles to seize a golden belt worn by Hippolyta, the queen of the Amazons. The Amazons, all female descendants of Ares, were large, aggressive women. The queen, however, willingly offered Heracles her belt. All would have gone smoothly had it not been for Hera, who tried for a third time to ruin Heracles. She disguised herself as an Amazon and spread rumors among the tribe that Heracles was going to kill Hippolyta. The Amazon warriors attacked Heracles, and in the ensuing battle Heracles killed many of them, including Hippolyta, before fleeing with the belt.

10. The tenth task was to seize the prized red cattle that belonged to Geryon, a monster with three torsos and three heads. For this task, Heracles used his brute strength to get rid of the huge two-headed dog, Orthos, who guarded the cattle, and his incredible endurance to drive the large herd from Spain all the way back to Greece.

11. For the eleventh task, Eurystheus asked Heracles to steal three golden apples from a tree Gaea had given to her granddaughter Hera on Hera's wedding day. The beautiful tree, guarded by nymphs known as the Hesperides, grew in the shadow of Atlas, the Titan assigned the task of holding up the heavens. After locating the Garden of the Hesperides, Heracles asked if Atlas could pick the apples while Heracles temporarily held the heavy sky.

Atlas gladly passed off his burden, got the fruit, and even offered to take the apples back to Tiryns himself. Heracles suspected, however, that the Titan was looking for a way to escape from his grueling task. So the wise hero claimed he did not have a firm enough hold on the heavens and needed a chance to reposition himself. As soon as the foolish Titan took back the heavens, he realized his mistake. Heracles fled, leaving Atlas to continue his backbreaking job.

On the way home, Heracles passed through the Caucasus Mountains and came upon Prometheus, who had been lashed to a rock for 30,000 years. Heracles killed the bird who had pecked the brave Titan's liver every day, and cut Prometheus' painful chains.

12. Eurystheus had saved the most difficult task for last, asking Heracles to bring him Cerberus, the three-headed dog who guarded the gates of the Underworld. Eager to complete his tasks, Heracles descended into Hades' realm, seized the dog by its throat, and wrestled it back to Tiryns. Eurystheus never expected Heracles to complete this task, so he was dumbfounded and terrified when Heracles showed up with the Nemean Lion's hide on his back and the gigantic three-headed, fire-breathing Cerberus under his arm. Eurystheus hurriedly announced that he had only wanted a glimpse of Cerberus and that after Heracles returned the dog to the Underworld, he would be a free man.

- Some say Amazon women lured men into their tribe to mate, and then saved only the female babies. Others say they kept all babies, but reared males to be their slaves.

- Remember how Zeus spared the Nemean Lion, the Hydra, and Orthos—all offspring of Echidna and Typhon—so they could be used as tests for heroes? Heracles killed all three of them.

- The male Hercules beetle from Central and South America can grow more than seven inches long and is shown here at its actual size.

◆ Atlas, who could not outsmart Heracles, was one of the few Titans not sent to Tartarus after being defeated by the Olympians. Images of Atlas holding a globe on his back are still common today. An **atlas**, a book containing maps of the world, got its name from this Titan.

After the Labors

The twelve labors had taken nearly ten years to complete, and Heracles was eager to move on with his life. After several failed relationships, he finally married a princess named Deianira. Several years later, the two were traveling and came upon a wide river. Nessus, a centaur, offered to carry Deianira across the river for a small fee. Heracles agreed and set off across the river, assuming Nessus would follow. He soon heard his wife's screams, however, and turned to see Nessus attacking Deianira. Heracles shot the centaur with one of the arrows poisoned by the blood of the Hydra.

In the moments before Nessus died, he quickly planned revenge. He filled a vial with his own oozing blood and secretly offered it to Deianira, promising it would keep Heracles faithful if ever he were tempted by another woman. Deianira accepted the token and tucked it away.

The Death of Heracles, the Hero

Years later, when Deianira wrongly suspected Heracles was falling in love with a young woman, she brought out the centaur's blood and sprinkled it on Heracles' tunic. She did not realize that as soon as her husband put on the shirt, the poisonous blood would burn his skin. When he tore at the fabric, his skin came off as well. He begged his sons to build him a funeral pyre and burn him on it to put him out of his misery. No one could bring himself to kill the great Heracles, however, until Philoctetes, a son of a shepherd, performed the deed. The grateful Heracles offered the mortal his bow and his quiver full of poisoned arrows.

◆ Philoctetes later used the poisoned arrows to kill Paris of Troy during the war between the Greeks and the Trojans.

The fire actually cleansed Heracles and burned away his mortality. He rose to Mount Olympus, where he was welcomed by his father. And Hera finally recognized Heracles' heroism and accepted him as a god.

" 'Trust horse-strength if you will, you'll not escape.
With wounds not feet I'll follow!' His last words
Were proved at once: an arrow flew and pierced
The fleeing centaur's back: out from his breast
The barbed point stuck. He wrenched the shaft away,
And blood from both wounds spurted, blood that bore
The Hydra's poison. Nessus caught it up.
'I'll not die unavenged', he thought and gave
His shirt soaked in warm gore to Deianira,
A talisman, he said, to kindle love."

OVID, *METAMORPHOSES*, BOOK IX, LINES 125-134

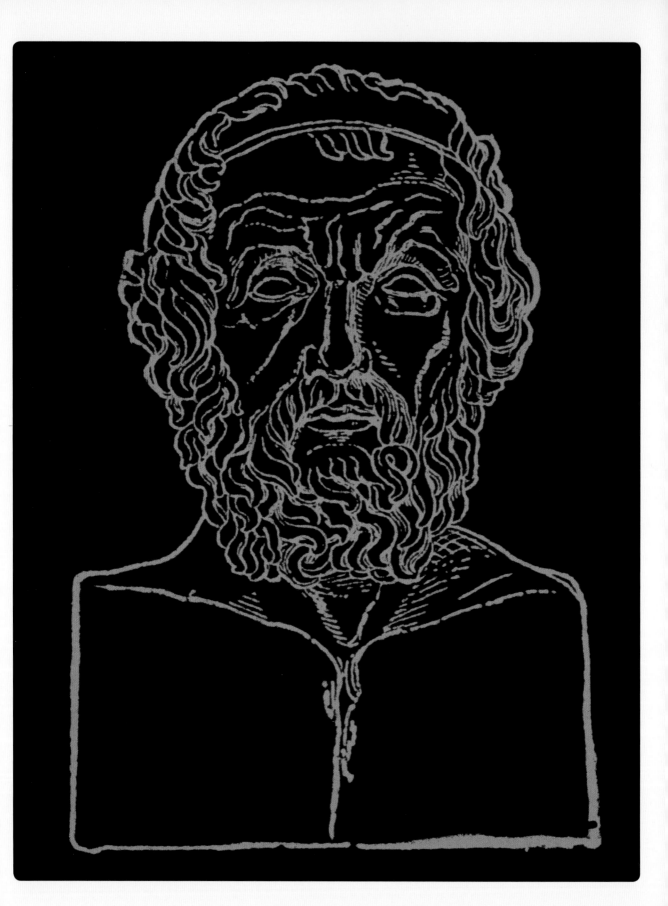

The Epics
of Homer

When introducing a famous work of literature, it helps to talk about the author. Unfortunately, no one knows much about Homer. In fact, there is no proof he ever existed. That said, scholars think the Greek poet may have lived in the eighth and seventh centuries BCE and produced the two epic masterpieces, the *Iliad* and the *Odyssey*. Many think Homer was blind, and many now agree that he, like most people in his era, was illiterate. It is likely, then, that his works were never actually recorded during his lifetime. But so many rhapsodes—men who "sang" works of poetry—continued to perform his works that both of his epic poems were written down years later and credited to Homer.

No matter how these works came into being so many centuries ago, the *Iliad* and the *Odyssey* are considered the earliest great works of Western literature, and they remain excellent studies of human beings and the critical choices they make. Although the *Iliad* is set thousands of years ago during a war between two massive armies, it focuses on timeless issues of the human spirit. And the *Odyssey* follows one man's difficult journey, but it actually represents a universal search for home, values, and a sense of self.

Homer

Sources

The retellings of Homer's *Iliad* and *Odyssey* are based on the translations of Robert Fagles.

Additional sources used to retell the events before and after Homer's *Iliad* include *The Library* (Apollodorus), *The Trojan Women* and *Hecuba* (Euripedes), *Metamorphoses* (Ovid), the *Aeneid* (Virgil), *The Judgment of the Goddesses* (Lucian), and *Agamemnon* (Aeschylus).

for the ILIAD

Main characters from Greece, known collectively as the Achaeans

Achilles *(uh KIL eez)*
Most skilled Greek warrior. His anger makes him a powerful fighter, but his pride causes great despair for the Achaeans. Achilles was the commander of a troop called the Myrmidons.

Agamemnon *(ag uh MEM non)*
Husband of Clytemnestra and the demanding, arrogant leader of the Achaeans. Older brother of Menelaus.

Menelaus *(men uh LAY us)*
Husband to Helen before Paris takes her to Troy. Younger brother of Agamemnon.

Patroclus *(pa TROH klus)*
Closest friend of Achilles.

Helen *(HEL en)*
Most beautiful mortal woman in the world. Married to Menelaus but taken by Paris to Troy. Helen's sister is Clytemnestra.

Odysseus *(o DIS ee us)*
Greek king best known for his intelligent strategies.

Ajax *(AY jaks)*
Ajax of Salamis, otherwise known as Great Ajax. He is second only to Achilles in terms of strength.

Clytemnestra *(klie tem NES truh)*
Bitter wife of Agamemnon and older sister to Helen.

Iphigenia *(if i juh NEE uh)*
Daughter of Agamemnon and Clytemnestra. She is sacrificed by Agamemnon in order to get fair winds to travel to Troy.

Main characters from Troy, called the "Trojans"

Paris (*PAIR us*)
Trojan who takes Helen from Menelaus with the help of Aphrodite. Paris is headstrong but cowardly in battle.

Hector (*HEK tor*)
Paris' older brother and the most skilled and dedicated Trojan warrior.

Priam (*PREE um*)
King of Troy and husband of Hecuba. Father of numerous children, including Paris, Hector, and Cassandra.

Hecuba (*HEK yoo buh*)
Queen of Troy and wife of Priam.

Chryseis (*krie SEE us*)
Daughter of one of Apollo's priests, taken as a slave girl by Agamemnon.

Briseis (*brih SEE us*)
Trojan girl awarded to Achilles. Agamemnon demands that Achilles give her up to him, however, after Agamemnon loses his own slave girl, Chryseis.

Andromache (*an DROM uh kee*)
Loving wife of Hector.

Cassandra (*kuh SAN druh*)
Sister of Paris and Hector. She predicts the future but is never believed.

Gods and goddesses

Aphrodite (*af ro DIE tee*)
Goddess of love and beauty who helps the Trojans.

Apollo (*uh PAWL oh*)
God of light who helps the Trojans.

Ares (*AIR eez*)
God of war who helps the Trojans.

Athena (*uh THEE nuh*)
Goddess of war and wisdom who prefers the Achaeans.

Hera (*HEER uh*)
Queen of the gods who prefers the Achaeans.

Poseidon (*poh SIE dun*)
God of the oceans who prefers the Achaeans.

Thetis (*THEE tis*)
Mother of Achilles and wife to the mortal Peleus.

Zeus (*ZOOS*)
King of the gods who intervenes in the war when pressured by other deities. Zeus, however, knows he must follow the decree of the Fates.

✦ Athena holding up Nike, the goddess of victory.

THE ILIAD
The Wrath of Achilles

About Homer's *Iliad*

Little is known about Homer, and only a little more is known about an epic battle between the Greeks and Trojans that may have taken place around 1250 BCE. Many had assumed the war was total fiction, but in 1870 CE, a wealthy German businessman named Heinrich Schliemann took his beloved copy of Homer's *Iliad* to Turkey. His intention was to use the book as a blueprint to locate ancient Troy, a city earlier known as Ilium after its founder, the legendary Ilos. Although Schliemann was ridiculed by professional archaeologists, his vast fortune allowed him to fund a massive dig, and he had surprising success.

What Schliemann discovered was not just one city, but the ruins of as many as nine cities stacked in layers like a cake. His teams dug until they found bronze, silver, and gold objects dating back to what Schliemann claimed was Homer's Ilium. Schliemann had his beautiful young Greek wife, Sophia, pose in the jewelry they had found, and the pair became international, eccentric celebrities. Although his methods were unusual and facts show his treasures were from the wrong "layer" of the city, author Caroline Moorehead writes that Schliemann's finds "sparked off the entire modern study of prehistory" and that the collection, referred to as "Priam's Treasure," is now worth over one billion dollars.

The *Iliad*—"a poem about Ilium" and 15,693 lines long in its original Greek text—is set in the period of Mycenaean Greece. The city of Troy, on the east coast of modern Turkey, would have been extremely wealthy because of its strategic location. It was a major center of overland trade and controlled the strait between the Aegean and Black Seas. Therefore, any battle that took place there would logically have involved trade routes and money, not a woman named Helen, as Homer's epic claims.

Homer, however, would likely object to any fuss over geography or the historical accuracy of his story. Rather than writing about the large-scale war or complex military strategy, he focuses on a tense psychological battle among just a few men. In fact, while the war raged on for ten years, his *Iliad* spans only a few weeks during the last year and ends before any victory is claimed.

In addition, readers should recognize that Homer takes no sides in the war. Instead, he portrays a battle in which both sides have arguable cause to fight, and he paints realistic pictures of the Greeks and Trojans, including their valiant heroism and their troubling faults. Homer sees himself as a mere narrator, stating in the first stanza that Calliope, the Muse of epic poetry, is simply using him to relay the tale. With this detached approach, Homer allows readers to draw conclusions about the choices the characters make and the events that unfold.

◆ An **epic** is a long poem that tells a complex story of a historical figure or hero and comes from the Greek *epos* (word or song). Homer's *Iliad* and *Odyssey* are two of eight epics about the Trojan War written during the seventh and sixth centuries BCE. They are known collectively as the Epic Cycle.

" The details of the Trojan War may no longer command attention, but the characters in Homer's epics still seem vitally alive, as if yesteryear were but yesterday. When we watch Homer's characters react to the problems in their lives, we realize that the people who lived in 800 [BCE] are basically the same as we are."

DONNA ROSENBERG,
WORLD MYTHOLOGY

Part 1: Events Leading Up to the *Iliad*

The Wedding of Thetis and Peleus

The oracle told the immortal sea nymph Thetis that any son born to her would become more powerful than his father. Zeus, although attracted to Thetis, avoided her because he feared being overthrown. He even made Thetis marry the mortal Peleus to ensure their son would not threaten the gods.

Many mortals and almost every god and goddess attended the wedding of Thetis and Peleus. Eris, however, the goddess of discord, was not invited because of her disagreeable temper. Out of spite, she inscribed the words "For the Fairest" on a golden apple and rolled it into the middle of the party. Her plan worked perfectly: Hera, Athena, and Aphrodite began feuding over the apple and disrupted the whole celebration.

The goddesses took their quarrel to Zeus, who wisely refused to choose among his wife and two of his own daughters. Instead, he told them to seek out a young man named Paris.

The Judgment of Paris

Years earlier, Paris had been born to King Priam and Queen Hecuba, the rulers of Troy, but an oracle had warned the royal couple that the child would ultimately cause the destruction of their kingdom. With overwhelming sadness, Priam and Hecuba gave their infant to servants with instructions to kill him. The servants, however, could not bring themselves to slay the baby and chose to abandon him. Paris was raised by shepherds and grew into a charming, handsome man.

Now, by Zeus' decree, Paris would choose the fairest of the Olympian goddesses. In an attempt to win his favor, the three goddesses offered him bribes. Hera promised him extraordinary wealth and power, and Athena vowed to make him a skilled and heroic warrior. But Aphrodite was wise about a young man's priorities and offered him Helen, who was considered the most beautiful woman in the world. Helen was already married to Menelaus, the king of Sparta, but that did not stop Paris. He handed the apple to Aphrodite.

Before claiming Helen, Paris learned of his royal heritage. He attended the funeral games that Priam and Hecuba held to honor the son they thought had died. When Paris won a prize for raising a bull, a prophetess told the royal family he was their son, and they welcomed Paris home.

Aphrodite soon arranged for Paris to visit Sparta, where he was a guest at the royal palace. When Menelaus left to conduct business on Crete, Paris took Helen back to Troy. Although her departure is sometimes called an abduction, it is clear in the *Iliad* that she had fallen in love with the handsome and romantic Paris, who was years younger than Menelaus.

- In their earliest written form, Homer's epics would have been copied by hand onto rolls of papyrus. And because of their length, there would have been a dozen or more rolls. Many believe the "books" of the poems were originally the individual rolls.

- The story of Paris is similar to that of Oedipus: Parents are told by an oracle that their infant son will cause some form of destruction, so they sadly send their child away to be killed. Servants spare the lives of both boys, however, and the oracles' predictions come true.

- Hera and Athena were furious when Paris gave the prized apple to Aphrodite, and both held a grudge against the Trojans from then on.

FOR THE FAIREST

Helen's Story

The drama Eris started with the golden apple had more far-reaching effects. Years earlier, when Helen came of age, dozens of princes from all over Greece sought her hand. Helen's mother, Leda, and Leda's husband, King Tyndareus, feared that all of the men not chosen would revolt and threaten their kingdom.

It was Odysseus, a suitor from Ithaca, who came up with an ingenious plan to help. Odysseus proposed that before a husband was chosen for Helen, all her suitors must vow that no matter what the outcome, they would always protect her. The suitors agreed to the conditions and accepted Tyndareus' choice of Menelaus of Sparta. Tyndareus showed his thanks to Odysseus by allowing him to marry Penelope, the king's wise and faithful niece.

When Helen was taken to Troy, Menelaus was angry, humiliated, and heartbroken. He knew, however, that he could count on the numerous Greek leaders who had sworn to protect Helen. Menelaus' older brother, King Agamemnon of Mycenae, eagerly took control of the situation and amassed armies of Greek men to go to Troy and reclaim Helen. The bellicose, power-hungry Agamemnon saw this as a great opportunity to wield his power and take down the city of Troy.

Recruiting Odysseus and Achilles

Ironically, the same man who devised the oath to protect Helen tried to avoid upholding it himself. An oracle had told Odysseus that if he left his home, he would be gone for twenty years. So when men came to his palace to recruit him, he pretended to be insane by wildly sowing salt in his fields using a donkey hitched to his plow. The men were suspicious, however, and placed Odysseus' infant son, Telemachus, in the path of the plow. Unable to harm his own child, Odysseus gave up the ruse. With a heavy heart, he left Penelope and Telemachus and went with the recruiters in search of Achilles.

The mortal son of Thetis and Peleus, Achilles was both strong and strong-willed. Thetis had been told her child was destined to live an adventurous but short life. To avoid this fate, Thetis tried to make her son immortal by placing him in a fire. When Peleus saw this, however, he yanked Achilles from the flames. The furious Thetis left and returned to the sea. Years later, when she heard men were going to battle against the powerful Trojans, she reappeared in a second attempt to protect her son. She sent Achilles to stay with a king who had a dozen daughters. The king agreed to dress Achilles as a young woman and hide him in his palace.

Odysseus and the recruiters had been told Achilles was somewhere in the palace, but the king denied it. Odysseus, knowing the mind of a young man, planned a scheme. He gathered all the king's "daughters" together and showed them a collection of jewelry and trinkets, as well as a golden sword. Odysseus then had servants shout that the palace was under attack. Achilles instinctively ripped off his disguise and grabbed the sword, ready to defend the palace. Achilles, who had been hiding only to please his mother, agreed to go to war against the Trojans.

+ Tyndareus was not Helen's father; Zeus had taken the form of a swan and seduced the mortal Leda, who gave birth to several children, including Helen. Zeus celebrated the birth by creating the constellation Cygnus, the Swan.

+ Agamemnon and Menelaus were the sons of Atreus. Atreus' father was Pelops, and his grandfather was Tantalus, the ungrateful man whose family became cursed when he played a trick on the Olympians.

+ A later Roman version of Achilles' story is more common: Thetis dipped Achilles into the River Styx to make him immortal, but the heel by which she held him was not touched by the sacred water. That heel was his only vulnerable spot.

+ The tendon on the back of the ankle is called the **Achilles' tendon**.

- The etching on the left shows Achilles after he ripped off his disguise and grabbed weapons in order to defend the palace.

- Achilles' father, Peleus, entrusted his son to Chiron, a wise centaur who also taught the heroes Jason, Theseus, and Heracles. While most centaurs were violent and irreverent, the civilized Chiron was known for his healing powers and can be seen on Achilles' aegis in this etching. When Chiron died, Zeus made him the constellation Sagittarius, which is a centaur holding a bow and arrow.

- It was at Thetis and Peleus' wedding that the goddesses quarreled over the golden apple. Therefore, it does not seem likely their son Achilles could be old enough to go to war. That, however, is the nature of mythology.

Setting Sail for Troy

All of the Greek ships were now gathered at the port of Aulis, but the winds would not blow in the right direction. Agamemnon finally consulted the oracle and learned that Artemis, the goddess of the hunt, was offended because the arrogant Agamemnon had bragged about his skills as a hunter. To appease the goddess and get favorable winds, Agamemnon lured his own daughter Iphigenia to Aulis by telling her she would marry Achilles. Instead, he sacrificed his innocent daughter to the goddess. Clytemnestra, Agamemnon's wife and the older half-sister to Helen, never forgave her husband for this unconscionable deed. Agamemnon's actions revealed just how far the powerful king would go to defend his family's honor, and how eager he was to prove his army's superiority over the Trojans.

- Artemis was said to have spared the innocent girl, and Iphigenia became one of her attendants.

Now, with favorable winds, the numerous troops of the Greek army—called the "Achaeans" by Homer—were ready. All told, one thousand ships set sail from Aulis and crossed the Aegean Sea to Troy in search of Helen, the most beautiful woman in the world.

The First Nine Years of War

The massive walls that surrounded Troy were said to have been twelve feet thick, and its strategic position overlooking the plains along the Aegean Sea gave the Trojans a clear view of oncoming invaders. Instead of attempting to conquer Troy, therefore, the Achaeans decided to methodically ransack all of the smaller surrounding cities that provided Troy with supplies. By taking the food and raw materials that would have gone to Troy, the invaders kept themselves alive and set up a massive camp on the beaches beneath the walls of Troy.

The Achaeans won many battles and were successful in their campaign to isolate Troy, but by the ninth year of war, they were exhausted. Because of their frustration, tensions were high among the Achaean leaders, and morale was low among the troops. Finally Agamemnon sought an oracle to learn why they could not achieve victory and why so many of their men were dying from a plague. The oracle revealed that Apollo was angry because Chryseis, the daughter of one of his favored priests, had been taken as a slave girl by Agamemnon. Until Chryseis was returned to her father, the Achaeans would not be victorious, and the plague would continue.

Homer chose to begin his story at this point, when the war seemed increasingly futile and tensions were extremely high in the Greek camp.

Part II: The *Iliad*

Achilles Refuses to Fight

When Agamemnon learned he would have to give up Chryseis, he was deeply offended. Such slave girls were important "prizes of honor" and were rewarded to those who performed with distinction on the battlefield. The proud Agamemnon refused to have his prize taken away without immediately getting another. After exchanging ugly words with Achilles, the king demanded that Achilles give him *his* prize of honor, Briseis, someone Achilles had come to care for very deeply.

For Achilles, who was already angry because he had fought so hard in battles while Agamemnon had taken all the glory, this was a humiliating outrage. He berated Agamemnon, accusing him of being an incompetent leader, of being greedy and cowardly. He went on to remind Agamemnon that he himself had no quarrel with the Trojans; he and thousands of other men were giving up years of their lives, even life itself, just to restore the honor of Agamemnon's brother. Achilles could barely contain his rage and longed to draw his sword and kill his leader right then and there. Instead, he agreed to give up Briseis. But he would also stop fighting. Achilles declared that he and his troops, the powerful Myrmidons, were on strike.

When two heralds came to get Briseis from Achilles the next day, Achilles left his tent in silence and went alone to the beach. Overwhelmed with frustration, he cried out to his mother, the sea nymph Thetis. When she appeared, she gathered him up in her arms and listened as he ranted about Agamemnon. With a vengeful heart, Achilles begged his mother to go to Zeus and ask him to punish the Achaeans.

♦ Achilles' Myrmidons were originally worker ants who had been transformed into strong, loyal humans by Zeus.

♦ Rather than supporting the Greeks or Trojans based on any particular moral principle, the gods and goddesses often favored one mortal or another for selfish reasons.

ACHILLES ANGERED BY AGAMEMNON

"The Trojans never did *me* damage, not in the least,
they never stole my cattle or my horses, never
in Phthia where the rich soil breeds strong men
did they lay waste my crops. How could they?
Look at the endless miles that lie between us . . .
shadowy mountain ranges, seas that surge and thunder.
No, you colossal, shameless—we all followed you,
to please you, to fight for you, to win your honor
back from the Trojans—Menelaus and you, you dog-face!
What do *you* care? Nothing. You don't look right or left."

HOMER, THE *ILIAD*, BOOK 1, LINES 180-189

AGAMEMNON BELITTLING ACHILLES

"But I, I will be there in person at your tents
to take Briseis in all her beauty, your own prize—
so you can learn just how much greater I am than you"

HOMER, THE *ILIAD*, BOOK 1, LINES 217-219

Thetis told her son again how she had always known he was destined to live a heroic but brief life, and she mourned with him that his life was filled with little else but anger and war. Then she slipped back into the sea, promising Achilles that she would talk to Zeus.

Agamemnon Tries to Rally the Troops

The desperate Agamemnon tried to rally his troops by telling them about their bleak situation, hoping they would roar into battle, determined to defend their honor and pride. Instead, Agamemnon only made the men panic, and they ran back toward their beached ships. After nine years of futile war, the men longed to go home. Indeed, they would have given up had it not been for Athena, the goddess who despised the Trojans. She silenced the troops so Odysseus could speak to the men and convince them to take the mighty walls of Troy.

Odysseus' speech worked, and Athena breathed new strength into the Achaean army. Even though Achilles was no longer in their ranks, the men marched by the thousands, ready to fight the Trojans once again.

"... And his loving father laughed,
his mother laughed as well, and glorious Hector,
quickly lifting the helmet from his head,
set it down on the ground, fiery in the sunlight,
and raising his son he kissed him, tossed him in his arms,"

HOMER, THE *ILIAD*, BOOK 6, LINES 562-566

♦ The grueling, gruesome, painful realities of the *Iliad* can be heart-wrenching for the reader. Thomas Cahill likened the characters to "swimmers in an undertow that is much stronger than their most strenuous strivings." And Johann Wolfgang von Goethe once wrote, "An inch beneath the *Iliad* is Hell."

Paris Challenges Menelaus

When the Trojans saw the enemy approaching, Paris strutted out of the ranks and dared any one of the Achaeans to challenge him. When Menelaus saw this, he jumped down from his chariot, determined to slay the man who had stolen his wife. Paris turned pale and slunk back into the Trojan lines.

Paris' older brother, Prince Hector, was appalled. Hector was exhausted from years of bearing the burden of protecting Troy, and he had just witnessed, again, how pathetic Paris made the Trojans look. Hector railed at his brother, blaming him for Troy's years of anguish and shaming him into bringing the battle to an end by challenging Menelaus in combat.

Paris conceded and both sides agreed that the outcome would determine who won the war. After the men began to battle, however, it became clear that Menelaus would easily kill Paris. Aphrodite, determined to protect Paris, intervened. She lifted Paris from the battlefield and placed him in his own bed within the protective walls of Troy. At first the Achaeans were bewildered, but then Agamemnon called out to the Trojans, saying Menelaus had clearly won and Helen must be returned.

Once again, the Olympians took action. Athena disguised herself and entered the Trojan lines, urging a soldier to shoot at Menelaus, who still stood alone on the battlefield. The goddess whispered promises, luring him with fame and fortune if only he would be brave enough to get rid of the hated Greek. The Trojan let loose an arrow, and although Menelaus was not killed, his injury enraged the Achaeans, and the truce was over.

Hector, Father and Warrior

After the mortals regrouped, the battle was taken up again, and the Trojans lost more ground. Before returning to the fight, Hector found his wife, Andromache, in tears, miserable with grief. She held up their infant son and begged Hector not to make him fatherless and her a widow. Hector stroked her cheek and tried to comfort her, explaining how his fate was already determined and stressing that his life was defined by how well he protected his beloved city. He picked up his son and kissed him and prayed with his wife for protection.

Hector and Paris returned to battle, and this time they had the gods on their side. Thetis kept her promise to Achilles and spoke to Zeus, convincing him to punish the Achaeans in the upcoming battle. Although Zeus was acting against the wishes of his wife, Hera, and his most beloved daughter, Athena, he orchestrated the actions of the mortals in favor of the Trojans.

The entire Achaean army was pushed back toward the beaches. If the Trojans reached the Achaean ships, they would burn the vessels and thus leave their enemies trapped in a hostile foreign land.

Agamemnon Tries to Make Amends

Without Achilles on the battlefield and with the will of the gods against them, Agamemnon was in a terrible predicament. He sent Ajax and Odysseus to Achilles' tent to try and lure him back into battle with gold, stallions, priceless gifts, and the hand of any one of Agamemnon's own daughters in marriage. Briseis would also be returned to Achilles with the solemn oath that Agamemnon had never touched her. Achilles listened quietly and then refused every gift. He had come to see them as empty rewards, and he was insulted that Agamemnon had sent other men to negotiate rather than coming himself with an apology.

Achilles then told Ajax and Odysseus about the prophecy that he was to lead an exciting but brief life. Why should he risk his life for a war he no longer cared about? Why should he fight battles to defend the honor of Agamemnon and Menelaus, two men he did not even respect? What if he just stopped fighting? What if he found a woman to love, the way he had found love with Briseis? The Muses might not sing about his heroism, but he could live a quiet and contented life.

Odysseus continued to plead with Achilles, but Ajax stood to leave and tried a different strategy: He called Achilles a deserter whose pride and anger would cost his comrades their lives. Achilles responded that he would never forgive Agamemnon, and that he would only fight if the Trojan Hector were to reach Achilles' own ship. Odysseus and Ajax left to relay Achilles' decision.

Patroclus Enters the Battle

For days the Trojans fought fiercely, slaying their enemy and gaining more ground. Although Hera, Athena, and Poseidon all tried to help the Achaeans, Zeus kept his promise to Thetis and allowed them to suffer.

Patroclus, Achilles' best friend since childhood, had tried desperately to help Achilles through his personal struggles and respected Achilles' decision not to fight. But Patroclus now saw how close the Achaeans were to death. Many of the men fought from the decks of their own ships, and Hector and the Trojans seemed unstoppable.

In tears, Patroclus arrived at Achilles' tent, reminding his friend that he had promised to fight when the Trojans were close. Patroclus begged Achilles to allow the Myrmidons back into the battle and suggested he wear Achilles' famous armor. If he led the men in that gear, the Trojans would think Achilles had rejoined the war. Achilles considered for a moment and then actually heard Hector's voice in the distance, bellowing commands to his powerful troops. Achilles helped Patroclus put

Throughout his epics, Homer made use of **epithets**, which are adjectives or phrases used to characterize a person or place. The word itself is from the Greek *epi-* (on or after) and *tithenai* (to put), and these epithets served three purposes: They allowed Homer's writing to be more descriptive; they were mnemonic devices for the singers who performed the epics; and they helped complete the rhythmic structures in the metered lines of the poem. Below are examples of Homer's most well-known epithets.

"far-famed Achaeans"
"swift-footed Achilles"
"Agamemnon, lord of men"
"Apollo, god of the silver bow"
"Athena, hope of soldiers"
"rosy-fingered Dawn"
"Hector, shepherd of the people"
"the wine-dark sea"

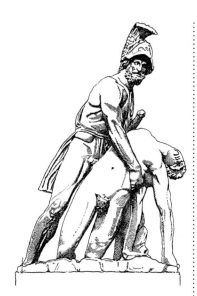

+ This etching shows Menelaus trying to protect Patroclus' body on the battlefield after Hector had stripped off his armor.

+ In Shakespeare's *Romeo and Juliet*, Romeo refuses to fight his enemy Tybalt. Romeo's dearest friend Mercutio battles him instead and gets killed. Like Achilles, Romeo feels overwhelming guilt for letting it happen and vows revenge.

+ The deceitful goddess Ruin was also known as Ate.

on the armor but told him that once Patroclus turned the enemy away from the ships, he was not to pursue them any further. Achilles knew the Olympians were assisting the Trojans, and he did not want Patroclus to die in the battle.

Patroclus stepped out onto the plains just as the first ship was being burned. With the strong and rested Myrmidons behind him, Patroclus let out a battle cry that terrified the Trojans: Achilles was back. The rejuvenated Achaeans succeeded in turning the Trojans away from their ships, and the Trojans retreated in a disorganized panic. Rather than heeding Achilles' advice, however, Patroclus, in a blind, proud fury, pushed the Trojans back to their own gates, and he even tried to scale the walls of Troy alone. Soon, the young warrior came face to face with Prince Hector.

Because the god Apollo wanted to assist the Trojans in their battle, he hid himself in a mist and crept up behind Patroclus, knocking off his helmet to reveal his true identity. Although relieved that the soldier was not Achilles, Hector could not dismiss the opportunity to kill Patroclus, his worst enemy's best friend. After Apollo injured Patroclus, Hector stabbed the Achaean, who cursed him with his dying breath.

Thus began a dreadful battle for Patroclus' body. Hector was able to strip off the armor—Achilles' prized possession—and put it on himself, but the Achaeans continued to defend the body. When a messenger told Achilles of the events on the battlefield, the great warrior was utterly destroyed. He went into a rage, covering himself in dirt and tearing at his hair. His wrenching cries were heard by his immortal mother, Thetis, who came to the beaches to see him.

Thetis tried to comfort her son and cradled him in her arms. She reminded him that he had gotten exactly what he had prayed for, because the Achaeans had suffered mightily without him. It was then that Achilles realized the cost of his pride, and he vowed to take revenge on Hector. But first he needed to retrieve Patroclus' body so he could provide his dearest friend with a proper burial. Wearing no armor except his own anger, the mighty Achilles stepped onto the battlefield. He let loose an enormous howl—and Athena echoed his cry from the heavens—and the Trojans retreated to safety behind the walls of their city. The Achaeans lifted Patroclus' body from the plain and carried it back to Achilles.

Achilles Rejoins the Battle

Achilles knew he had to make amends with Agamemnon and return to battle. Although Thetis was devastated by her son's choice, she returned to Mount Olympus and asked Hephaestus to make new armor for Achilles. The next morning, Thetis delivered the brilliant armor to her beloved son.

Now ready to enter the battle, Achilles approached Agamemnon with outstretched arms, a sign of peace. Achilles spoke, saying he now saw how their feud had only benefited the Trojans, and he admitted he had held his rage too long. The Achaeans roared with enthusiasm, relieved and elated to have Achilles rejoin their ranks. Agamemnon, annoyed by the sound of the applause, stood and began a long speech, blaming Zeus' malicious daughter Ruin for blinding him into madness

"'O dear mother, true! All those burning desires Olympian Zeus has brought to pass for me— but what joy to me now? My dear comrade's dead—"

HOMER, THE *ILIAD*, BOOK 18, LINES 92-94

the day he seized Achilles' prize girl and providing examples of how others had succumbed to this goddess' trickery. Finally, he offered to return Briseis to Achilles.

Achilles was ready to explode with impatience; he did not care about gifts now and felt the Achaeans were only wasting precious time. Odysseus, desperate to stop another feud between Agamemnon and Achilles, came up with a compromise. He said the Achaeans should feast first to regain their strength, and then make appropriate sacrifices to the gods before they met the Trojans on the battlefield.

The seething Achilles waited but refused to eat until he had killed the man who had taken his friend. Athena, however, flew down to fill the angry warrior with nectar and ambrosia. The wrath of Achilles was no longer directed toward Agamemnon; it was now focused on his enemy. With renewed strength and purpose, Achilles and the Achaean army stormed toward Troy.

A NOTE *about* ACHILLES' ARMOR

Armor was, for the majority of warriors, their most valuable possession. Even more importantly, armor represented personal strength and honor. When a warrior killed an opponent, he would try to strip off his victim's armor so he could keep it as a sign of triumph.

Although the armor Hephaestus crafted for Achilles was designed to protect the Achaean in his battle against Hector, the handiwork went far beyond thick metal and a strong sword. The masterful blacksmith created a scene on the massive shield that symbolized the very essence of the human struggle by showing two cities, one at war and another in peace. The people at war fight for their existence, surrounded by slaughter. But the majority of the shield shows a peaceful city, with weddings, harvests, musicians, and dancing children.

Homer dedicated more than 150 lines of the *Iliad* to the description of Hephaestus' exquisite work, and his attention to the idyllic scenes was a way of raising a crucial question: Who would the characters in the *Iliad* have become had they lived their lives in a peaceful city?

Bloodthirsty Achilles

When Zeus saw the raging Achilles rush onto the battlefield, he knew the mortal was capable of storming the walls of Troy alone. Because this was not the fate of the city, however, Zeus instructed the Olympians to keep the battle balanced by providing assistance to the Trojans. Even with this help, Achilles blazed across the battlefield, brutally slaying countless enemies. He killed so many men, in fact, that the nearby Xanthus River became choked with Trojan bodies. When the river rose up in anger, the maniacal Achilles turned and actually started to fight against Xanthus itself, getting caught up in its raging, torrential, bloody waters.

Again Zeus recognized the will of the Fates and sent Poseidon and Athena to help Achilles out of the waters. As Achilles continued on his bloody rampage toward the gates of Troy, King Priam watched from a tower as his soldiers streamed back inside Troy's walls. Apollo took the form of a mortal to distract Achilles, allowing all of the Trojans to escape from the battlefield. All, that is, except Hector.

Achilles and Hector Finally Meet

Despite the cries and pleas of King Priam and Queen Hecuba, Hector refused to come inside the city's gates. But when he saw the great Achilles running toward him, Hector thought briefly of trying to offer Achilles some terms. In his heart, however, Hector knew this bitter foe, this crazed warrior, would scoff at any proposal of peace. Although Hector desperately wanted to take a stand against the mighty Achilles to protect his beloved city, to protect his parents, his wife, and his infant son, he panicked and began to run.

✦ While Zeus held great power, he had no choice but to follow what the Fates decreed.

In fact, Hector ran at full speed three times around the city's great walls with Achilles at his heels, pursuing him like prey. When Zeus and the other Olympians looked down and saw this strange sight, they knew it was time for the Fates to have their say. Zeus held up his golden scale—with Hector's destiny on one side and Achilles' on the other—and watched Hector's life sink.

Athena, taking the form of one of Hector's brothers, appeared next to the fleeing Trojan and convinced him to stop so they could turn and face Achilles together. The grateful Hector halted and announced he would run no further, but asked Achilles to agree that no matter who won, the victor would return the victim's body for a proper burial. Achilles growled his refusal, saying that wolves and lambs have no

"...So he triumphed
and now he was bent on outrage, on shaming noble Hector.
Piercing the tendons, ankle to heel behind both feet,
he knotted straps of rawhide through them both,
lashed them to his chariot, left the head to drag
and mounting the car, hoisting the famous arms aboard,
he whipped his team to a run and breakneck on they flew,
holding nothing back. ..."

HOMER, THE *ILIAD*, BOOK 22, LINES 465-472

such agreement. He hurled the first spear, and Hector threw one of his own. But when Hector turned to his brother for assistance, he had vanished. Hector knew he had been tricked by the gods and that his end was near.

Although Hector fought valiantly, Achilles had the advantage of knowing Hector's armor because it had been his own. Aiming for a small hole near the collarbone, Achilles drove a spear straight through Hector's neck. The dying Hector pleaded again to have his body given to his father, King Priam, but Achilles would hear none of it. In a violent rage, Achilles stripped the dead Hector of the armor and lashed his legs to the back of his chariot, dragging him around the walls of Troy three times while King Priam and Queen Hecuba wailed from the towers. After this shocking and reprehensible act, Achilles took Hector's battered corpse back to his own camp, flinging it down for the dogs to eat.

Achilles and King Priam

Mysteriously, no animal would touch Hector's body: Apollo and Aphrodite were protecting it. But now that Achilles had exacted revenge on Hector, he could finally bring himself to bury his beloved friend, Patroclus. He made elaborate preparations for the funeral, including a magnificent pyre of wood, sacrificed animals, and, gruesomely, twelve Trojans Achilles had killed at the Xanthus River. Achilles then presided over an array of athletic competitions, all in honor of Patroclus.

The last contest was to be a javelin throw, and Agamemnon stepped forward to compete with the other men. But Achilles stood up to acknowledge that Agamemnon was the best thrower in the army and that no man could ever compete with him. Achilles offered Agamemnon the prize, and the Achaean leader accepted it graciously.

Even with this closure—Hector slain, Patroclus buried, and his feud with Agamemnon put to rest—Achilles was still wracked with guilt and struggling to

King Priam kneeling before Achilles

"'I have endured what no one on earth has ever done before—
I put to my lips the hands of the man who killed my son.'"

HOMER, THE *ILIAD*, BOOK 24, LINES 590-591

+ **Supplication** is the act of praying or humbly asking someone a favor. The word comes from the Latin *sub-* (under) and *plicare* (to fold, double up). Priam would have had to kneel before Achilles and rest his hands on Achilles' knees. It was a sign of utter surrender and would have been humiliating for Priam.

come to terms with his role in the war. He refused to give Hector's body back to the Trojans and continued to drag it around Patroclus' grave. Finally, the gods decided enough was enough. Thetis was called to speak to her son, to calm him and convince him that he must relinquish Hector's body. And Hermes was asked to lead Priam to Achilles' tent to request his son's body.

In Hermes' care, King Priam entered the Achaean camp undetected. In ten long years of war, Achilles had never seen King Priam this close, and now, here he was kneeling before him in supplication. Achilles was moved by the sight of the old man weakened with grief, and he realized Priam felt the same pain his own father would soon face: Achilles now knew he would die fighting the Trojans.

The wrath of Achilles subsided, and he granted Priam his wish. Achilles ordered his servants to bathe Hector's body and wrap it in fine linens. He offered to share a meal with Priam and invited him to spend the night before returning to his city in the morning. The two men agreed to suspend all fighting until Priam could hold the funeral rites for his son. For ten days the Trojans mourned Hector's death before burning his body on a pyre, just as the Achaeans had done for Patroclus.

Part III: After the *Iliad*

Homer chose to end his epic tale here, at a point when both the Achaeans and the Trojans had suffered deeply. He does not describe the much-anticipated death of Achilles, nor does he conclude with any victory. Achilles' anger toward Agamemnon was gone, but the epic tale ends the same way it began, with two enemies entrenched in war. It was other Greek and Roman writers who continued the Epic Cycle, creating other stories and poems about what surrounded the "wrath of Achilles."

The Death of Achilles

Despite his grief, or perhaps because of it, Achilles remained the strongest of the Achaean warriors. After fulfilling the agreement to suspend battle for ten days, Achilles continued to threaten the Trojan forces. Ironically, his life would end at the hands of the meek Trojan Paris. Despite the fact that Paris was the initial cause of the war, and despite losing many of his own brothers and countrymen to the Greek army, he had never been an aggressive force in battle. But finally, with the divine assistance of Apollo, Paris was able to shoot an arrow directly into Achilles' heel, which, according to a Roman version of the story, was his only vulnerable spot.

 The Greeks put Achilles' body on a funeral pyre, and Thetis rose from the sea to mix her son's ashes with those of Patroclus, which had been Patroclus' dying wish.

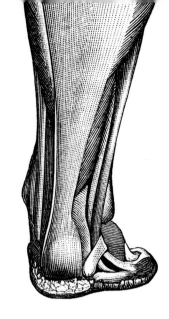

APOLLO TELLS PARIS

" ' If you would serve your side, aim at Achilles,
 And take your vengeance for your brothers' deaths!'
[Apollo] pointed to Achilles laying low
The troops of Troy, and turned the bow on him
And guided the sure shaft with deadly aim.
This, after Hector, was a thing to make
Old Priam glad. And so Achilles fell,
Victor of mighty triumphs, vanquished by
The craven ravisher of that Greek wife:
If in a woman's fight he had to fall,
He'd have preferred the Amazon's double axe.
 And now that terror of the ranks of Troy,
The grace and guardian of the name of Greece,
Achilles, prince unconquerable in war,
Had burned upon the pyre. "

BOOK XII OF OVID'S *METAMORPHOSES*, LINES 609-623

- An **Achilles' heel** is a flaw or weakness, like being overly sensitive or too jealous. While Achilles' physical weakness was his heel, his psychological weakness, or **tragic flaw**, was his pride.

- Achilles is the first **tragic hero** in Western literature: He had the potential for greatness but was doomed because of a tragic flaw. Unlike an antagonist, a tragic hero stills earns respect because he recognizes his role in his own downfall and takes responsibility for the outcome.

- When Achilles was killed, the great Ajax risked his life to carry his body off the battlefield, while Odysseus defended Ajax against attack. Ajax wanted Achilles' armor as a reward, but the gods gave the prize to Odysseus. This made Ajax go mad, and when he returned to his senses, he killed himself in shame.

- Paris was killed by Philoctetes, the man who had lit Heracles' funeral pyre. Heracles had given Philoctetes an arrow poisoned with the Hydra's blood, and it was this arrow that killed Paris.

The Destruction of Troy

Having lost their most powerful warrior, the Achaeans were struggling. They had already attempted to isolate Troy. They had already tried to scale Troy's walls. What if they tried deceit?

Odysseus, known for his intelligent schemes, came up with a risky but brilliant plan. He instructed the Achaeans to build an enormous wooden horse, and then he and a dozen of his best warriors hid inside its hollow belly. The other Achaeans struck the camp and set sail so that the Trojans would think they were admitting defeat and leaving.

When the Trojans tentatively approached the horse on the deserted beaches, they found a man with his ankles and wrists bound. Acting enraged, the man, Sinon, claimed he had been left behind as a human sacrifice to Athena and explained how the horse had been built to appease Athena so she would lead the Achaeans safely home. Finally, Sinon told the Trojans that the Achaeans had purposely built the horse too large to fit through Troy's gates because they hoped the Trojans would destroy it, thus offending Athena.

Although several prophets tried to dissuade them from believing Sinon's story, the Trojans leaders were convinced they should not harm the horse. They dragged it into their city and even removed a section of their walls so the horse could pass through.

Later that night, after the Trojans had celebrated their victory and the city was quiet, Odysseus and his men crept from the horse and signaled for the ships to return. By dawn the next morning, Menelaus had taken back his wife, and Troy was utterly destroyed. The Achaeans slaughtered the men, enslaved the women, desecrated the temples, and looted priceless treasure. The prophecy predicting that Paris would ultimately cause the ruin of Troy had come true.

The Achaeans Sail Home

After ten years away from home, the exhausted Achaeans were grateful to be going home. The gods, however, saw how ruthlessly the Achaeans had destroyed sacred temples and abused the Trojans, and they made their return voyages difficult. Menelaus and the prized Helen were blown off course. It took Odysseus ten long years to return to his wife and son in Ithaca, a tale related by Homer in his second epic, the *Odyssey*.

Agamemnon met a more gruesome fate. Although he reached his home uneventfully, he did not survive his welcome. His wife, Clytemnestra, had been seething with anger the whole time her husband was in Troy. Not only had he killed her first husband and forced her into marriage, he had later sacrificed Clytemnestra's beloved daughter, Iphigenia. To get revenge, Clytemnestra took Agamemnon's hated cousin as a lover and then, while servants washed Agamemnon on the day of his return, she and her lover killed him while he was defenseless in the bathtub. Like his great-grandfather Tantalus, Agamemnon had killed his own child and died as a consequence.

- Achilles' son, Neoptolemus, arrived in Troy after his father had been killed. He was the first to climb up inside the wooden horse, he killed King Priam, and he took Andromache as a slave girl.

- Sinon may have inherited his ability to lie from his father, Sisyphus. Here, Sinon used **reverse psychology** by telling the Trojans that the Greeks wanted them to destroy the horse, which made them do the exact opposite.

- When suspicious of another's kindness, someone might say, **"Beware of Greeks bearing gifts."** This saying originates from the Trojan Horse, which seemed like a gift from the Greeks but ultimately caused tragedy.

Agamemnon was not the only one to die at the hands of Clytemnestra. The king brought the Trojan priestess Cassandra back from Troy, and she had repeatedly warned him about her horrific visions of destruction. He did not believe her, of course, and she, too, was killed by Agamemnon's bitter wife.

A Final Word on Homer's Iliad

Although thousands of people were involved in Homer's story of the Trojan War, the *Iliad* focuses on relatively few men and women. Indeed, the choices and actions of a handful of core characters—Achilles, Agamemnon, Menelaus, Hector, Paris, Helen, and Priam—critically affect the lives of the remaining thousands. Homer did not choose sides in the war, and readers (or, in ancient times, listeners) must absorb the content, reflect on the characters' actions, and then make their own decisions about the epic's lessons.

Did Achilles have good reason to refuse to fight? Should Agamemnon have done more to get Achilles back in the war? Should Achilles have allowed Patroclus to enter the battle in his place? Was it cowardice or wisdom that made Hector run? Should Menelaus and Paris have assumed more active roles in their fight over Helen? Could Helen be held responsible for the deaths of thousands of men?

These issues—cause and effect, personal responsibility, passion, honor, jealousy, duty—faced people of the ancient world, and they remain the realities for people today. People still deal with temptation, loss, grief, and anger. They face times of crisis when their strengths are tested and their weaknesses are painfully revealed. They are still aware of the value of reputation, and they can be fiercely protective of their own interests. And one of the biggest quandaries people still struggle with is an enduring one: How much control does a person have over his or her own life?

The *Iliad* is over 2,700 years old and was likely composed by a blind man who could have no vision of the future. The story, however, remains remarkably timeless, and its impact still resonates today.

+ Of the one thousand Greek ships that had arrived in Troy, only one hundred sailed away. And many of these ships would never reach their intended shores.

+ While the Achaeans who survived the harrowing Trojan War were glad to be going home, they bore much sorrow. They knew, too, that many things would be different when they returned because they had been gone for so long. The word **nostalgia**, from the Greek *nostos* ("homecoming") and *algos* ("pain") has come to mean "a sad longing for the past."

THE IMPORTANCE OF HOMER'S WORK

"Everything currently suggests that Homer should be taken seriously, that his story of a military conflict between Greeks and the inhabitants of Troy is based on a memory of historical events—whatever these may have been. If someone came up to me at the excavation one day and expressed his or her belief that the Trojan War did indeed happen here, my response as an archaeologist working at Troy would be: Why not?"

MANFRED KORFMANN, "WAS THERE A TROJAN WAR?", *ARCHAEOLOGY*

THE ODYSSEY
A Long Journey Home

A Comparison of Homer's Epics

The *Odyssey*—12,109 lines long in its original Greek text—differs on so many levels from the *Iliad* that some scholars have questioned whether the epics actually came from the same author. Traditionally, however, it is believed that Homer first devised his account of the Trojan War and then years later crafted the *Odyssey* to describe Odysseus' return home. While the poems are set in the same historic time period and share many of the same characters, they have several obvious differences.

First, the *Iliad* is a gritty piece that takes place over just a few weeks, and details graphic violence and a series of day-to-day decisions. The passionate fury of Achilles' wrath and the results of his actions, then, are something like a metaphorical sprint. In contrast, the *Odyssey* is a lavish adventure story spanning ten years. Odysseus' arduous journey culminates when he reaches home and reclaims his throne, and it is by comparison a metaphorical marathon.

Second, the *Iliad* involves the Olympians, but the story focuses on the actions of a handful of humans. Furthermore, Homer does not assign clear roles in the conflict; there is no single enemy or "bad guy." The *Odyssey*'s character list, on the other hand, includes a one-eyed giant, a six-headed monster, dead spirits, a wicked whirlpool, a sneaky sorceress, and a god who relentlessly punishes the protagonist. Odysseus faces specific and unmistakable enemies, including beasts, humans, and immortals.

Third, the *Iliad* focuses mainly on men and presents the women mainly as prizes to be won or lost. The many dominant female characters in the *Odyssey*, however, play more pivotal roles. The wise goddess Athena, for example, assists Odysseus, the sorceress Circe wields great power, and the goddess Calypso holds Odysseus captive. Perhaps most important, however, is Penelope, Odysseus' wife, who is depicted as loyal, independent, and capable. Indeed, it can be successfully argued that she has more heroic traits than her husband.

Finally, in the *Iliad*, Homer rifles through the complex layers of human psychology and purposely ends the work on a tragic note with many issues left unresolved. In its last scene, when the aged King Priam meets the godlike Achilles, both men come face to face with the tragic realities of their lives and the war that rages around them. The *Odyssey* begins after the war, and while Odysseus must face a series of hardships, the epic ends at a peaceful time for the hero, when he reclaims his home and is reunited with his wife, son, and father.

Despite their differences, both of Homer's works have survived with remarkably lasting relevance. The *Iliad* takes its reader on a grueling psychological journey, and the *Odyssey* follows its hero on an exhausting physical journey. But both epics explore timeless issues of honor, love, death, and passion, and they both explore the difficult choices humans must make.

The "Homeric epic—the *Odyssey* in particular—has retained a primacy of various sorts, as the first and probably the finest example of its genre, the beginning of the Western literary tradition, and the ideal introduction to literature, so simple and so profound, so obvious and so mysterious, so accessible and so elusive."

HOWARD W. CLARKE,
THE ART OF THE ODYSSEY

Prologue to the Odyssey

Odysseus' plan to use the wooden horse to get inside the walls of Troy succeeded. After ten arduous years, the Achaeans had finally defeated the Trojans. Menelaus, Agamemnon, and other leaders organized their troops and set sail for various kingdoms in Greece. Odysseus was to lead a total of twelve ships, each carrying sixty men, back to the western shores of Greece. He longed to see his wife, Penelope, and their son, Telemachus, who were waiting for him in Ithaca.

As with Homer's *Iliad*, the *Odyssey* begins *in medias res*, a Latin phrase that means "into the middle of things." So instead of starting when Odysseus sets sail from Troy, the tale opens nine years later in Ithaca, where Telemachus and Penelope are struggling to keep the peace. Telemachus has grown up with no father to guide him, and Penelope is finally resigning herself to the fact that she must choose a husband from among the throng of suitors who have taken over her palace.

Readers then learn of Odysseus' whereabouts and hear his treacherous tale in the first person, as the hero relates his adventures to a royal family who has found him washed up on their shores. Finally, readers follow Odysseus back to Ithaca to learn how he and his son, all grown, restore peace to their palace.

⋆ Homer starts his *Iliad* by asking the Muse of epic poetry, Calliope, to begin her story with the argument between Achilles and Agamemnon. In the *Odyssey*, Homer recognizes the vast amount of information that Calliope, pictured below, must cover and tells her, "start from where you will…"
(Book I, Line 12)

THE FIRST LINES OF HOMER'S *ODYSSEY*

"Sing to me of the man, Muse, the man of twists and turns
driven time and again off course, once he had plundered
the hallowed heights of Troy.
Many cities of men he saw and learned their minds,
many pains he suffered, heartsick on the open sea,
fighting to save his life and bring his comrades home."

BOOK 1, LINES 1-6

for the

ODYSSEY

Greek mortals

Odysseus (*oh DISS ee us*)
A mortal man who spends ten years trying to return to his home in Ithaca after the Trojan War. The Romans referred to him as "Ulysses."

Penelope (*pe NEL oh pee*)
Odysseus' faithful wife who, always hopeful that her husband will return, spends years fending off swarms of suitors.

Telemachus (*tuh LEM e kiss*)
Odysseus' only son. Telemachus was only an infant when Odysseus left for the war in Troy, and at the start of the *Odyssey*, he is coming of age under difficult circumstances.

Alcinous (*al SIN oh us*)
King of Phaeacia who offers to help Odysseus.

Nausicaa (*noh SIK ay uh*)
Daughter of King Alcinous, and the girl who finds the weary Odysseus on the shores of Phaeacia.

Eurylochus (*yoo RIL oh kus*)
Second in command to Odysseus.

Tiresias (*tie REE see us*)
Dead prophet who advises Odysseus in the Underworld.

Eumaeus (*yoo MEE us*)
Loyal farmer who helps the disguised Odysseus in Ithaca.

Antinous (*an TIN oh us*)
Arrogant leader of the suitors who pursue Penelope in Odysseus' absence.

Eurycleia (*yoo ri KLEE uh*)
Penelope's servant, once a nurse to Odysseus.

Monsters

The Cyclops (*SIE klops*)
A powerful giant with only one eye. While Cyclopes were also born to Gaea and Uranus, the monster in the *Odyssey* is the offspring of the sea god Poseidon and is named Polyphemus.

Laestrygonians (*lee strie GOH nee unz*)
A race of giants who despise men.

Sirens (*SIE renz*)
Beautiful female creatures who try to lure men to their deaths by singing tempting songs.

Scylla (*SIL uh*)
A six-headed beast who lives in a cave on a huge rock.

Charybdis (*ka RIB diss*)
A whirlpool monster who lives across from Scylla's rock.

Gods and goddesses

Athena *(uh THEE nuh)*
The goddess of wisdom who tries to protect Odysseus.

Poseidon *(poh SIE dun)*
The god of the sea who despises Odysseus.

Zeus *(ZOOS)*
Olympian leader who often aids Odysseus but also punishes him and his crew when they disobey.

Aeolus *(ee OH lus)*
The god who is the keeper of the winds.

Hades *(HAY deez)*
The god of the Underworld, which is itself often called Hades.

Circe *(SUR see)*
A powerful sorceress who loves to play tricks on men. In the Odyssey, she turns Odysseus' men into pigs.

Helios *(HEE lee ohs)*
The sun god who keeps sacred cattle on Thrinacia Island.

Calypso *(kuh LIP soh)*
A beautiful goddess who falls in love with Odysseus and wants to make him immortal so he can stay with her forever.

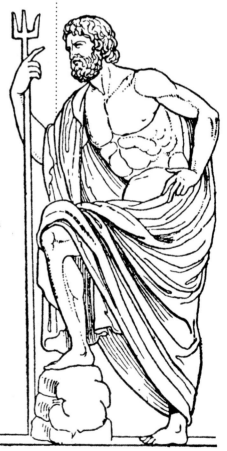

◆ Poseidon, god of
the sea, wielding his
powerful trident.

Part I: Ten Years after the Trojan War

The Situation in Ithaca

It had been almost twenty years since Odysseus had feigned madness to avoid following Agamemnon and Menelaus to Troy and fighting for Helen's return. Forced to choose between harming his newborn son, Telemachus, or continuing to act mad, he had given up the ruse and left his beloved Ithaca for Troy.

Telemachus was now a man, and although he had no memory of his father, he knew Odysseus was famous for his part in the destruction of Troy. Telemachus was struggling to come of age with no father figure and to live up to the expectations of being the son of such a legendary king. His life was made even more difficult when the Ithacan palace was taken over by arrogant men who wished to marry his mother, Penelope.

Seven years after the fall of Troy, after all of the other Greeks had found their way back across the Aegean Sea, Odysseus had still not returned. Men from neighboring cities had come to Ithaca to seek Penelope's hand, and she had politely refused. But suitors kept coming, and their numbers rose until well over one hundred men had settled into the palace, abusing the rules of hospitality so valued by the Greeks.

Throughout Odysseus' long and frustrating absence, Telemachus and Penelope devised numerous schemes to foil the suitors. At one point, Penelope agreed to choose a suitor as soon as she finished weaving a burial shroud for her elderly father-in-law, Laertes. But though she wove by day, she secretly pulled out most of her work at night.

- This etching shows Penelope at her loom, discussing her dire situation with Telemachus. Although looms are constructed differently, they all allow a weaver to pass a weft yarn over and under a set of warp yarns to construct fabric.

- Another word for fabric is **textile**, a word that derives from the Latin *textus*, "fabric or structure." **Text**—the words structured by a writer—shares this root, so in essence a weaver and a writer each take separate strands of material and arrange them into a whole and meaningful piece. And when something is in **context**, it is connected to that which surrounds it (*com-* means "with").

For three long years, these unwelcome guests feasted on the palace's livestock and depleted Odysseus' wealth, and the great city of Ithaca was unstable without a ruler. Unfortunately, many of Penelope's servants had fallen in love with the suitors, so they, too, were becoming unruly. Penelope knew she had to choose a suitor soon.

Telemachus Sets Sail

Telemachus grew more frustrated with the situation and attempted to assert himself. He lectured the suitors harshly and told them to leave, and when they tried to blame the situation on Penelope, Telemachus defended his mother. Encouraged by Athena, he set sail for Sparta to ask King Menelaus if he had news about Odysseus.

When he reached Sparta, Telemachus was overjoyed to learn that a prophet had told Menelaus that Odysseus was still alive and being held captive by the goddess Calypso. Telemachus readied himself to return to Ithaca and share the good news with his mother.

Meanwhile, Penelope was at the palace dreading her son's return. The suitors had found out about Telemachus' journey and were scheming to kill him when he came back. Penelope feared she would lose her beloved son just as she had lost her husband. The goddess Athena, however, sent word to Penelope that young Telemachus would be protected.

Odysseus on Calypso's Island

Athena was taking care of Odysseus as well. The goddess, who had always been fond of the intelligent and determined mortal and respected his actions in wartime, had grown impatient with Poseidon and Zeus, who, for reasons that will become clear, had kept Odysseus from his home for so many years. Athena went to Zeus to defend the mortal and plead his case.

The lovely Calypso had indeed found the injured warrior on the shores of her private island seven years earlier and had nursed him back to health. She had also fallen in love with the strong hero and refused to let him leave, even promising him immortality if he would stay with her on her island. But while Odysseus felt some contentment on the beautiful island, closed off from the rest of the world, he longed for his wife, his son, and his homeland, and he grew more miserable every year of his captivity.

Zeus agreed with Athena that Odysseus should be allowed to leave, and he called on Hermes to deliver his decision. Although Calypso was hurt and saddened, she agreed to give Odysseus the tools he would need to build a raft so he might continue on his journey toward the shores of Ithaca. She watched with a heavy heart as he worked on his small raft, and she gave him provisions and good winds. Thus the strange relationship between Odysseus and his captor, a beautiful, powerful, and adoring nymph, came to an end.

+ Calypso was a daughter of Atlas. Her name comes from the Greek word that means "to hide," and she tried to sequester Odysseus on her beautiful Greek island, known as Ogygia.

+ *Calypso* was the name the famous French oceanographer Jacques Cousteau gave to his beloved ship in the 1960s.

The Kindness of the Phaeacians

When Poseidon learned what Zeus had done to free Odysseus, he was outraged and stirred up yet another storm to destroy Odysseus' raft. But Zeus had a sea goddess give Odysseus a magic scarf that would keep him afloat until he reached the island of the Phaeacians. When the bedraggled traveler reached the shores, Nausicaa, a kind daughter of King Alcinous, helped him back to her father's palace and had the stranger bathed and fed.

At dinner, Odysseus finally revealed his identity to the royal family, and they were awestruck. Here at their table was the famed Odysseus, long thought to have perished at sea. The Phaeacians pleaded with him to tell them about his journeys since the Trojan War, and Odysseus complied, describing all the details of his frightening adventures and devastating losses.

Part II: Odysseus Recounts His Travels

The Island of the Lotus Eaters

Odysseus first told the Phaeacians how he and his men—720 in all—had been blown by harsh seas for many days. When they finally landed on an island for fresh provisions, Odysseus sent three men inland to see if the inhabitants of the island were friendly. Indeed they were. The island turned out to be the dreamlike land of the Lotus Eaters, people who ate nothing but the sweet, tempting fruit of the lotus plant.

When Odysseus' men tasted the delicious fruit, they lost their memory and any ambition to return home. They wanted nothing more than to stay on the island, eating the lotus to forget their problems and their difficult journey home. But Odysseus dragged them back to the ships and ordered the fleet to set sail.

- The edible lotus flower holds significance in cultures throughout the world. Hindus associate it with creation myths, and it is the national flower of both India and Vietnam. In yoga, the cross-legged **lotus position** allows for deep breathing.

- A flower called the Egyptian blue lotus was found in the tomb of Tutankhamen and is known to contain a hypnotic drug. This is likely the flower Homer referenced when he talked about a powerful plant that made Odysseus' men want to stay on the island.

"Why are we weigh'd upon with heaviness,
And utterly consumed with sharp distress,
While all things else have rest from weariness?
...Surely, surely, slumber is more sweet than toil, the shore
Than labour in the deep mid-ocean, wind and wave and oar;
Oh rest ye, brother mariners, we will not wander more."

ALFRED, LORD TENNYSON, "THE LOTUS-EATERS"

The Cave of the Cyclops

Odysseus and his crew reached another island several days later. After the bad experience with the Lotus Eaters, Odysseus himself chose to lead a dozen men in search of provisions, and took bags of his best wine to offer the inhabitants. Moving cautiously through the woods, Odysseus and his men came upon a huge cave and marveled at the bounty of cheese and fruit and pens for sheep they found inside. Hoping the owner would return and offer them hospitality, the men began to eat.

Toward nightfall, a giant shadow fell across the opening of the cave. The terrified sailors recognized the one-eyed Cyclops Polyphemus, a son of the mighty Poseidon, and crept into dark corners of the cave. Polyphemus, unaware of his guests, herded his sheep into the cave and moved an enormous boulder across the entrance, trapping the animals—and the men—inside.

Odysseus stepped forward into the light of the fire, revealing himself to Polyphemus and pleading with him to follow the rules of hospitality, in which hosts treat their guests kindly. But the huge beast just laughed and said he and the other Cyclopes paid no mind to rules. Rather than offering to stock the ships, the massive Polyphemus lurched forward and grabbed two of the men, smashed their heads against the rocky floor of the cave, and swallowed them whole. The beast then fell into a deep slumber.

Odysseus' first instinct was to kill the beast, but he knew that only the Cyclops could move the massive boulder. He therefore spent a sleepless night with the snoring Cyclops, devising a plan. In the morning, Polyphemus ate two more men for breakfast, herded his sheep out of the cave, and replaced the boulder at the entrance. The wily Odysseus immediately put a plan into action. He had his men hone the end of one of Polyphemus' huge shepherd staffs into a sharp point and harden it in the flames of the fire. Then they poured the strong wine Odysseus had brought into large bowls.

When Polyphemus returned to his cave that evening, he herded his flock inside and snatched up two more men for dinner, threatening to kill even more. But Odysseus stepped forward and offered him the wine. The beast swallowed one bowl

- The name Cyclops comes from the Greek *kyklos*, meaning "round or wheel," and refers to the beast's round eye. Over time, the *k* became a *c*, so *cyclos* is a root for words like bicycle, cyclical, recycle, and cyclone. An **encyclopedia** is a book that contains helpful information and comes from *cyclos* and *paideia*, a Greek word that describes the process of getting a good education.

- One beast is known as a Cyclops (SIE klops). The plural is Cyclopes (sie KLOPE eez).

- The Polyphemus moth gets its name because of the large, singular eye spots on each of its wings.

• The etching above shows three of Odysseus' men clinging to the bellies of rams in order to escape unnoticed from Polyphemus' cave. The need to escape from someone or something is a common element in many story genres, and the word comes from the Latin *excapparae*, "to leave one's cape (or cloak) behind."

and demanded another. Softened by the drink, he asked Odysseus his name. The crafty Greek replied, "My name is Nobody," and held up a third bowl of the strong wine. The beast gulped it down and slumped to the floor in a drunken stupor.

Odysseus and his men retrieved the hidden staff and heated its sharpened end in the fire until it was white-hot. Then, with a tremendous effort, they plunged the stake into Polyphemus' single eye. The blinded beast thrashed in pain and screamed for help. Although several other Cyclopes were gathered just outside the cave, Odysseus' plan had worked brilliantly: Polyphemus kept yelling, "Nobody is killing me!" and his neighbors assumed he was dreaming.

In agony, Polyphemus groped his way toward the entrance of the cave and slid the boulder aside. He then knelt down with outstretched hands, waiting to catch his prisoners as they fled. In the meantime, Odysseus and his men had crawled under the bellies of the Cyclops' rams and grabbed onto their thick wool. As the rams trotted out of the cave, Polyphemus felt along their backs but did not notice the men underneath. Thus the men escaped—and even managed to herd the rams back to their ships for later provisions.

By the time Polyphemus heard the men in the distance, they were already back on their ships. He hurled large boulders in their direction screaming, "Nobody!" over and over. Now that they had escaped the Cyclops, Odysseus could not resist revealing his true identity. So he cupped his hands to his mouth and cried, "It was I, King Odysseus of Ithaca, who blinded you, Polyphemus!"

Odysseus may have had the last word, but as he sailed away, Polyphemus stretched his massive arms toward the sea in anguish. His father, Poseidon, heard him and vowed revenge. From that moment on, although Poseidon had supported the Achaeans in battle against the Trojans, Odysseus became Poseidon's worst enemy.

> "... 'Cyclops—
> if any man on the face of the earth should ask you
> who blinded you, shamed you so—say Odysseus,
> raider of cities, *he* gouged out your eye,
> Laertes' son who makes his home in Ithaca!'"

HOMER, THE *ODYSSEY*, BOOK 9, LINES 558-562

The Winds of Aeolus

Odysseus and his men grieved for their dead comrades, and a full week passed before they reached the island of Aeolus, the keeper of the winds. The hospitable god allowed the mortals to rest there, and after several weeks, Aeolus gave Odysseus a large bag tied tightly with twine. He explained that the bag held all the storm winds, leaving Zephyrus, the west wind, to blow Odysseus' fleet toward Ithaca. Odysseus thanked Aeolus and hid the bag in the hollow of his ship.

For nine days and nights, the twelve ships sped smoothly across a calm sea. When Odysseus finally saw the shores of Ithaca in the distance, he ordered his men to prepare for landing. The exhausted leader then allowed himself to fall asleep.

Tragically, Odysseus' men were suspicious. They thought Aeolus' bag contained gold and Odysseus was hoarding the riches for himself. They seized the bag and opened it just off the shore of Ithaca. Out gushed howling winds that swept the ships all the way back to Aeolus' island.

Aeolus' gift had guaranteed a safe trip back to Ithaca, so the god of the winds was shocked to see Odysseus on his island again. Convinced that Odysseus was truly cursed by the gods, Aeolus refused to assist him again and sent him away.

The Laestrygonians

With heavy hearts, the men set sail again on the twelve ships. When they came upon an unfamiliar island, Odysseus ordered eleven of the ships to dock together in a safe harbor hidden from view, while he moored his own ship further away. Then he took several of his men to explore the island.

Unfortunately, they had come to the land of the Laestrygonians, ruthless giants who despised humans. Odysseus and his men escaped, but the other eleven ships were doomed. Rather than being safe in the harbor, they became easy targets as the giants hurled boulders at them from the cliffs above. The boats were smashed, and the men—well over six hundred of them—either drowned or were speared from the water and eaten by the giants.

Odysseus and his men, sickened by the gruesome sight, could do nothing to save their comrades. Their journey had begun with twelve ships carrying over seven hundred men. Now one lone ship remained with fewer than sixty men on board.

✦ The only wind Aeolus did not put in the bag was Zephyrus, the west wind. The modern word **zephyr** means "a gentle breeze."

+ Circe was a daughter of Helios, the sun god. Circe's brother was Aeetes, the owner of the Golden Fleece until his daughter Medea helped Jason steal it. Circe, then, is Medea's aunt.

Queen Circe

The Phaeacians listened, still rapt, as Odysseus told how he and his remaining men had rowed on. When they again spotted land, Odysseus divided his crew in half and assigned Eurylochus, his second in command, to lead one half while he led the other. Seeing smoke in the distance, they drew lots to see which group would investigate. Eurylochus lost, so he and his men went to explore.

They came upon an elegant palace surrounded by lush gardens and waterfalls. As the men began to climb the stairs, they were startled to see several lions. The men turned to run, but a beautiful woman appeared, and the beasts dropped to the floor and began to purr. The woman invited the men inside. Although Eurylochus tried to dissuade his men by reminding them of their tragic misfortune on the other islands, they were too tempted by the woman—really the sorceress Circe—and her enchanting palace. They followed their hostess inside while Eurylochus slipped to the back of the group and hid outside the door.

As Eurylochus watched, Circe offered the men wine. Then, raising her wand, Circe transformed the men into swine. Snorting and squealing in panic, the men tried to escape, but the palace gates were closed. Eurylochus dashed back to the ship and told Odysseus what he had seen, and Odysseus grabbed his sword and set off in the direction of the palace.

As he ran through the woods, however, the god Hermes suddenly appeared. He warned the mortal that if he acted rashly, which he had been known to do, he too would be turned into a pig. Hermes gave Odysseus a magic herb to swallow that would ward off Circe's magic, and Odysseus listened closely to Hermes' advice.

Odysseus approached the palace, and Circe prepared to welcome another unsuspecting guest. But when her magic did not change Odysseus into a pig, she recoiled. Following Hermes' instructions, Odysseus pressed his sword to her throat. Circe had been warned that a powerful man would come to her one day, a man who could not be weakened by her spells. Recognizing Odysseus as that man, she respectfully returned the crew to human form.

The goddess and her attendants were so welcoming, and Odysseus and his crew so weary of traveling, that the men stayed on Circe's beautiful island. After a year, however, the men reminded Odysseus that it was time to continue their journey. Circe told Odysseus that if he wanted to survive future hardships, he must first travel to the Underworld and listen to the advice of the dead prophet Tiresias. She gave him instructions for entering into Hades' realm and then bade him safe travel.

The prophecy of Tiresias

"'And even if *you* escape, you'll come home late
and come a broken man—all shipmates lost,
alone in a stranger's ship—
and you will find a world of pain at home,
crude, arrogant men devouring all your goods,
courting your noble wife, offering gifts to win her.'"

HOMER, THE *ODYSSEY*, BOOK 11, LINES 129-134

In Hades, the Land of the Dead

The North Wind blew Odysseus' ship to the edge of the world and they went ashore. Then, following Circe's instructions, they dug a trough in the sand, poured wine, honey, and milk into it, and filled it with the blood of two ewes. The men returned to the ship and left Odysseus to face the ghosts of the Underworld.

Within minutes, dozens of silent spirits swarmed around Odysseus. He held them off, though, because Circe had instructed him to let Tiresias drink first from the offering. When the prophet appeared, he drank deeply and then spoke to Odysseus in a hoarse whisper.

Tiresias explained that Poseidon was still furious with Odysseus for blinding Polyphemus and that he would continue to punish him on his journey. Odysseus had already deeply offended one god, and Tiresias warned the traveler to avoid offending another: When Odysseus landed on Helios' island of Thrinacia, he and his men must not, under any circumstance, eat the sacred cattle.

With that, Tiresias faded into the dark fog. Odysseus then let other spirits drink from the sacrificial trough so he could hear their stories. First, he spoke with his tearful mother, Anticlea, who had died of grief because her son never returned from Troy. Anticlea assured him that Penelope had remained faithful in his absence and that she and Telemachus waited for his return. Odysseus also met the ghost of Agamemnon, who explained how his jealous wife had killed him upon his return from Troy. He advised Odysseus to land in Ithaca secretly and not reveal his plans until he was sure of his wife's loyalty and the safety of his palace.

Odysseus then saw the ghost of the great Achilles, who even in death stood tall among the other spirits. As Achilles approached, however, Odysseus could see the sorrow in his face. Achilles had lived the life of a legendary warrior, but he told Odysseus if he had known what death would be like, he would have chosen to live as a humble slave. Still, Achilles was proud to learn how valiantly his son, Neoptolamus, had fought for the Achaeans at Troy.

Odysseus saw others in the Underworld—Sisyphus futilely pushing a boulder up a hill, and Tantalus standing in a pool of water—but he was too shaken to stay any longer.

Circe's Advice

Sweating with fear, Odysseus ran back to his ship and ordered his men to set sail immediately. They returned to Circe's island to thank the goddess, and she invited them to eat and rest before they left the next morning. As the sun set, Circe took Odysseus aside and warned him of the Sirens, creatures who lured sailors with their beautiful songs but killed them if they came too close to their island. She also told him of the dangers of passing between Scylla, a six-headed, dragonlike monster who lived on a rock, and Charybdis, a powerful whirlpool that sucked in victims and devoured them. With a sad embrace, Odysseus took his leave from Circe and went back to the angry seas.

The Sirens

As the men sailed toward Ithaca, they heard faint singing in the distance. Remembering Circe's warning, Odysseus plugged his men's ears with wax. But Odysseus longed to hear the song of the Sirens, so he ordered his men to tie him to the mast of the ship. They were instructed not to free him, no matter how much he begged.

As the songs became louder, Odysseus saw beautiful women on an island's rocky shore. Their voices were undoubtedly the loveliest sound he had ever heard. In delicate harmony, they promised that if he came ashore, they would sing him songs of praise, as well as songs to make him wiser. Odysseus was desperate to go ashore and struggled to get free, but his men tightened the ropes that bound him and rowed on.

As the ship sailed away, Odysseus turned to see the Sirens, angry that they could not tempt him, turn into their true forms of hideous, flightless birds. Their voices changed as well, becoming horrible, dissonant noise. The men then untied Odysseus, the only mortal to ever hear the Sirens' song and live.

- The Sirens were once mortal women who had refused to sing for the gods. So Aphrodite turned them into ugly birds.

- A **siren song** is something that is dangerous yet difficult to resist, and an emergency vehicle's **siren** earned its name because its sound demands attention.

- When Orpheus sailed with the hero Jason, he had played his lyre to drown out the songs of the Sirens so that the Argonauts could pass without being tempted.

- The French word *siréne* means mermaid, and many paintings and sculptures portray the Sirens as mermaids and not birds. The logo for Starbucks Coffee Company is a double-tailed mermaid, like the one in the etching above. The idea behind this logo is that the coffee is as alluring and irresistible as a siren.

Scylla kills six of Odysseus' crew

"But now, fearing death, all eyes fixed on Charybdis—
now Scylla snatched six men from our hollow ship,
the toughest, strongest hands I had, and glancing
backward over the decks, searching for my crew
I could see their hands and feet already hoisted,
flailing, high, higher, over my head, look—
wailing down at me, comrades riven in agony,
shrieking out my name for one last time!"

HOMER, THE *ODYSSEY*, BOOK 12, LINES 263-270

Scylla and Charybdis

As Odysseus was being untied, he saw the narrow channel Circe had described. On the left, a craggy rock rose straight up from the sea, and on the right, water spewed up from a whirlpool. He had not yet told his men of these dangers; he did not want to frighten them. Even now, he only warned them of Charybdis, the whirlpool, and instructed them to row past it with every ounce of energy they had. He chose not to tell them of Scylla, the six-headed monster who lived on the rock, for he worried they would become paralyzed with fear.

The men trusted their leader and rowed with all their might. Focusing on Charybdis, they did not see the ghastly heads of Scylla lash out toward them. The crew could only watch in horror as Scylla yanked six screaming men inside her cave. Terrified, the rowers pulled frantically on the oars and managed to pass the swirling Charybdis. But the loss of more comrades took a heavy toll on Odysseus' crew. They were overwhelmed with grief and exhaustion.

On Helios' Island

Odysseus and his weary crew saw the beautiful island of Thrinacia on the horizon, the island where Helios kept his sacred cattle. Odysseus pleaded with his men not to land, but they were so shaken and tired after their ordeal with Scylla that he feared a mutiny. Before they landed, however, Odysseus made each of his men take a Stygian Oath not to kill any of the sacred animals.

The men held to their promise and ate only the food Circe had provided. But stormy weather raged for an entire month, thanks to the vengeful Poseidon, and the men could not even attempt to leave the island. They grew restless and hungry. Finally Odysseus made his way to the highest peak on the island and prayed to the gods of Olympus for help. But then the exhausted leader fell into a deep sleep. It was then that Eurylochus convinced the starving men to slaughter several sacred

• The etching above shows the monstrous Scylla, who has ensnared several victims.

• Odysseus was caught between Scylla, who lived on a rock, and the dangerous Charybdis. His plight is the origin of the phrase "caught between a rock and a hard place," used when someone must choose between two undesirable options.

animals. When Odysseus awoke and returned to camp, he saw smoke rising from the shores and smelled the tantalizing fragrance of meat. Every one of his men had eaten some of Helios' cattle.

Helios told Zeus what had happened, and Zeus punished the men. He calmed the storms and let the men set sail from Thrinacia, but then showered the ship with lightning bolts, killing every man except Odysseus. Odysseus gripped the mast and was tossed all the way back toward Scylla and Charybdis. He was sucked toward the whirlpool but was able to cling to a tree limb, waiting for hours until Charybdis spewed out a gush of water, and with it, the mast. He then drifted at sea for ten lonely days until he washed ashore on Calypso's island.

Odysseus Reaches Ithaca

At the palace of King Alcinous, Odysseus had reached the end of his long story. He had already told the Phaeacians about being held captive on Calypso's island, and it was just days after Calypso released him that the princess Nausicaa found him on Phaeacia's shore. Now Odysseus' audience, amazed by his tale, promised to help him reach his home. King Alcinous ordered a crew of his finest sailors to take Odysseus to Ithaca, and he gave the weary traveler loads of gifts to take as well.

Once on board, the weary Odysseus fell into such a deep sleep that he was oblivious to the journey. The Phaeacians simply lifted him off the ship and placed him on the sands of Ithaca.

Part III: Odysseus Reclaims His Throne

Father and Son

Odysseus woke up disoriented. He thought at first that the Phaeacians had tricked him and taken him to yet another unfamiliar island. But then gentle Athena appeared and assured him he was finally home. She warned him of the barbaric suitors who swarmed around his palace, and she disguised Odysseus as an old beggar to protect his identity until they could devise a plan. Athena led him to the hut of Eumaeus, one of his former swineherds, who gladly offered to take care of the stranger. Athena then arranged for Telemachus' swift return from Sparta; he would come to the swineherd's hut rather than the palace, thus thwarting the suitors' plan to attack the prince.

Telemachus first saw Odysseus disguised as a beggar and showed the stranger kindness and respect. Odysseus was proud to see that his son had grown into such a respectable man. When the swineherd left the hut to tell Penelope that Telemachus had returned, Odysseus revealed his identity to his son.

They embraced with an overwhelming mixture of sadness and joy, weeping for lost years and smiling with the relief of reunion. Unfortunately, their conversation soon turned to the suitors. Odysseus decided to go to his palace as a beggar, allowing him to get close to the unwelcome guests. With Athena's protection, Telemachus was to return first and pretend as if nothing had happened.

+ Poseidon was so angry with the Phaeacians for helping Odysseus that he turned their ship to stone just before they could land on Phaeacia.

Odysseus at His Palace

Odysseus was astonished when he reached the grounds of his palace. The boisterous suitors strutted about as if they belonged there, and the few remaining loyal servants struggled in vain to keep the palace clean. Odysseus' anger deepened when the suitors, led by the pretentious Antinous, treated him rudely when he asked for food. Antinous even hurled a stool at the beggar. Although Odysseus was furious, he managed to stay calm. He knew he had to remain disguised if he wanted his plan to work.

That night, Penelope made it a point to find the beggar and apologize to him for the suitors' despicable behavior. She treated the stranger kindly, listening to his elaborate stories and instructing her loyal nurse, Eurycleia, to bathe his feet. The old nurse had spent her life in the palace and had attended to Odysseus in his youth. When she held up the beggar's leg to wash it, she recognized a scar Odysseus had received in a hunting incident. Startled, she dropped his leg and spilled the bowl of water. She whispered his name, but Athena made sure Penelope did not hear her, and the loyal nurse promised to keep Odysseus' identity a secret.

After the bath, Penelope explained to the beggar that she could not wait any longer to choose a suitor. Although it pained her to think of marrying another man, she had to take a new husband to restore order to the kingdom. She also told the beggar of her plan to hold a competition to choose a new husband: She would marry the first man who could string her husband's bow and shoot an arrow through the handles of twelve axes. When Odysseus assured Penelope that her husband would be present for the competition, the sad queen smiled and turned away.

◆ In this etching, Eurycleia bathes Odysseus' foot, and he covers her mouth to keep her from revealing his identity. Under Odysseus' stool is his aged dog, Argos, who immediately recognized his master. Homer writes that Argos died soon after greeting Odysseus.

"so with his virtuoso ease Odysseus strung his mighty bow.
Quickly his right hand plucked the string to test its pitch
and under his touch it sang out clear and sharp as a swallow's cry.
Horror swept through the suitors, faces blanching white,
and Zeus cracked the sky with a bolt, his blazing sign,
and the great man who had borne so much rejoiced at last
that the son of cunning Cronus flung that omen down for *him*."

HOMER, THE *ODYSSEY*, BOOK 21, LINES 456-462

The Death of the Suitors

The next morning, Penelope called the suitors into the great hall. She silently brought forth Odysseus' bow and a quiver of his arrows, and lined up the twelve axes. In a clear, steady voice she promised to marry the first man who could string the bow and shoot an arrow straight through the handles. The men scoffed at the easy competition, but one after another, the embarrassed suitors failed. Not one of them could even string the massive bow.

Then Odysseus, still disguised as the beggar, quietly stepped forward. When he requested a turn, the men in the great hall roared with laughter. Penelope held up her hand, however, and lectured the suitors, shaming them for not allowing him to try. When she finished, Telemachus told his mother that the contest was meant for the men alone and that she should leave the room.

As Odysseus took up the bow and arrows, Telemachus quietly locked the doors of the great hall. All the suitors' eyes were fixed on the old beggar, who slowly ran his hands over the worn, familiar bow. Then, in one swift movement, he strung the bow and sent an arrow flying through all twelve handles. A moment later, he sent another arrow through Antinous' throat.

The men gasped as the beggar transformed into the great Odysseus. Telemachus and several loyal servants, including Eumaeus, stepped up beside Odysseus, and a vicious, gruesome battle ensued. With divine assistance from Athena and Zeus, the small band of men succeeded in slaying the suitors and then hanged the disloyal servants.

Penelope and Odysseus Reunite

When Penelope was told Odysseus was alive and had killed the suitors, she would not accept the news. She approached her husband, but overwhelmed with emotion, she turned away from his gaze. Telemachus was surprised and angry that his mother would not rush to welcome his father, but she assured her son that if the man was indeed Odysseus, she would welcome him soon enough. Telemachus then left his parents alone.

Penelope had always worried that a man might come claiming to be her husband. Now the wise queen calmly asked Eurycleia to move the bed out from her chamber so the stranger could rest on it for the night. Odysseus became argumentative, repeatedly saying that no one could possibly move the bed; he himself had crafted it as part of a living olive tree that had grown in the courtyard! He went on to describe the tree, the room, and the intricate details of the bed itself.

These were the words that Penelope needed to hear, and they filled her weary heart with joy. Odysseus was the only man to have ever seen their bed chamber, so his response proved his identity. She threw her arms around his neck with strength she had stored for twenty years, and he wrapped his arms around her waist, sobbing, thankful and humbled for having such a loyal wife.

Peace in Ithaca

Penelope and Odysseus spent the night together, and Athena even delayed the dawn for the two mortals. Penelope told her husband of the troubles she faced in Ithaca, and she listened intently as he described his long journey to reach home. Odysseus also explained that the prophet Tiresias had instructed him to travel to a town in the middle of Greece and plant an oar in the earth. In this way, the great god Poseidon would finally be appeased. As soon as he did this, Odysseus would be able to live peacefully until he died a gentle death in his old age.

Although all seemed well, the next day brought trouble. While Odysseus visited his aged father, Laertes, the devious goddess Rumor spread the news that Odysseus and Telemachus had slain over one hundred men. The families of the suitors came from neighboring towns, swarming the palace to seek revenge. Odysseus, still

◆ The devious Rumor was Zeus' messenger, and she loved to tattle. The word **rumor** comes from the Latin word for "noise" and refers to gossip or personal details that should not be shared with others.

PENELOPE TRIES TO ASSURE TELEMACHUS

"Penelope, well-aware, explained, 'I'm stunned with wonder,
powerless. Cannot speak to him, ask him questions,
look him in the eyes . . . But if he is truly
Odysseus, home at last, make no mistake:
we two will know each other, even better—
we two have secret signs,
known to us but hidden from the world.'"

HOMER, THE *ODYSSEY*, BOOK 23, LINES 119-125

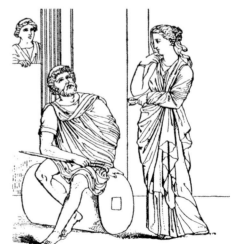

A **mentor** is a counselor or guide, and it is also the root for **monitor** ("to oversee" when used as a verb, or "something that watches over" when used as a noun).

angered, was willing to fight, but Zeus sent down a lightning bolt that landed at Odysseus' feet.

Athena then took the form of Mentor, a respected sage of Ithaca who had helped raise Telemachus in Odysseus' absence. She spoke calmly to Odysseus, Telemachus, and the suitors' families and convinced them all that after the losses in Troy, on the seas, and in Ithaca, it was finally time for peace.

A Final Word on Homer's *Odyssey*

Scholars have shown the many differences between the *Iliad* and the *Odyssey*. But at their core, both epics trace the paths of critical choices, and readers are challenged to decide for themselves the wisdom and rationale of the characters' actions.

While the *Iliad* has a larger cast of main characters whose choices affect others, the *Odyssey* really focuses on Odysseus. Like Achilles in the *Iliad*, Odysseus is inconsistent. He sometimes acts wisely, pausing to consider the long-range effects of his actions and looking out for the interest of others. Too often, however, his actions are rash and costly to those around him.

The *Odyssey* leaves a number of questions open for debate. Should Odysseus have revealed his name to the Cyclops? Why did his crew distrust him so much that they opened Aeolus' bag of winds? Was it wise or irresponsible for Odysseus not to tell his crew about the danger of Scylla? And did Odysseus and Telemachus have just cause to slay the suitors and servants?

Whatever readers may decide, few can doubt that one of the most remarkable, heroic actions Odysseus takes is to sail away from Calypso's island on a tiny raft. By turning down the goddess' offer to make him immortal, Odysseus proved without a doubt that he was willing to face hardships and an unknown journey for the chance to be with his wife and his son again in the homeland he loved. The word *odyssey* has come to describe a long and challenging journey; one can hardly imagine a more arduous one than Odysseus'.

Mark Twain

An **odyssey** is a long journey that is full of adventure. The theme of journeying is common in myths and other stories. Gilgamesh was a Babylonian man who set out on an odyssey seeking answers about mortality. And numerous modern works feature characters on some sort of odyssey, including *The Wizard of Oz*, by Frank Baum, and *Huckleberry Finn*, by Mark Twain.

In the nineteenth century, the English poet Alfred, Lord Tennyson wrote a piece titled "Ulysses" (Odysseus' Roman name) in which he describes the hero's urge to persevere:

"How dull it is to pause, to make an end,
To rust unburnish'd, not to shine in use!
As tho' to breathe were life...
...that which we are, we are;
One equal temper of heroic hearts,
Made weak by time and fate, but strong in will
To strive, to seek, to find, and not to yield."

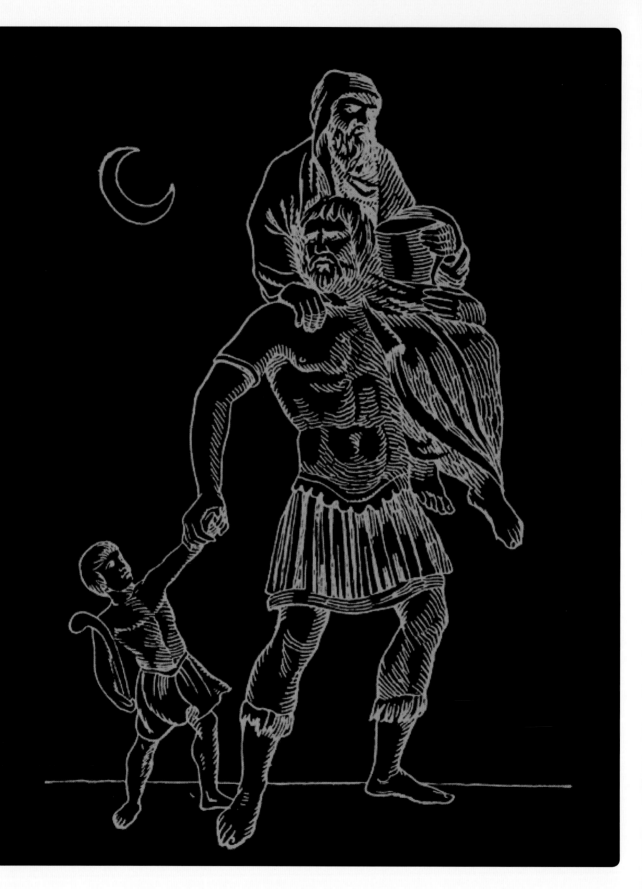

Virgil's Epic, *the Aeneid*

While historians have been able to collect only a smattering of information about the Greek poet Homer, they know a considerable amount about Publius Vergilius Maro, the Roman poet who wrote the *Aeneid*. Born October 15, 70 BCE in northern Italy near modern-day Mantua, he was called Vergil. The more common spelling, Virgil, originated with the later belief that poets had magical powers: The Latin word *virga* means "wand," and so Vergil began to be spelled "Virgil" as a way for people to honor his brilliant powers of writing.

Although Virgil was very well respected during his lifetime, the posthumous publication of his most elaborate work, the *Aeneid*, made him famous throughout the Roman Empire. Even after Christianity was adopted as an official religion and people considered Jupiter and Juno to be pagan gods, the *Aeneid* continued to be celebrated and studied. Today the epic is still seen as an exemplary work of both Latin grammar and written expression.

✦ **Posthumous** refers to something that comes after death. The Latin *post* means "after" and *humus* means "ground."

SOURCES

The retelling of Virgil's *Aeneid* in this chapter is based on the translation by Robert Fitzgerald.

The Life of Virgil

Virgil was born into a successful family, and his father prepared him for a career in law. Virgil did study law and rhetoric in Rome for several years, but after taking on just one case, he began to pursue his interest in philosophy and writing.

When Julius Caesar marched into Rome to seize power in 49 BCE, Virgil escaped the political upheaval by leaving Rome and moving south to Naples. He studied with several philosophers there, and in 37 BCE, he published his first collection of poems. The work, titled *Eclogues*, focused on the beauty of pastoral life and was followed seven years later with a poem of more than two thousand lines titled *Georgica*, "About Farming." *Georgica* was an educational work that taught readers about agriculture and raising animals, but it was also a poetic celebration of the natural world.

Georgica was published in 30 BCE, just three years before Caesar Augustus was named Rome's first emperor. Virgil had actually become friends with Augustus—known then by his given name, Gaius Octavius—when they studied law together. And it was Augustus who had become Virgil's patron and encouraged him to write a national epic for Rome. So, with all the funds he needed, Virgil was able to dedicate over ten years of his life to researching and writing the *Aeneid*, which was just under 10,000 lines long.

Virgil had planned to spend several more years polishing the poem, but his health began to fail. Knowing he would die soon, he wrote his own epitaph, including the words "I sang of pastures, farms, leaders," a reference to his three significant works. Unhappy that he had not perfected the *Aeneid*, however, Virgil stated that he wanted the manuscript to be destroyed. But after his death in September of 19 BCE, Augustus had two of Virgil's friends edit the latest draft. The masterpiece was released to the awaiting public one year later and was eagerly adopted as the work that defined the Roman world.

The Impact of Virgil's *Aeneid*

The *Aeneid* was celebrated because, simply put, it was written to glorify Rome. Virgil crafted the piece during the same years that the chaotic Roman Republic was being reborn as the more structured, more unified Roman Empire. Rome's Golden Age emerged under Augustus' rule, and who better to represent the sacred Roman virtues than the heroic character of Aeneas? Bound by his strong sense of duty—termed *pietas* in Latin—Aeneas was obedient to the gods, did what was best for his countrymen, and was an admirable son and father.

Virgil accomplished exactly what he set out to do when he wrote the *Aeneid*. Romans needed a hero to emulate, and Virgil gave them Aeneas. Romans wanted their own story, written in their own language, and Virgil proved poetry could be written in Latin as well as it had been written in Greek. Romans sought validation for the struggles they had endured during the civil unrest of the Republic, and Virgil provided them with an interesting history—based on fascinating myths—along with the promise of a glorious future.

* Most of the biographical information about Virgil comes from *Life of Virgil*, by Aelius Donatus, a grammarian and teacher who lived in the late 4th century CE.

* Augustus acted as Virgil's patron in the sense that he provided for him and protected him. The word originates from the Latin word for father: *pater*.

* *Pietas* is related to both **piety** (a noun meaning devotion to religious duties, parents, or family) and **pious** (an adjective that refers to a very moral person, often used in a negative way if the person is overtly zealous or hypocritical).

The Epics of Homer and Virgil

Before beginning the *Aeneid*, it may be helpful to understand the connections between Virgil's work and Homer's two epics. First, readers will see the same basic structure except that the main plots are flipped: Virgil tracks Aeneas' journey from Troy to Italy first—his odyssey—and then focuses on Aeneas' physical battle against the Italians, a war not unlike the one described in Homer's *Iliad*.

All three epics start *in medias res*, Latin for "in the middle of things," which establishes immediate tension and intrigue. The *Iliad* begins more than nine years into a war between the Greeks and Trojans, the *Odyssey* opens nine years after Odysseus left Troy for his homeland, and the *Aeneid* begins seven years into Aeneas' journeys. And just as Odysseus relates his tale to the Phaeacians who find him washed up on their shores, Aeneas describes his travels to Queen Dido and her audience at a banquet in Carthage.

In addition to these structural similarities, Aeneas faces many of the same situations as Homer's heroes to test his strength and his honor. Aeneas is delayed by a love interest on his journey, just as Achilles was affected by his love for Briseis and Odysseus was distracted by Circe and Calypso. Aeneas meets with many of the same monsters as Odysseus, including the Cyclops Polyphemus and the twin threats Scylla and Charybdis. And Aeneas must battle a nemesis in order to win the hand of a woman, a situation that harkens back to Paris and Menelaus' fight over Helen, and Odysseus' battle against Penelope's suitors.

Finally, the lives of the main characters in the epics are all altered by divine intervention. While one goddess in particular is obsessed with ruining Aeneas, other immortals, including his own mother, root for him. Homer's characters, too, were whisked off the battlefield for protection, tricked or advised by gods who had assumed mortal form, or hurled against monstrous waves as punishment. Ultimately, the three epics prove the power of the Fates because all the heroes reach their true destinies.

The ancient Greeks had embraced Homer's *Iliad* and *Odyssey*, and the Romans were proud when Virgil wrote an epic they could call their own. Later, during the Renaissance that began in Italy in the early 1400s CE, Homer and Virgil were again celebrated and revered for their remarkable contributions to literature. Now, thousands of years after these epics were created, modern readers can continue to appreciate how these works show humans facing the timeless issues of power, pride, duty, loss, longing, and love.

◆ A reminder that when Odysseus appears in the *Aeneid*, he will be called "Ulysses," his Roman name.

Virgil

The Trojans

Aeneas (*ee NEE us*)
Son of the goddess Venus and the mortal Anchises. Aeneas flees Troy and journeys west to Italy in search of a new home for his followers. Though he falls in love with Queen Dido and faces many obstacles along his journey, he remains determined to fulfill his destiny.

Anchises (*an KIE seez*)
Wise and respected father of Aeneas.

Ascanius (*as KAY nee us*)
Son of Aeneas by his first wife, Creusa, a daughter of King Priam and Queen Hecuba. Ascanius is sometimes called Iulus.

Priam (*PREE um*)
Aged king of Troy and husband of Hecuba. Father of numerous children, including Creusa, Hector, Paris, and Helenus.

Hector (*HEK tor*)
Commander of the Trojan forces who was killed by Achilles before the fall of Troy.

Paris (*PAIR us*)
Trojan prince who took Helen from her husband, the Greek king Menelaus.

Helenus (*he LAY nus*)
Trojan prince who offers advice to Aeneas during his journey.

The Greeks

Sinon (*SEE non*)
Greek soldier who tricks the Trojans into taking a huge wooden horse into their walled city.

Ulysses (*yoo LIS eez*)
The best Greek strategist during their war against the Trojans. Ulysses, whom the Greeks called Odysseus, spends ten years sailing home after the war, and meets many of the same obstacles as Aeneas.

The Carthaginians

Dido (*DIE doh*)
The founder and queen of Carthage, who falls madly in love with Aeneas.

Anna (*AN uh*)
Queen Dido's loyal sister.

The Italians

Latinus *(luh TIE nus)*
King of Latium who welcomes Aeneas and believes he should marry his daughter, Lavinia. Latinus is quick to seek peace.

Amata *(uh MAH tuh)*
Wife of King Latinus, who is set against Aeneas' marriage to her daughter. Juno works through Amata to ruin Aeneas' plans and delay his destiny.

Lavinia *(luh VIN ee uh)*
Only surviving child of King Latinus and Queen Amata. Her mother wants her to marry Turnus, but her father believes her destiny is to marry Aeneas.

Turnus *(TUR nus)*
Italian king who was told he would marry Lavinia. Turnus becomes Aeneas' nemesis.

Evander *(ee VAN dur)*
Aged king of Pallenteum who becomes an ally to Aeneas.

Pallas *(PAL us)*
Son of King Evander who befriends Aeneas and joins him in his fight against the Italians.

The Olympians and other immortals

Juno *(JOO noh)*
Queen of the Olympians who hates all Trojans. She tries again and again to exact revenge on Aeneas, setting up obstacles to delay his destiny.

Jupiter *(JOO pi tur)*
King of the gods who is caught between the will of the Fates and the fury of his wife, Juno.

Venus *(VEE nus)*
Roman goddess of beauty and the protective mother of Aeneas.

Harpies *(HAR peez)*
Horrible winged creatures that attack Aeneas and tell him confusing prophecies.

♦ Venus, Aeneas' immortal mother, in a chariot being pulled by doves.

THE AENEID
Seeking One's Destiny

Prologue

Just as Poseidon was determined to punish Odysseus on his way home to Ithaca, Juno seeks revenge on Aeneas in Virgil's *Aeneid*. The jealous queen never forgot that it was the Trojan Paris who had given Venus the golden apple inscribed with the words "For the Fairest." Furthermore, Juno knew that a group of Trojan men was destined to destroy her favorite city, Carthage. So she held a bitter grudge against Aeneas and tried to stop him and his followers from settling a new city. The *Aeneid* begins *in medias res*, after Aeneas has traveled for seven years and is about to face another of Juno's plots against him.

Part I: The Deities Get Involved in Aeneas' Journey
Juno's Anger

From high atop Mount Olympus, Juno saw Aeneas and his twenty ships still sailing westward toward Italy. She called upon Aeolus, controller of the winds, to create a storm so violent that it would sink every one of Aeneas' vessels. Aeolus dutifully obeyed her command and released both the East and West Winds, which howled toward the ships. Many men drowned in the colossal waves, and many ships seemed to disappear completely. The terrified Aeneas raised his arms toward the skies and proclaimed that the men who died on the fields of Troy were far luckier than he.

♦ Works by Homer, Virgil, and others included **epic similes**, lengthy and complex comparisons that often likened human acts to something in nature: Men running on a battlefield would be compared to scattering leaves, for instance. In the first book of the *Aeneid*, an epic simile likens Neptune to a wise statesmen (Augustus) who can calm a riotous sea (civil unrest).

When Neptune heard the storm raging over his head, he emerged from the water and saw Aeneas and his ravaged fleet. He recognized Juno's work and reprimanded the winds for causing the storm at sea without his authority. Neptune immediately calmed the waters and sent the dark clouds away. With the help of his son, Triton, Neptune righted the ships that had become caught on cliffs or sandbars and then rode away on his horses.

Aeneas led his seven remaining ships to the nearest shore, which turned out to be Libya on the northern coast of Africa. He and his companion, Achates, scaled the highest peak to look for their lost ships but could see no sign of them. They did, however, manage to kill several stag to take back to their hungry comrades.

Jupiter Assures Venus about Her Son's Fate

Watching the scene from Olympus, the goddess Venus felt overwhelming grief for her son. She approached her father, the great god Jupiter, and asked what the Trojans had done to anger him so. Had he not promised that Aeneas would reach Italy and found a magnificent city? Was this how he rewarded his grandson's virtue?

Jupiter smiled at his daughter to reassure her and told her what would become of Aeneas and his Trojan followers. Aeneas would wage war in Italy and succeed in uniting the people there under his rule for three years. Then his son Ascanius would take command and lead for another thirty years. During that time, Ascanius would move the seat of power from the city of Lavinium to a new fortress called Alba Longa. For three hundred years, the Trojans' descendants would reign until a queen bore twin sons by the god Mars. One of these sons, Romulus, would grow up to found the city of Rome, which would become the center of an empire with no end.

Jupiter went on to tell Venus that even though Juno's anger toward the Trojans consumed her now, she would eventually accept and love the Romans. Finally, he explained that a great man named Julius Caesar would lead the Romans and become a star in the heavens upon his death. To assure Aeneas' success in the next step of his journey, Jupiter sent his son Mercury to the Libyan city of Carthage to tell the people and their queen, Dido, about the arrival of the Trojans.

Aeneas and Queen Dido Meet

The next morning, Aeneas and Achates set out to explore the land and were met by Venus, who had disguised herself as a huntress. She asked the men who they were, and they explained that they were Trojans who feared they had lost more than half of their ships in the previous day's storm.

Venus kindly told the men to follow the path into Carthage, a city being built by Queen Dido. She also told them that their lost ships were safe and their shipmates were already in the city. Venus then shrouded Aeneas and Achates in a fog so they could arrive without being questioned. As the men neared the city, they marveled at the paved roads, the strong walls, and the many buildings being constructed. The progress they saw made them long for the destroyed city they had loved so much.

- Twin boys Romulus and Remus were fathered by Mars and the Vestal Virgin Rhea Silvia. Their grandfather, Amulius, feared they would overthrow him and ordered servants to kill them. The servants spared the innocent babies, and they were suckled by a she-wolf and raised by a shepherd and his wife. As a young man, Romulus killed his brother in a quarrel and became the legendary leader of the city named Rome.

- Dido's brother, a king named Pygmalion, savagely killed her beloved husband, Sychaeus, in an attempt to get his wealth. Sychaeus' ghost later appeared to tell Dido what had happened. The ghost revealed where his great treasure was buried and urged Dido to gather followers and flee, using his money to build a new city called Carthage.

Aeneas and Achates soon found Queen Dido inside a temple built to honor Juno, and moments later their shipmates arrived. One of the Trojans bowed before the queen and related the story of how he and his fellow travelers had just lost their king, the great Aeneas, in a storm. Queen Dido told the soldiers they were welcome to stay as long as they needed to repair their ships, and she offered to send men out to search for Aeneas.

As she spoke these words, the fog that surrounded Aeneas dispersed, and he regally stepped forth. The Trojans were reunited and Aeneas gratefully acknowledged Dido's kindnesses. Dido had a feast prepared for the men, and Aeneas sent for his son, Ascanius, as well as for gifts from his ship to offer the kind queen.

As Venus looked down on this scene, she worried that Juno would again ruin Aeneas' plans. She cast a spell on Ascanius that put him to sleep and sent a disguised Cupid to take the place of the young boy. That night, as Dido talked to Aeneas and embraced the boy she thought to be his son, Cupid breathed love into her. Dido had been overwhelmed after the tragic death of her first husband, but now she felt the sadness being replaced with admiration and passion for Aeneas. Wanting to know everything about this brave man, Dido asked him to share what had happened to King Priam and the great city of Troy. So with a heavy heart, Aeneas shared his story with Queen Dido and the banquet guests.

Part II: Aeneas Tells his Tale
The Trojans Believe They Are Victorious

Aeneas began by telling his audience that after many tiresome years of battle, King Priam and the Trojans were astonished to see all of the Greek ships sailing west toward their homes. And they were even more surprised to find a massive wooden horse left on the shore. Making their way through the abandoned Greek camps, the Trojans cautiously approached the magnificent beast.

Baffled by the horse, the Trojans debated what to do with it. Then the priest Laocoon came running from within the walls of Troy, warning them about the deceitful Greeks and begging them to destroy the monstrous creation. In desperation, he even hurled a spear at the horse, which simply bounced off its leg.

At that moment, several Trojans came upon the scene, dragging a stranger beside them. The man identified himself as Sinon, a Greek, and explained angrily that he had been left behind as a human sacrifice to Athena. The Greeks, he said, had built the horse as a gift to the Trojans to appease Athena, hoping she would see them safely home. But they had built the horse too large to fit through Troy's gates because they wanted the Trojans to destroy it, thus offending Athena.

The Trojans were still arguing over what they should do with the horse when two monstrous serpents rose out of the sea and seized Laocoon and his two sons. Athena had sent the snakes to silence Laocoon, but her actions worked even more effectively than she had planned: The Trojans interpreted the serpents as

- Aeneas is asked to share the details of his journey with the people of Carthage, just as Odysseus was asked to share his tale with the Phaeacians. This allows the main character of each epic to tell his story in his own words.

- Sinon uses **reverse psychology**, telling the Trojans that the Greeks wanted them to destroy the horse, hoping they would do the opposite. Sinon was the son of the wily Sisyphus.

- In computer terminology, a **Trojan horse virus** is software that someone assumes will perform a helpful function but has been designed to unload hidden programs or scripts to ruin the user's computer.

punishment for Laocoon's attack on the horse. They were now determined to take the horse inside their walled city.

King Priam's daughter Cassandra, a priestess, begged her father to reconsider, but her pleas fell on deaf ears. Years earlier, Cassandra had offended Apollo when she refused his love. As punishment, he had given her the gift of prophecy—along with the curse of never being believed. So despite her tearful warnings, the Trojans dragged the beast toward their city and even tore down a portion of the massive walls so the horse could pass through.

THE TROJANS' FATEFUL DECISION

"New terrors
Ran in the shaken crowd: the word went round
Laocoon had paid, and rightfully,
For profanation of the sacred hulk
With his offending spear hurled at its flank.
'The offering must be hauled to its true home,'
They clamored."

VIRGIL, THE *AENEID*, BOOK II, LINES 306-312

- 191 -

The Devastating Fall of Troy

Aeneas explained to his audience how the Trojans had moved the immense horse with joy powered by victory. After ten grueling years of tension and war, they had won, and they celebrated with food and wine. That night, the sleeping Trojans did not notice Ulysses and his small army of Greek men sneak out of the hollow belly of the wooden horse. No longer on guard, the Trojans never saw the fleet of enemy ships returning silently in the darkness.

As the Greeks' plan was being carried out, Aeneas was sleeping soundly at home with his family. In his dreams, however, he was visited by the great Trojan prince, Hector, still bloodied and covered in black dust from his ghastly battle with Achilles. Hector screamed at Aeneas, urging him to wake and flee the city. Then Hector's ghost presented Aeneas with the household gods and treasures of Troy, telling him it was now his responsibility to find a new home for them.

Aeneas awoke to the sickening sounds of crashing armor and battle cries. He looked out to see Troy in flames and readied himself to fight. As he made his way to King Priam's palace, he witnessed Neoptolemus, Achilles' son who was as strong and furious as his father, brutally kill one of Priam's sons and then King Priam himself.

Recognizing the futility of trying to defend Troy, Aeneas' thoughts turned to his own family, unprotected in their home. Determined now to save them and flee the city as Hector had instructed, Aeneas turned to leave the palace. In the light of the flames, however, he saw Helen, trembling alone behind a statue of Vesta. The terrified woman blamed herself for the destruction of Troy, and she also feared the wrath of her husband, the spurned Menelaus, who had spent ten long years trying to reclaim her from Prince Paris.

Aeneas wanted nothing more than to destroy this woman who had caused the bloodshed of so many countless Trojans. But his mother, Venus, appeared before him to stay his sword. She assured her son that Troy was burning because of Fates and the gods, not because of any action by a mortal woman. She urged her son to return to his home and save his family.

Aeneas Flees Troy

Aeneas then told Dido how he left Helen behind and raced back toward his house. There he found his wife, Creusa, clutching their small son, Ascanius. Aeneas told Creusa to gather what food they had and get ready to leave, and Aeneas then offered to carry his father, Anchises. But the aged man refused, saying he would rather stay behind and die in his beloved city. As they argued, a crown of harmless flames danced around Ascanius' head.

Anchises saw this as an omen, and he prayed for another sign of favor from Jupiter. Before he had even finished speaking, a bolt of lightning lit up the eerie darkness, and a shooting star streaked across the sky. Anchises was now convinced he should flee with his son. Aeneas hoisted his father onto his back and gave him

- Aeneas' son, Ascanius, was born in Troy, which the Romans called Ilium. Ascanius, therefore, was also known as Iulus or Julus. As a way to stress his family's heritage, Caesar Augustus had Virgil emphasize these names to connect Julius Caesar to Ascanius, Aeneas, Venus, and Jupiter.

- The Penates ("the inner ones") were gods associated with food. Over time, they became gods of the household and were linked to Vesta, the goddess of the hearth. Roman mythology claims the statues that Anchises rescued from Troy eventually came to Rome.

the sacred household statues to hold. Then Aeneas grabbed his small son's hand and told his wife to stay close behind.

The city was in complete chaos, filled with the sounds of crackling flames, clanging armor, screaming women, and crying children. Aeneas dodged this way and that, trying desperately to keep his family safe. When he finally reached a temple outside the walls, he turned in horror to find his wife was not behind him. Leaving Anchises and Ascanius at the temple, Aeneas rushed back inside Troy, frantically retracing his steps in an attempt to find Creusa.

Suddenly, Creusa's ghost appeared before him, and she tried to assure her husband that it was not fated for her to survive the city's destruction. Aeneas was destined to travel to new shores and find a new bride. Aeneas tried to embrace his love, but her shadow slipped away. As dawn broke on a new day, the heartbroken Aeneas joined the other survivors, who were waiting for him to lead them to safety.

Attack of the Harpies

Aeneas' twenty ships left Troy and sailed first to Thrace, then to the small island of Delos, and then to Crete. In each place, however, they met with bad luck and heard prophecies that they were not meant to settle there. After they were told to go to Italy, a storm blew the Trojans off course to the Strophades, islands in the Ionian Sea. The starving men and women set about killing and cooking some of the animals they found on the shores. But just as they began to eat, huge shadows passed over the ground, and horrible shrieks pierced the sky. They were under attack by the ferocious Harpies.

Aeneas shuddered as he described these monstrous creatures, which had the faces and torsos of women, wings with bronze feathers, and huge talons. They snatched food from the Trojans and befouled what remained, leaving behind a horrendous stench. When Aeneas' men tried to get rid of the birds, their spears bounced off the impenetrable wings.

Before she flew away, the leader of the Harpies squawked out a prophecy from Apollo and Jupiter: Aeneas and his comrades would reach Italy, but not until they had suffered greatly and had to resort to eating their tables.

◆ The American harpy eagle, first described in 1758, was named for the mythological Harpies. Considered the most powerful raptor in the Americas, the female stands over 3 feet tall, has a 6-foot wingspan, and can weigh up to 20 pounds. The birds' talons, excellent for catching prey, are longer than the claws of a grizzly bear.

VIRGIL'S DESCRIPTION OF THE HARPIES

"No gloomier monster, no more savage pest
And scourge sent by the gods' wrath ever mounted
From the black Stygian water—flying things
With young girls' faces, but foul ooze below,
Talons for hands, pale famished nightmare mouths."

VIRGIL, THE *AENEID*, BOOK III, LINES 297-301

The Prophecy of Helenus

Disturbed by this confusing prophecy, Aeneas ordered his followers back to the ships. After weeks at sea, the Trojans finally landed near a city ruled by Helenus, one of the surviving sons of King Priam and Queen Hecuba. Aeneas was thrilled to see Helenus again and was glad to learn he had married Andromache, the widow of Helenus' brother Hector.

Helenus had been given the gift of prophecy by Apollo, just like his sister Cassandra. But unlike Cassandra, he had not been cursed with not being believed. Determined to help Aeneas in his journey, Helenus warned him about Scylla and Charybdis, two monsters who threatened passing ships off the coast of Sicily. The six-headed Scylla darted out of her cave to eat the sailors, while the monstrous whirlpool Charybdis waited just across the channel to swallow the ships. Helenus also advised Aeneas to seek a Sibyl in Italy who would tell him about the wars he must fight in his new land.

The Land of the Cyclopes

With Helenus' guidance, Aeneas and the Trojans avoided Scylla and Charybdis off the western coast of Italy and safely reached the island of Sicily. Although frightened by Mount Aetna's fiery bellows, the survivors found provisions and prepared to head south along the coast of the island. Before they departed, however, they saw a man emerge from the forest, half-starved, with tired eyes begging for mercy.

This pitiable man, a Greek named Acheamindes, had been left behind accidentally by Ulysses and his crew when they had escaped the island of the Cyclopes. For three long months, he had been forced to hide from hundreds of the beastly, one-eyed giants. Acheamindes recounted the horror he and Ulysses' men had witnessed when trapped in a cave with Polyphemus, and he explained how they had escaped after stabbing the beast in his eye. Although Acheamindes risked his life by revealing himself to the Trojans, he claimed he would rather die at their hands by any method they chose than be eaten by Polyphemus as his comrades had.

Aeneas allowed Acheamindes to come aboard his ships, and they raised their sails in silence after seeing the blinded Polyphemus lumber down to the shore. Hearing the splashing of their oars alerted the beast to the ships, but the Trojans were a safe distance from shore when they heard Polyphemus let loose an angry roar. So after avoiding Scylla and Charybdis off the eastern coast of Sicily and then escaping from the island of the Cyclopes, the Trojans moved on.

Unfortunately, tragedy struck the next time they reached land: Anchises, Aeneas' beloved father, died in Drepanum on the western coast of Sicily, a sorrow that neither the Harpy nor Helenus had revealed in their prophecies.

This was where Aeneas ended his story, because it was just after his father's death that Juno's storm forced their frail ships to land on the shores of Carthage.

◆ Scylla and Charybdis were the creatures who killed so many of the crew in Homer's *Odyssey*.

◆ Virgil gives a powerful account of the volcanic Mount Aetna in his *Aeneid*, a way for him to offer reverence to the geography and natural elements of Italy. Mount Aetna (more commonly spelled "Etna") was the mountain Zeus used to trap the beastly Typhon, and it remains one of the most active volcanoes in the world.

Part III: The Passionate Queen

Dido in Love

If Dido loved Aeneas a little before he had begun his tale, she now loved him completely. At dawn the next day, she confided her feelings to her sister Anna. Dido had always vowed she would not remarry after the death of her beloved husband, Sychaeus. But she felt such passion for this new man! The sympathetic Anna suggested that it may have been Juno's plan to lead this man here. Was their devious brother Pygmalion not still a threat to them? Would an alliance with the Trojans not help strengthen the city of Carthage and ensure its survival? Did Dido not deserve love and a chance to become a mother?

Empowered by her sister's words, Dido spent as much time as possible with Aeneas. She gave him so much of her attention, in fact, that she completely ignored the building projects in Carthage that she had kept under her watchful eye. She was helplessly in love, and this caught the attention of the ever-scheming Juno.

Seeing a union between Dido and Aeneas as a way to delay Aeneas from reaching Italy, Juno coyly approached Venus. Aeneas' immortal mother also saw the benefit in the union, but only because she hoped it would keep Aeneas in a safe place. So Juno caused a rainstorm while Aeneas and Dido were hunting together. The couple sought shelter in a cave, surrendered to their passion, and consummated their love. Afterwards, Dido considered herself married to Aeneas because she cared for him so deeply, but also because she was desperate to protect her reputation.

The Gods Intervene

The unstoppable goddess Rumor wasted no time in spreading word about Dido's actions and her disregard for the city she was building. Soon, a former suitor whom Dido had refused to marry heard about Dido and complained in a prayer to Jupiter. The all-powerful god knew that Aeneas, despite his grief over the fall of his beloved Troy and the deaths of his wife and father, could not tarry any longer in Carthage.

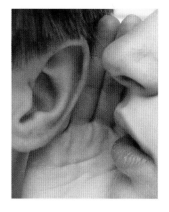

A DESCRIPTION OF THE GODDESS RUMOR

> "Pinioned, with
> An eye beneath for every body feather,
> And, strange to say, as many tongues and buzzing
> Mouths as eyes, as many pricked-up ears,
> By night she flies between the earth and heaven
> Shrieking through darkness, and she never turns
> Her eye-lids down to sleep."

VIRGIL, THE *AENEID*, BOOK IV, LINES 249-255

- A **rumor** (Latin for "noise") is an unconfirmed story that gets repeated to others. While Virgil describes the ancient Rumor as a strange creature with "buzzing mouths," many would say that she now takes the form of modern technology, where false stories and hurtful gossip can be passed along very quickly.

- Rumor was also the goddess who spread the news about the deaths of the suitors in Homer's *Odyssey*.

This was simply not his destiny, nor was it the destiny for his son, Ascanius, who was to grow up and lead the Trojans to greatness in their new land.

Jupiter had Mercury deliver this message to Aeneas. As if awakened from a dream, the mortal man felt a renewed determination to continue on his fated path, but he dreaded how he would explain his actions to Dido. He ordered his men to prepare the Trojan ships but to work in secrecy so he would have more time to plan his discussion with the vulnerable queen.

Rumor, however, had no patience for such a thoughtful plan, and the shameless goddess told Dido that Aeneas was leaving. In a fury, Dido berated Aeneas, screaming that she had given up her honor and had lost the trust of many in her own city because of him. How could he leave her? Aeneas tried to keep calm and focused on the divine message from Mercury. He explained that although he did love her, he was not able to design his life; his duty was to lead his followers to Italy. Dido continued to rant, so hurt and so angry that she cursed him and threatened to haunt him after she died. She left in tears, and Aeneas, torn between his love for Dido and his responsibility to his followers, sadly continued with his preparations.

Dido Cannot Be Consoled

Dido became so crazed and desperate that she instructed Anna to build a pyre on which to burn all the items Aeneas left behind. Anna followed her grieving sister's orders, and Dido herself heaped Aeneas' clothing, his portrait, and his sword onto the pyre. Tossing in her bed that night, Dido's mind raced. Could she marry one of her former suitors for protection? Should she leave her city and follow Aeneas to Italy? Would he even take her back? Her choices left her feeling so hopeless that she decided to take her own life on top of the pyre.

- Rome and Carthage had a lasting and bitter rivalry. During the three Punic Wars, which occurred between 264 and 146 BCE, hundreds of thousands of soldiers died on both sides. In the end, Carthage fell to the powerful Roman state.

- The etching on this page shows Dido and her sister Anna, along with several attendants, watching Aeneas' ship sail away from Carthage.

- English playwright Christopher Marlowe wrote the play *Dido, Queen of Carthage* in the late 1500s, and 200 years later, the work became the basis of an opera by English composer Stephen Storace.

Aeneas, still on the moored ships, had such disturbing dreams that he awoke in a panic and ordered his fleet to sail immediately. When Dido awoke to see the Trojans on the horizon, she cursed Aeneas and his descendents, climbed atop the pyre, and stabbed herself with Aeneas' sword. As Rumor's news reached Anna, the loyal sister clamored atop the pyre and held Dido as she suffered a painful death. When Aeneas saw the funeral flames rise from within the walls of Carthage, he knew in his heart that Dido was dead.

Part IV: Aeneas Is Bound for Italy
Leaving Some Trojans Behind
Because they had set sail during unfavorable weather, the Trojans needed to land quickly. They chose to try and reach the shores of Sicily where Aeneas' father had died a year earlier. Once on land, the men held athletic competitions to honor the late Anchises, and Juno saw this as the perfect opportunity to further disrupt Aeneas' journey.

Juno instructed her messenger, Iris, to go to the Trojan women and stir up their discontent. So Iris disguised herself as an elder Trojan and joined the other women on the beach. She lamented that after seven grueling years, they still had no control of their own lives and no place to call their home, and she inspired such rage in the women that they grabbed torches and set fire to their own ships.

When Aeneas saw the flames, he begged Jupiter to send a storm to extinguish them. The god obliged and the women were soon restored to their senses. Still, Aeneas was left feeling uncertain about his followers. That night, his father appeared in his dreams and advised Aeneas to leave behind those Trojans who did not wish to continue on; only the strongest and bravest would be of help during the wars awaiting him in Italy. Anchises also said that Aeneas must reach the Sibyl of Cumae and then travel to the Underworld so he could tell him more about his future.

The Sibyl
Although it was difficult to leave any of the Trojans behind, Aeneas and his most loyal followers made their decision to set sail and bade tearful farewells. After reaching Italy, Aeneas found the Sibyl's cave and entered, asking only to learn the destiny he had been given.

The Sibyl informed Aeneas that his next step was to fight in a war, but she also said he would ultimately be helped by a Greek city. She added that if he were to reach the Underworld to find his father, he needed a gift—a branch with golden leaves—to present to Proserpine, the wife of Pluto.

Heading alone into an expanse of woods, Aeneas did not know how he would ever find a single bough with golden leaves. But doves, his mother's birds, appeared before him and led him to a tree with bright gold shimmering among its green. Armed with this gift, Aeneas returned to the Sibyl, who led him into the depths of her cave.

• The Latin *sibyl* derives from the Greek *sibylla*, which means "prophetess." At least ten sibyls are referenced in classical mythology, each identified with a specific location. This Italian postage stamp depicts an image of the Delphic Sibyl as painted by Michelangelo on the ceiling of Rome's famous Sistine Chapel. And in author J.K. Rowling's *Harry Potter* series, the name of Hogwarts' divination professor is Sybil Trelawney.

Following the Sibyl, Aeneas reached the entrance to Pluto's world and passed through Grief, Discord, War, and all other evils that affect humans. He then saw the beasts that had been killed by heroes, including the hissing Hydra, the Chimaera, and Medusa. Aeneas also winced when he saw a throng of human ghosts begging for passage across the River Styx, only to be turned away by the ferryman Charon.

When Charon spotted Aeneas in the dismal crowd, he asked why a living man would seek passage; Charon had taken the likes of Hercules and Theseus across, but only because their fathers were gods. The Sibyl assured him that Venus had borne this man, and Aeneas held up the golden bough to prove his divine birth.

After being rowed safely across the black river, Aeneas saw the shade of Dido. He cried out to her, apologizing through tears and assuring her over and over that he had truly loved her. Dido would not look at him, however, and turned away, running back to join the ghost of her husband, Sychaeus.

The dejected Aeneas moved on, following the Sibyl through passages until they reached the beautiful Elysium, with its peaceful woods and valleys, its own sun and stars. After offering up his golden bough, Aeneas was allowed to enter. The beleaguered son was overjoyed to see his father, but then saddened again when his arms, so eager for an embrace, passed right through his father's shade.

Anchises tried to cheer him, however, encouraging him to embrace his destiny. And then, to give Aeneas strength, Anchises revealed the truth about the souls in Elysium: After spending one thousand years in the Underworld, these souls would drink water from the River Lethe to forget their pasts, and then be given new bodies so they could return to life on earth. Anchises began pointing excitedly to certain men in the crowd.

"There," said Anchises, "that soul will become the son born to your new wife, Lavinia. And there, that one will become Romulus, a son of Mars and the founder of the great city of Rome. There is the soul who will become the great Julius Caesar, and over there is Augustus, a descendent of the gods who will oversee a powerful Golden Age." Anchises went on to point out who would become the great leaders of an empire, kings who would rule with honor and great skill.

Emboldened with this clear vision of his future, Aeneas offered thanks to his father and to the Sibyl, and returned to his comrades who were waiting for him on the ships.

ANCHISES POINTS OUT THE DESTINED SOULS TO AENEAS

"'What famous children in your line will come,
Souls of the future, living in our name,
I shall tell clearly now, and in the telling
Teach you your destiny.'"

VIRGIL, THE *AENEID*, BOOK VI, LINES 1017-1020

+ Elysium, or the **Elysian Fields**, is the resting place for human souls who have shown heroism and virtue, and can be likened to the idea of a paradise. A part of the fairway at the famous St. Andrew's golf course in Scotland is called the Elysian Fields. And in his play *A Streetcar Named Desire*, Tennessee Williams adds a twist of irony by naming a street in a run-down neighborhood "Elysian Fields."

+ The Lethe was a river in the Underworld, and those who drank from it forgot their pasts. **Lethargy** is a dullness or a lack of energy and comes from *lethe* (forgetful) and *argos* (inactive).

The Harpy's Prophecy Comes True

The men, now full of hope and determination, set sail. Neptune gave them favorable winds and helped them sail safely past Circe's island. Circe was the powerful sorceress who had turned so many of Ulysses' men into swine, but Aeneas and his men luckily met no such fate.

Soon after, Aeneas turned his ships into the wide opening of a river, the Tiber. He and his men went ashore and found a bounty of delicious wild fruits. As they rested along the shores of the tranquil river, they piled the fine fruit on top of hardened grain cakes that were as large as platters. Then, after eating the fruit, they broke apart the cakes and ate them, too. Young Ascanius, laughing, pointed out how funny it was that they had just eaten their tables. Aeneas remembered the Harpy's prophecy and smiled at his son. He then announced to his crew that they had reached the country they would call home.

King Latinus, the ruler of the Italian region known as Latium, had just been told by an oracle that his only daughter, Lavinia, was destined to marry a foreigner and, after lengthy battles, their descendants would go on to form a great empire. So when Aeneas sent one hundred Trojan men to announce their arrival and offer up gifts to Latinus, the king welcomed Aeneas, believing him to be the foreigner who would marry his daughter.

Juno's Fury Continues

Juno, still determined to delay Aeneas' destiny for as long as possible, called upon the Fury Allecto to cause trouble. Allecto first sought Queen Amata, Lavinia's mother, and roused her into a rage, reminding her that Latinus had already promised Lavinia to a man named Turnus. Although Turnus lived in Italy, he had been born in Greece, so he would also fit the description of a foreigner. King Latinus refused to listen to his wife, however, which made the queen even more angry and more determined to denounce Aeneas as a suitor.

The Fury also went to Turnus himself, appearing in his dream and telling him of Latinus' plans for his daughter. Allecto made Turnus view the Trojans as invaders, and she also caused a fight between the Italians and the Trojans. Although the aged King Latinus refused to declare war on the Trojans, Juno flew down from Olympus and threw open the doors of Janus' temple herself. Turnus raised the flag of war, and troops began to arrive from all the surrounding regions to fight against the Trojans.

In his dreams that night, Aeneas received divine instructions to travel north on the Tiber River toward the city of Pallenteum. Following these orders, Aeneas found King Evander, who as a younger man had known both King Priam and Anchises. Aeneas explained his situation to the king, who said with sadness that he was too old to fight in battles any longer. He promised to send his own son Pallas to help the Trojans, however, along with four hundred other warriors. King Evander wanted Pallas to learn from the great Aeneas, and he expressed his hope that he would live to welcome his son back home.

- The passage about the Trojans eating their tables contains an error in Virgil's text. Anchises is said to have told this prophecy to Aeneas, when it was actually the Harpies who squawked out this confusing warning. Virgil would have likely found the error had he lived to make his final revisions.

- The Furies—Allecto (Endless), Tisiphone (Punishment), and Megaera (Rage)—were female spirits of justice and vengeance. They tortured damned souls in the Underworld and also punished mortals on the earth. One of the teachers in J.K. Rowling's *Harry Potter* series is named Alecto Carrow, and she assigns particularly harsh punishments to her students.

- The doors to Janus' temples were thrown open during wartime to allow him to witness the conflict, and they were then ceremoniously closed during peacetime.

+ There is a clear connection between Aeneas' shield and the one Vulcan had forged for Achilles: Both depict scenes of peace that point out the tragedy and loss involved in bitter war.

Venus, knowing that Aeneas would soon enter battle, asked her husband, Vulcan, to forge a magnificent suit of armor. Vulcan used his great skills to create a helmet, a sword and spear, a bronzed breastplate, and a huge shield that depicted scenes from the beautiful future city of Rome.

The Trojans Fight the Italians

In Aeneas' absence, war broke out between the Trojans and the Italians. Aeneas' son, Ascanius, stepped onto the battlefield for the first time in his young life, and with the help of Apollo was able to slay Turnus' brother-in-law. Although eager to continue fighting, Ascanius listened to the divine voice of Apollo and put down his weapons.

After many losses on both sides, the Trojans surrounded Turnus. Still furious but recognizing he was outnumbered, Turnus leapt into the Tiber River and floated back to his own camp. Soon, Aeneas and Pallas, along with an army of new allies, arrived from Pallenteum. After a bloody battle, Turnus and Pallas faced one another. Pallas fought valiantly, but the more skilled Turnus killed him. He stripped off the young warrior's sword belt and slung it casually over his shoulder, showing great disrespect for his enemy.

When Aeneas learned about Pallas, he felt responsible for the death of his young charge. He went after Turnus, but in yet another attempt to foil Aeneas, Juno whisked Turnus to safety. By this time, both the Trojans and the Italians had lost so many men, they declared a truce of twelve days to give themselves time to bury their dead.

The first matter that Aeneas tended to during the peace was to return Pallas' body to King Evander. The mournful Evander lamented that he himself had not died in his son's place but insisted he held no ill will toward the Trojans. The proud king said his son's death would not have been in vain if the Trojans achieved their destiny in settling Latium. But he did send a message: Aeneas' debt to him would be paid only with Turnus' life.

THE CLASSICAL HISTORY *of a* COMMON IMAGE

Ascanius says, "*Jupiter omnipotens, audacibus annue coeptis*" in Book IX of Virgil's *Aeneid* before he uses his weapon in battle for the first time. The translation is "All powerful Jupiter, give consent to [my] venture." **Annuit coeptis** has become a motto for the United States and is part of the Great Seal of the United States, which can be seen on the back of the dollar bill. In this usage, the words translate to "Providence has approved of [our] undertaking." A direct quote from Virgil's *Eclogues* is used on the ribbon under the pyramid: *novus ordo seclorum*, "a new order of the ages." And the Roman numerals at the base of the pyramid? They represent 1776, the year the Declaration of Independence was signed.

"'Come now, at last
Have done, and heed our pleading, and give way.
Let yourself no longer be consumed
Without relief by all that inward burning;
Let care and trouble not forever come to me
From your sweet lips. The finish is at hand.'"

VIRGIL, THE *AENEID*, BOOK XII, LINES 1083-1088

Attempts to End the Battles

King Latinus and Queen Amata both recognized that the Italians were losing ground, and they pleaded with Turnus to concede. But the warrior was determined to fight. Latinus then approached Aeneas and made an agreement: If Turnus and the Italians won, Aeneas would retreat to the city of King Evander, but if Aeneas was victorious, Aeneas would marry Lavinia, and the Trojans and Italians would rule together as equals.

The battle raged on, with Juno continuing to help the Italians and Venus and Mars inspiring Aeneas and his men. When Queen Amata saw the Trojans invading her city, which was now engulfed in flames, she hanged herself for playing a part in its ruin. Finally, Jupiter approached Juno and calmly questioned her reasons for holding on to her bitterness for so long. Did she not see how this had eaten away at her? Could she not accept that Aeneas' destiny was to found a new city?

Juno lowered her head and quietly admitted she had already abandoned Turnus on the battlefield. She knew he was fated to die at the hand of Aeneas, and she would let go of her grudge. Her one condition was that the Italians would keep their identity, their language, and their customs, and not simply become new Trojans; the city of Troy had been destroyed and did not deserve to be revived. Jupiter agreed and assured Juno the people who would be born from this union between the Trojans and Italians would honor her dutifully.

Turnus and Aeneas

Left alone on the battlefield without divine assistance, Turnus and Aeneas faced one other. Turnus had lost his chariot and his weapons, so he stood before his enemy unarmed. He caught sight of a boulder nearby, one so huge it would normally take a dozen men to lift. But with such rage in his heart, he was able to lift the rock over his head, and he tried to hurl it at Aeneas. As he moved forward, however, his knees gave out. When he let go of the boulder, it soared far, but not nearly far enough.

Then Aeneas cast his spear and hit Turnus' thigh with such force that the great man fell backward. Clutching his leg, Turnus groaned in pain and begged for mercy.

◆ The Romans wanted their city to have risen from honor and peace, believing their civilization was a cooperation between Italians and the Trojans. So King Latinus was portrayed as being very ready to marry Lavinia to Aeneas.

"Then to his glance appeared
The accurst swordbelt surmounting Turnus' shoulder,
Shining with its familiar studs—the strap
Young Pallas wore when Turnus wounded him
And left him dead upon the field; now Turnus
Bore that enemy token on his shoulder—
Enemy still."

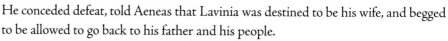

VIRGIL, THE *AENEID*, BOOK XII, LINES 1281-1287

He conceded defeat, told Aeneas that Lavinia was destined to be his wife, and begged to be allowed to go back to his father and his people.

Aeneas, who had lost so much at Troy, who had journeyed so long and endured such pain, considered sparing Turnus' life. But as he backed away, he recognized Pallas' sword belt dangling over his enemy's shoulder. Announcing that the next wound he would inflict was to honor Pallas, Aeneas plunged his sword into Turnus' chest and watched his soul fall down to the shadows.

A Final Word on Virgil's *Aeneid*

Homer's *Iliad* ends tragically, with war still looming and Achilles doomed to die. The *Odyssey* ends more happily because the hero is reunited with his loyal wife, and they preside over a peaceful Ithaca. The last notes of Virgil's epic fall somewhere between the two: The protagonist stands over the dead body of an enemy and knows his efforts will lead to a greater destiny, but he has not yet met the woman he will marry, and he will never see the rewards for his efforts during his lifetime.

Virgil did not give his fellow Romans a trite, happily-ever-after story when he wrote the *Aeneid*, nor did he provide an accurate history lesson. In fact, he spent years crafting a poem using bits and pieces of reality sprinkled together with myths and his own imagination. What he did offer the Romans, though, was more useful than any promise of happiness or collection of facts: He gave them the encouragement to believe in a greater purpose.

After the tumultuous years of the Roman Republic, the Roman people welcomed Augustus as a man destined to lead their divinely chosen land into a golden age, and Virgil delivered a story and a hero to inspire them. While Homer's epics had showcased the rugged determination of Achilles and of Odysseus, both strong-willed men who questioned authority, the hero of the *Aeneid* demonstrates *pietas* and makes many personal sacrifices for the greater good. Is one type of hero, by definition, better than the other? Not necessarily. But Aeneas was exactly the right hero to help Augustus inspire the Romans and strengthen their resolve at a critical point in their culture's history.

Augustus

Chapter Notes

Grateful acknowledgment is made for the following permissions:

- All quotes from Ovid are from *Metamorphoses* by Ovid, translated by A.D. Melville, © 1986 by A.D. Melville. Used by permission from Oxford University Press.

- All quotes from Hesiod are from *Theogony, Works and Days* by Hesiod, translated by M.L. West, © 1988 by M.L. West. Used by permission from Oxford University Press.

- All quotes from the *Iliad* are from the *Iliad* by Homer, translated by Robert Fagles, © 1990 by Robert Fagles. Used by permission of Viking Penguin, a division of Penguin Group (USA) Inc.

- All quotes from the *Odyssey* are from the *Odyssey* by Homer, translated by Robert Fagles, © 1996 by Robert Fagles. Used by permission of Viking Penguin, a division of Penguin Group (USA) Inc.

- All quotes from the *Aeneid* are from the *Aeneid* by Virgil, translated by Robert Fitzgerald, translation copyright © 1980, 1982, 1983 by Robert Fitzgerald. Used by permission of Random House, Inc.

Following are other sources quoted in *Panorama*:

Preface
2   Joseph Campbell, *The Power of Myth* (New York: Anchor, 1991), 185.

Introduction
5   Donna Rosenberg, *World Mythology: An Anthology of the Great Myths and Epics* (Chicago: National Textbook Company, 1994), xxii.
7   Robert Ingersoll, *The Works of Robert G. Ingersoll—Volume 2—Lectures (Some Mistakes of Moses)* (Reprint Services Corp; 1879 edition, 2007), Preface.

Chapter 1
9   Campbell, *The Power of Myth*, 45.
9   David Sansone, *Ancient Greek Civilization* (New Jersey: Wiley-Blackwell, 2003), 81.
10   Ellen Datlow and Terri Windling, eds., *Snow White, Blood Red* (New York: Eos Books, 1993), 10.
13   Claude Lévi-Strauss, *The Raw and the Cooked: Introduction to a Science of Mythology*, translated by John and Doreen Weightman (New York: Harper & Row, 1969), 12.
13   Jay D'Ambrosio, *Rethinking Adolescence: Using Story to Navigate Life's Uncharted Years* (Lanham, Maryland: Rowman & Littlefield Education, 2006), xvii.
17   Campbell, *The Power of Myth*, 87.
17   Joseph Campbell, *The Hero with a Thousand Faces* (New York: Pantheon Books, 1949), 30.

Chapter 2

26 Thomas Cahill, *Sailing the Wine-Dark Sea: Why the Greeks Matter* (New York: Anchor Books, 2004), 88.

27 Cahill, 145.

30 Cahill, 264.

34 W. Willard Wirtz, Former Secretary of Labor, as quoted on the Classical Association of the Middle West and South's website, www.camws.org. Originally published in "The Forum," *The Classical Journal* 64, 4 (January 1969) 162-166.

36 William Shakespeare, *Julius Caesar* (New York: Signet Classics, 1963).

38 Randolph Nesse, *The Greatest Inventions of the Past 2,000 Years* (New York: Simon & Schuster, 2000), 53.

Chapter 3

48 E.D. Hirsch, Jr., Joseph F. Kett, James Trefil, *The Dictionary of Cultural Literacy* (Boston: Houghton Mifflin, 1993), 28.

53 Homer, the *Iliad*, translated by Robert Fagles (New York: Penguin Books, 1996), 41.

64 William E. Burrows, *This New Ocean: The Story of the First Space Age* (New York: Modern Library, 1999).

65 Peter Whitfield, *The Mapping of the Heavens* (San Francisco: Pomegranate Artbooks, 1995), 11.

Chapter 4

108 William Shakespeare, *The Tragedy of Romeo and Juliet* (New York: Washington Square Press, 1959).

Chapter 5

123 Rosenberg, xvii.

127 Apollodorus, *The Library of Greek Mythology* (New York: Oxford University Press, 1998).

129 Apollonius, *Jason and the Golden Fleece*, translated by Richard Hunter (New York: Oxford University Press, 1998).

131 Christa Wolf, *Medea: A Modern Retelling* (New York: Nan A. Talese, 1998), xiv.

Chapter 6

146 Rosenberg, 37.

146 Caroline Moorehead, *Lost and Found: The 9,000 Treasures of Troy* (New York: Penguin, 1997).

152 Cahill, 24.

161 Manfred Korfmann, "Was There a Trojan War?" *Archaeology*, Volume 57, Number 3, May/June 2004.

162 Howard W. Clarke, *The Art of the Odyssey* (Wauconda, IL: Bolchazy-Carducci Publishers, 1999), introduction.

About the images used in *Panorama*:

All photographs were purchased from stock photography or available in the public domain. The one exception is the image on page 95, a photo of the author's father, Navy Lieutenant Junior Grade Richard Zuberbuhler (on the left) with friend Steve Graffam, a Marine Corps Lieutenant. The picture was taken in 1958 in front of the King George Hotel in Beirut, Lebanon.

The etchings can be found in the public domain from sources available before 1923. Many can be seen at http://etc.usf.edu/clipart, a service of Florida's Educational Technology Clearinghouse.

ACKNOWLEDGMENTS

You know when you're on a roller coaster, and it's fun and you feel really happy, but then every once in a while, you think that your head might explode? Yes? Well, writing this book was kind of like that. My family, friends, and colleagues were a constant source of inspiration, though, and thanks to them, I managed to stay on the ride until it came to a complete stop.

My earliest mentors include Judy Lackner, who taught me how to write; Professor Dan Chambliss, who taught me how to think; and the late Sally Smith, who taught me how to teach. And then came Roy Parker, who always just did the "next right thing." Roy, along with the supportive Kristin Smith and our eighth graders at Sewickley Academy, helped this project take form.

David Sansone, Penny Cipolone, Diana Nixon, Scott Stickney, and Jay D'Ambrosio were under absolutely no obligation to be nice to me, but they all willingly helped move this project forward. Their advice and encouraging words were priceless.

I am indebted to Julie Long for all the hours she spent hunkered down next to me in coffee shops and cannot begin to thank her for her friendship, enthusiasm, and encouragement. My appreciation also goes to Lisa Selzman Greenberg for her soulful inspiration, the witty Alan Lopuszynski for his extra set of eyes, Christine Trebilcock and brother-in-law Andy Klaber for sound legal guidance, Beth Polen for her attention to detail, and Vince Maffensanti and Jason Dancisin for production and interactive support. And with a heavy heart, I thank the lovely Helen Croft, whose interest in this project meant the world to me.

Kevin and I are lucky to be surrounded by amazing friends like Alisa and Josh Blatter, Sielke and David Caparelli, Rachel and Stephen Catanzarite, Paula and Gary Cercone, Jacqueline and Chris Davis, Kathy and Zoot Dwyer, Johnette and Alan Lopuszynski, Holly and Dave McKissock, Michelle and Neil Medic, Laurie and Victor Mizrahi, Contenta and Erik Schoenman, Christine and Paul Swann, Kathleen and Tony Trehy, and Monica and Russ Walsh. We thank those of you who would bravely ask, "So how is the book coming along?" and then stick around to listen.

Love also to our siblings and their broods—the Klabers, Campbells, Schrecengosts, Kelmans, and two sets of Kennedys—and to the rest of our families for offering support along the way.

For my parents, Rae Nancy and Richard Zuberbuhler: I managed to string together over 80,000 words to write this book, but if given the task of expressing the love and admiration I have for you, I would fail. What has mattered to me has always mattered to you, and I know there are no two people who are prouder to hold this book in their hands.

To Grace and Megan—my sweet, funny, brilliant little Muses—this is the book I have been working on since you can both remember. And so I thank you for taking an interest in my writing, for playing together under my desk while I worked, and for listening closely to every story I have ever told you. It's an honor to be your Mom.

And to Kevin: You handed me a thread outside a labyrinth and gave me the confidence to start this project. Then you heroically stepped into the maze with me, devising plans, pulling us out of dead ends, and lighting our way. You are an excellent designer, but you are, more importantly, an incredible husband and a wonderful father to our girls. I am so lucky to be in this world with you.

GLOSSARY *of* MYTHOLOGICAL NAMES

After each name in this glossary is a series of syllables that act as a pronunciation guide. Most of the names should be pronounced just how they look, but the following key can serve as a reference. The syllable written in capital letters should be stressed when the name is said aloud. And remember that some pronunciations vary.

a = hat	e = set	i = sit	u = us	o = hot
ay = day	ee = green	ie = pie	ur = hurt	oh = hose
				oo = moon

A

Achaeans (*uh KEE anz*)—Achaea was a province in Greece's Peloponnesian region, and the Achaeans were once the dominant people in ancient Greece. In his account of the Trojan War, Homer referred to all the Greeks who fought against the Trojans as Achaeans because the war likely took place during the peak of their rule.

Achilles (*uh KIL eez*)—A son of the sea goddess Thetis and the mortal Peleus, Achilles was the most skilled Greek warrior in the Trojan War. His anger made him an incredibly powerful fighter, but his pride cost him dearly. Although Thetis tried to make her son immortal, he was destined to live a heroic but brief life.

Acrisius (*uh KRIS ee us*)—King of Argos who was frightened when an oracle told him that any child born to his daughter, Danae, would cause his death. He tried to keep his daughter from becoming pregnant, but she bore Perseus, who led a heroic life but did unintentionally kill Acrisius.

Actaeon (*ak TEE on*)—Hunter who accidentally saw the goddess Artemis bathing in her sacred spring. The fiercely private goddess turned him into a stag, and the condemned Actaeon was killed by his own hunting dogs.

Aeetes (*ee EE teez*)—King of Colchis who possessed the famed Golden Fleece. The hero Jason took the fleece with help from Aeetes' daughter Medea.

Aegeus (*EE jee us*)—King of Athens and father of the hero Theseus. When Theseus forgot to raise his ship's white sail after slaying the Minotaur, Aegeus thought his son had died and drowned himself in what is now called the Aegean Sea.

Aeneas (*ee NEE us*)—Son of the goddess Venus and the mortal Anchises. Aeneas fled from Troy after the Greeks sacked the city and traveled west to Italy in search of a new home for his followers. The hero fell in love with Queen Dido and faced many obstacles along his journey, but he was determined to fulfill his destiny. His descendants ultimately founded the city of Rome.

Aeolus (*EE oh lus*)—God of the winds. Aeolus helped Odysseus on his voyage home, but when Odysseus asked for help a second time, Aeolus was convinced the hero was cursed and turned him away. Aeolus also helped Juno delay Aeneas during the Trojans' voyage by causing a storm at sea.

Aeson (*EE son*)—Father of Jason who fought with his own half-brother, Pelias, over the throne of Iolcus. Aeson conceded the throne but insisted that when Jason came of age, he would inherit it.

Although Pelias later sent Jason on a dangerous mission and had Aeson killed, Medea helped Jason gain power and restored Aeson to life.

Aethra (*EETH ruh*)—Mother of Theseus. Aethra showed Theseus where his father, Aegeus, had hidden a pair of sandals and a sword under a heavy stone. Aethra told Theseus that as soon as he was strong enough to lift the stone, he could go to Athens to claim the throne from Aegeus.

Agamemnon (*ag uh MEM non*)—Son of Atreus, older brother of Menelaus, and husband of Clytemnestra. Agamemnon became the commander of the Achaeans and led one thousand ships from Greece to Troy to get Menelaus' wife, Helen, back from the Trojans. Agamemnon's bitter feud with Achilles was the crux of Homer's *Iliad*, and the arrogance of both men caused anguish for the Achaeans. Agamemnon was ultimately killed by his angry wife.

Aglaia (*uh GLAY uh*)—Youngest of the three Graces. See **Graces**.

Ajax (*AY jaks*)—Greek warrior who fought valiantly at Troy. He was known as "Great Ajax" and was second only to Achilles in terms of strength. When he was not chosen to receive Achilles' prized armor, Ajax went temporarily insane.

Alcinous (*al SIN oh us*)—King of Phaeacia, husband of Arete, and father of Nausicaa. Alcinous listened to Odysseus' account of his journey back from the Trojan War and helped the hero return home to Ithaca.

Alcmene (*alk MEE nee*)—Mortal woman who carried twin sons, one fathered by her mortal husband and the other, Heracles, fathered by Zeus.

Allecto (*uh LEK toh*)—One of the three Furies. When the goddess Juno wanted to punish Aeneas in Virgil's *Aeneid*, she sent Allecto to make the Italians see Aeneas as an enemy. See **Furies**.

Amata (*uh MAH tuh*)—In Virgil's *Aeneid*, she is the wife of King Latinus in Italy, and opposed the marriage between her daughter, Lavinia, and the Trojan Aeneas. Juno worked through Amata to try and ruin Aeneas' plans.

Amazons (*AM uh zonz*)—A tribe of huge women warriors. One of Heracles' tasks was to take a belt from the queen of the Amazons, Hippolyta.

Amphion (*am FEE on*)—Husband of Niobe, who killed himself when he learned that all seven of his sons had been slain by Apollo as punishment for Niobe's extreme hubris.

Anchises (*an KIE seez*)—Wise and respected father of the hero Aeneas by the goddess Venus. When Aeneas wanted him to flee the burning city of Troy, Anchises refused. But after witnessing an omen, Anchises collected the sacred household statues and allowed his son to carry him on his shoulders. Anchises eventually died during Aeneas' journey toward Italy.

Andromache (*an DROM uh kee*)—Wife of the Trojan warrior Hector. She was terrified every time Hector entered battle and witnessed his gruesome death at the hands of the Greek Achilles.

Andromeda (*an DRAWM e duh*)—Daughter of King Cepheus and Queen Cassiopeia. Andromeda's parents had to sacrifice her by chaining her to a rock, but the hero Perseus rescued her from a sea monster and married her.

Anna (*AN uh*)—In Virgil's *Aeneid*, Anna was Queen Dido's loyal sister. She encouraged Dido to pursue her passion for Aeneas, but later held her dying sister, who burned herself on a pyre.

Antinous (*an TIN oh us*)—In Homer's *Odyssey*, Antinous was the cruel and arrogant leader of the one hundred suitors who pursued Penelope, the queen of Ithaca, in Odysseus' absence. Years later, Odysseus shot Antinous through his neck as punishment.

Antiope (*an TIE oh pee*)—The hero Theseus' first wife and the mother of Hippolytus.

Aphrodite (*af roh DIE tee*)—Greek goddess of love and beauty whose Roman name was Venus. Said to be born of the sea's foam, she was married to Hephaestus, although she loved many others, including Ares. She was the mother of several children, including Eros and the hero Aeneas. Aphrodite was awarded the golden apple inscribed with the words "For the Fairest" by the young Paris and so helped him win over Helen, known as the most beautiful mortal woman in the world.

Apollo (*uh PAWL oh*)—Greek god of light, medicine, poetry, music, and prophecy. While the Romans changed the names of all the other Olympians, they felt Apollo represented perfection and did not alter his Greek name. Apollo and his twin sister, Artemis, were born to Leto and Zeus. Apollo is often depicted wearing a crown of laurel and holding a lyre.

Apsyrtus (*ap SER tus*)—Son of King Aeetes of Colchis and brother of the sorceress Medea. When Medea helped Jason and the Argonauts escape with the Golden Fleece, she murdered Apsyrtus and threw his limbs into the ocean so the Colchians would have to stop and collect them.

Arachne (*uh RAK nee*)—Mortal girl who boasted that she was a better weaver than Athena. In a contest with the goddess, Arachne wove a beautiful tapestry that slandered the Olympians. As punishment, Athena turned her into a spider so she and her descendents could weave forever.

Ares (*AIR eez*)—Aggressive Greek god of war. While he was played down in Greek myths, the Romans, who renamed him Mars, revered him. His chariot was pulled by his sons Phobos and Deimos, gods who represented fear and dread. Ares had a long affair with Aphrodite, and he favored the Trojans during the Trojan War.

Argonauts (*AR goh nots*)—Sailors who traveled with the hero Jason on the *Argo* in search of the Golden Fleece. Some of the most famous Argonauts included Heracles, Theseus, and Peleus.

Argos (*AR gohs*)—Man who built the *Argo* for Jason when he went in search of the Golden Fleece. Argos was also the name of Odysseus' loyal dog, who still recognized his master after twenty years.

Argus (*AR gus*)—Beast with one hundred eyes who often helped Hera. Argus was given the job of guarding Io when she was transformed into a white cow, but Hermes got Argus to fall asleep and beheaded him. Out of respect, Hera placed Argus' eyes on the ends of her peacock's feathers.

Ariadne (*air ee AD nee*)—Daughter of King Minos of Crete. When Theseus came to Crete to kill the Minotaur, Ariadne helped him through the Minotaur's Labyrinth by giving him a ball of string to unravel. Theseus escaped with Ariadne, but he then left her on the island of Naxos, and she later married the god Dionysus.

Artemis (*AR te miss*)—Greek goddess of the hunt whose Roman name was Diana. The daughter of Leto by Zeus, Artemis represented the moon while her twin brother, Apollo, was associated with the sun. Women who wished to remain unmarried were followers of Artemis. The goddess was so protective of her independence that when the mortal Actaeon accidentally saw her bathing, she turned him into a stag so his own hunting dogs would kill him.

Ascanius (*as KAY nee us*)—Son of Aeneas by his first wife, Creusa. Ascanius, sometimes called Iulus, was rescued by his father from the burning city of Troy. He ultimately succeeded his father and moved their kingdom from Lavinium to Alba Longa, which eventually became Rome.

Atalanta (*at uh LAN tuh*)—Mortal woman who said she would only marry a man who could beat her in a foot race. Atalanta happily defeated all her suitors until she met Hippomenes. She allowed herself to be distracted and he won, but then he forgot to thank Aphrodite for her help in wooing Atalanta. As punishment, the mortals were turned into lions and made to pull Rhea's chariot.

Athena (*uh THEE nuh*)—Greek goddess of war and wisdom who sprang fully grown from Zeus' head. The Romans called her Minerva, and she was associated with the owl and the olive tree and was the patron of Athens. She is often shown with Medusa's head on her aegis or armor, for she helped the hero Perseus slay the snake-haired beast. Athena supported the Greeks when they fought against the Trojans and protected the hero Odysseus on his return to Ithaca.

Atlas (*AT les*)—One of the few Titans spared by the Olympians. Rather than being sent to Tartarus, Atlas was given the task of holding up the sky so it would not crush the earth. Sometimes Atlas is shown holding the entire globe on his back, and thus an atlas is a book showing maps of the world.

Atropos (*AT roh pohs*)—See **Fates**.

Augeas (*OH jee us*)—King who owned the massive stables that were cleaned by the hero Heracles.

Aurora (*oh ROH ruh*)—Roman goddess of the dawn whose Greek name was Eos. The bands of brilliant light that appear in the night skies in the northern hemisphere are called the aurora borealis, a name combining Aurora's lights and the movement of Boreas, the god of the north winds.

Bacchae (*BAK ee*)—Mortals who worshipped Dionysus, the god of wine and drama, whose Roman name was Bacchus. Their celebrations often became shockingly savage.

Bacchus (*BAK us*)—Roman name for Dionysus, god of wine and drama. See **Dionysus**.

Baucis (*BOW kiss*)—Old woman who, along with her husband, Philemon, provided hospitality to the disguised Zeus and Hermes. As a reward, their tiny home was turned into a temple; they were granted their wish of dying at the same time; and they were transformed into intertwining trees.

Bellerophon (*be LER uh fon*)—Mortal boy who was allowed to ride the winged horse Pegasus. After slaying the Chimaera, Bellerophon succumbed to hubris and attempted to fly to Mount Olympus. Zeus struck him down with a lightning both, and Bellerophon was maimed.

Briseis (*brih SEE us*)—Trojan girl who was awarded to the great Achaean warrior Achilles. When the Achaean leader, Agamemnon, insisted Achilles give her up, a bitter quarrel began, and Achilles refused to take part in the Trojan War.

Calliope (*kuh LIE oh pee*)—See **Muses**.

Calypso (*kuh LIP soh*)—Daughter of Atlas whose name comes from the Greek "to hide." She fell in love with Odysseus when he washed ashore on her private island and offered him immortality. Odysseus wanted to return to Ithaca, however, and Zeus made Calypso release the hero.

Cassandra (*kuh SAN druh*)—One of the twelve daughters of King Priam and Queen Hecuba of Troy. Apollo gave Cassandra the gift of prophecy but cursed her with never being believed. Although she predicted many of the events that led to the fall of Troy, her warnings were all ignored.

Cassiopeia *(kas ee oh PEE uh)*—Ethiopian queen who bragged that her daughter Andromeda was more beautiful than the sea nymphs. Poseidon made Cassiopeia sacrifice Andromeda to a sea monster, but the hero Perseus rescued her. Cassiopeia was punished by being turned into a constellation that is often tipped at an awkward angle in the sky.

Centaurs *(SEN torz)*—Mythological creatures with the bodies and legs of horses and the torsos, arms, and heads of humans. Centaurs were usually frightening, but the gentle and wise centaur Chiron helped train many of the best-known heroes.

Cepheus *(SEE feh us)*—Ethiopian king whose wife, Cassiopeia, bragged that their daughter Andromeda was more beautiful than the sea nymphs. Poseidon made the royal couple offer their daughter as a sacrifice to a sea monster, but the hero Perseus rescued her.

Cerberus *(SER ber us)*—Vicious three-headed dog who guarded the gates of the Underworld and served Hades, the god of the dead.

Ceres *(SEE reez)*—Roman name for Demeter, goddess of grain. See **Demeter**.

Chaos *(KAY os)*—The first entity that existed in the universe, according to the Greeks. The earth, heavens, sea, mountains, and gods all descended from Chaos and the universe took shape.

Charites *(KAR i teez)*—Greek name for the Graces. See **Graces**.

Charon *(KAIR on)*—The ferryman who rowed the dead across the River Styx and into the Underworld. Many ancients placed coins on the eyes of the deceased as payment for Charon's service. The few living mortals to ever ride in his boat included Orpheus, Heracles, Aeneas, and Odysseus.

Charybdis *(ka RIB diss)*—A monster in the form of a whirlpool that lived across from Scylla's cave. Both Odysseus and Aeneas faced this beast, and both lived to tell their tales.

Chimaera *(kie MEE ruh)*—Creature killed by Bellerophon. It had the head of a lion, the body of a goat, and the tail of a dragon, and it breathed a deadly fire. The Chimaera had terrorized the land of Lycia until Bellerophon rode on Pegasus' back and killed it in a battle.

Chiron *(KIE ron)*—Wisest and gentlest of the centaurs. Chiron helped educate many of classical mythology's greatest heroes, including Heracles, Perseus, Achilles, and Aeneas.

Chryseis *(krie SEE us)*—Trojan girl who was the daughter of one of Apollo's priests. She was awarded to the Achaean leader Agamemnon, but when Apollo punished the army with a plague, Chryseis was returned to her father. Agamemnon then insisted Achilles give him *his* slave girl, Briseis, and this situation sparked a bitter quarrel between the two men.

Circe *(SUR see)*—Sorceress who was the daughter of the sun god Helios. She used her magic to play cruel tricks on others, and she turned Odysseus' crew into swine. Her spell did not work on Odysseus, however, and she ended up falling in love with him and assisting him on his journey.

Clio *(KLEE oh)*—See **Muses**.

Clotho *(KLO tho)*—See **Fates**.

Clymene *(KLIM uh nee)*—Oceanid who fell in love with the sun god Helios. She raised their son, Phaethon, and when he was older, she allowed him to travel to meet his father. Unfortunately, Phaethon insisted on driving Helios' sun chariot and died after losing control of the horses.

Clytemnestra *(klie tem NES truh)*—Bitter wife of Agamemnon and older half-sister to Helen. Clytemnestra was furious when Agamemnon sacrificed their daughter Iphigenia before setting sail to Troy. When Agamemnon returned from Troy more than ten years later, Clytemnestra and her lover killed him as he sat defenseless in his bath.

Cronus *(KROH nus)*—King of the Titans whose Roman name was Saturn. Son of Gaea and Uranus, and husband to his sister Rhea. When Rhea bore children, Cronus swallowed them to protect his power. Rhea hid their sixth child, Zeus, who later forced his father to vomit up his five siblings. These six Olympians then overthrew him.

Cupid *(KEW pid)*—Roman name for Eros, the god of love. See **Eros**.

Cyclopes *(sie KLOPE eez)*—Monstrous one-eyed creatures. The singular form is Cyclops (SIE klops). Several Cyclopes were born to Gaea and Uranus and were called upon by the Olympians to help fight their battle against the Titans. The Cyclops Polyphemus, a son of Poseidon, became enraged when he was blinded by the hero Odysseus; as punishment, Poseidon persecuted Odysseus on his journey back to Ithaca.

Daedalus *(DEED uh lus)*—Greek inventor best known for constructing the Labyrinth for King Minos to imprison the Minotaur on the island of Crete. When Minos tried to keep Daedalus from leaving, the inventor made wings for himself and his son, Icarus. Unfortunately, Icarus flew too high, and the heat of the sun melted the wax that held his feathered wings together. He drowned, and Daedalus vowed he would never fly again.

Damon *(DAY mon)*—Young man who offered to be jailed so that his best friend, Pythias, could take care of his own affairs before being wrongfully executed by King Dionysius. Damon and Pythias' friendship so impressed the cold-hearted ruler that he pardoned Pythias and set both men free.

Danae *(DAN a ee)*—Daughter of King Acrisius of Argo. Acrisius tried to prevent Danae from getting pregnant because he was told his daughter's son would cause his death, but Danae was impregnated by Zeus and later bore a son, Perseus. Perseus lived heroically and saved Danae from having to marry the evil King Polydectes. But he fulfilled the prophecy by accidentally killing his grandfather.

Daphne *(DAF nee)*—Nymph who wanted to remain unmarried. When Daphne was pursued by Apollo, her father, Peneus, turned her into a laurel tree so she could remain chaste. Apollo was thereafter associated with laurel and wore a wreath of it on his head.

Deianira *(dee ya NIE ruh)*—Heracles' second wife, who was attacked by the centaur Nessus. Nessus tricked her by giving her a vial of his blood, saying it would keep Heracles faithful. The blood was poisonous, however, and Deianira unintentionally burned Heracles with it years later.

Deimos *(DEE mos)*—The personification of dread and the son, along with Phobos, of the god of war, Ares. Deimos is the name of one of the moons of Mars.

Demeter *(de MEE tur)*—Olympian goddess of fertility and the harvest whose Roman name was Ceres. Hades kidnapped her daughter Persephone and took her to be his queen in the Underworld. Persephone was eventually allowed to return to earth for part of the year. In spring and summer the mother and daughter lived happily together and plants flourished, but in fall and winter, the lonely Demeter did not allow crops to grow.

D

Deucalion (*doo KAY li on*)—Man who received a warning from his father, Prometheus, that Zeus would punish mortals with a great flood. Deucalion and his wife, Pyrrha, survived by building a large ship and later repopulated the world by throwing stones that formed new men and women.

Diana (*die AN uh*)—Roman name for Artemis, goddess of the hunt. See **Artemis.**

Dictys (*DIK tiss*)—Kind fisherman who found Danae and her baby, Perseus, washed ashore in a chest. He and his wife helped Danae raise Perseus, and the hero later overthrew Dictys' tyrannical brother, Polydectes, and Dictys became a king.

Dido (*DIE doh*)—Founder of Carthage who fell madly in love with Aeneas. When he left her to fulfill his obligations, she became so overwhelmed with anger and grief that she killed herself.

Dionysius (*die oh NEE see us*)—Tyrannical ruler of Syracuse on the island of Sicily. He wrongfully sentenced the young man Pythias to die, but when he witnessed Pythias' friendship with another youth named Damon, Dionysius pardoned Pythias and set both men free.

Dionysus (*die oh NEE sus*)—Greek god of wine and drama whose Roman name was Bacchus. The son of Zeus and Semele, Dionysus later took Hestia's place on Mount Olympus. While Apollo was known as the god of moderation, Dionysus was associated with excess.

Discordia (*dis KOR dee uh*)—Roman name for Eris, goddess of discord and strife. See **Eris.**

Echidna (*e KID nuh*)—Beastly serpent with the head of a woman. She and her partner, Typhon, created the Nemean Lion, the Hydra, Orthos, Cerberus, the Sphinx, and the Chimaera. While Zeus could have killed Echidna and her offspring, he chose to spare them so they could be used as tests for heroes.

Echo (*EK oh*)—Nymph whose voice was taken away by the jealous goddess Hera; Echo could only repeat the last few words spoken by others. After being shunned by Narcissus, Echo's body withered away and all that was left was her faint voice.

Eos (*EE ohs*)—Greek goddess of the dawn.

Epimetheus (*ep i MEE thee us*)—A Titan and brother to Prometheus. While Prometheus showed foresight, Epimetheus only had hindsight. After marrying the curious Pandora and ignoring his brother's warnings, Epimetheus gave Pandora access to the box of evils, and she opened it.

Erato (*AIR uh toh*)—See **Muses.**

Erebus (*AIR uh bus*)—Offspring of Chaos and the father of Nyx. Erebus personified the darkness of the Underworld and fathered Hemera (Day) and Aether (Light).

Eris (*AIR iss*)—Daughter of Nyx; the Greek goddess of strife whose Roman name was Discordia. Eris rolled a golden apple inscribed with the words "For the Fairest" into the wedding of Thetis and Peleus, thus starting a battle among the goddesses that ultimately led to the Trojan War.

Eros (*AIR os*)—A force produced from Chaos that personified love. Eros was also the Greek god of love, the son of Aphrodite, who later married the mortal Psyche. Eros' Roman name was Cupid.

Eumaeus (*yoo MEE us*)—Loyal swineherd who protected Odysseus when he returned to Ithaca and helped him kill the suitors.

Euphemus *(YOO fuh mus)*—One of the Argonauts who released a bird between the Clashing Rocks to ensure that the *Argo* could pass safely through.

Euphrosyne *(yoo FROS i nee)*—See **Graces**.

Eurycleia *(yoo ri KLEE uh)*—Odysseus' elderly nurse who, while giving a beggar a bath in Ithaca, recognized a scar on his leg and realized the beggar was actually Odysseus in disguise.

Eurydice *(yoo RID i see)*—Wife of Orpheus who was killed by a snake bite. Orpheus descended into the Underworld and begged Hades to release her, and Hades agreed on the condition that Orpheus walk ahead of Eurydice and not look back until he reached the light. At the last moment, Orpheus turned, and Eurydice was lost forever.

Eurylochus *(yoo RIL oh kus)*—Second in command to Odysseus and the only other man not turned into a pig by Circe.

Eurystheus *(yoo RIS thee us)*—King who assigned twelve labors to his cousin Heracles because the hero wanted to atone for killing his own family.

Euterpe *(yoo TUR pee)*—See **Muses**.

Evander *(ee VAN dur)*—Aged king of Pallenteum who became an ally to Aeneas upon the hero's arrival in Italy. Evander's beloved son Pallas died while supporting Aeneas and his troops, but Aeneas exacted revenge on Pallas' killer, Turnus.

Fates *(FAYTS)*—Three sisters, also called the Moirai, who were daughters of Erebus and Nyx. Clotho carried a spindle and spun the yarn of life, Lachesis used a ruler to measure its length, and Atropos held shears to cut it.

Faunus *(FAW nus)*—Roman name for Pan, the god of the forest. See **Pan**.

Furies *(FYOOR eez)*—Three sisters who doled out punishment. Allecto (Endless) was the Fury who helped Juno cause trouble for the hero Aeneas in Virgil's *Aeneid*. Her sisters were Tisiphone (Punishment) and Megaera (Rage). The Furies are also known as the Erinyes (e RIN i eez).

Gaea *(GAY uh)*—Greek Earth goddess who was actually Earth itself. Mother of Uranus (Sky), the Sea, the Mountains, the Hecatonchires, the Cyclopes, and the Titans. Sometimes spelled Gaia.

Genius *(JEE nee us)*—Roman guiding spirits who granted men energy, joy, and intelligence. A Roman man would offer gifts to his genius each year, just as a woman would make an offering to her juno.

Glauce *(GLAW see)*—Younger woman whom Jason planned to marry. Glauce was brutally killed by Jason's jealous wife, Medea.

Gorgons *(GOR gonz)*—Female creatures with snakes for hair. They were so hideous that anyone who looked at them turned to stone. Medusa, the only mortal Gorgon, was killed by the hero Perseus.

Graces *(GRAY ses)*—Three sisters, daughters of Zeus, who were responsible for the pleasures and beauties of nature and life. Their names were Aglaia (Brilliance), Euphrosyne (Joy), and Thalia (Bloom), and they were Aphrodite's attendants. The Greeks called these three sisters Charites.

Graeae *(GREE ee)*—Three "gray women" who were sisters of the Gorgons. They shared just one eye and one tooth and were tricked by the hero Perseus into revealing the location of Medusa's cave.

F

G

H

Hades (*HAY deez*)—Brother to Zeus and Poseidon who became god of the Underworld. He spent so much time away from Mount Olympus that he was not considered an Olympian; in fact, the Underworld was often referred to as "Hades." Hades kidnapped Persephone and married her, but he eventually allowed her to return to the earth for part of the year.

Harpies (*HAR peez*)—Vengeful birdlike women who stole food from others and left behind their droppings and a horrible stench. These creatures appear in the myth of Jason, and others attack Aeneas and his crew in Virgil's *Aeneid*.

Hecatonchires (*hek uh ton KEE reez*)—The hundred-handed monsters born to Uranus and Gaea.

Hector (*HEK tor*)—Son of King Priam and Queen Hecuba of Troy, older brother to Prince Paris, and husband to Andromache. Hector was the commander of the Trojan forces in their ten-year battle against the Greek army. After Hector killed Achilles' best friend, Patroclus, Achilles killed Hector and dragged his body around the walls of Troy.

Hecuba (*HEK yoo buh*)—Queen of Troy and wife of Priam.

Helen (*HEL en*)—The most beautiful mortal woman in the world. She was married to King Menelaus and then taken by Paris to Troy. Menelaus and his brother Agamemnon (who was married to Helen's sister Clytemnestra) led one thousand Greek ships to Troy to get her back, which was the origin of the Trojan War.

Helenus (*he LAY nus*)—A Trojan prince and twin brother of Cassandra. He was the only son of King Priam to survive the Trojan War, and he offered advice to Aeneas during his journey.

Helios (*HEE lee ohs*)—The god of the sun whose crown was the sun itself. Helios' son, Phaethon, tried to drive his father's sun chariot but could not control it and had to be shot down. Helios' Roman name was Sol.

Hemera (*HEM er uh*)—Daughter of Nyx and Erebus; personification of day.

Hephaestus (*he FAY stus*)—Greek god of the forge whose Roman name was Vulcan. Hephaestus was said to be born to Hera, but when Hephaestus was born lame, Hera threw him off Mount Olympus. Years later he reconciled with Hera and was welcomed on Olympus. Hephaestus crafted houses for the Olympians, armor for worthy heroes, and lightning bolts for Zeus. He was married to the beautiful Aphrodite, but their marriage was not a happy one.

Hera (*HEER uh*)—Greek goddess whose Roman name was Juno. After marrying her brother Zeus, she became queen of the Olympians. She was known as the goddess of childbirth and of marriage, but ironically, her own marriage to Zeus was marred by his numerous infidelities. She often tormented Zeus' lovers and offspring, most notably his son Heracles.

Heracles (*HAIR uh kleez*)—Son of Zeus and Alcmene; called Hercules by the Romans. When Hera made Heracles go mad, he killed his family. To atone, Heracles performed twelve labors for his cousin, Eurystheus. His second wife, Deianira, accidentally burned him when she gave him a tunic soaked in poison. Heracles rose to Mount Olympus, where he was forgiven by Hera and regarded as a hero.

Hercules (*HUR kyoo leez*)—Roman name for Heracles. See **Heracles**.

Hermes (*HUR meez*)—Messenger to the gods whose Roman name was Mercury. He was also the patron god of travelers and thieves. He wore winged sandals and a winged cap and always carried the caduceus, a staff entwined with snakes, which was a gift from his half-brother, Apollo.

Hestia (*HES tee uh*)—Greek goddess of the hearth whose Roman name was Vesta. She was a first-generation Olympian but disliked the activity of Mount Olympus and was eventually replaced by Dionysus. Although Hestia does not appear in many myths, every hearth in Greek homes was a tribute to this goddess, and Vestal Virgins were highly respected priestesses in ancient Rome.

Hippolyta (*hi POL i tuh*)—A daughter of Ares and the queen of the Amazons. She was accidentally killed by the hero Heracles when he was sent to get her golden belt for his ninth task.

Hippolytus (*hi POL i tus*)—Son of the hero Theseus who was wrongfully accused of molesting his stepmother, Phaedra. Theseus only realized his son's innocence after Hippolytus' death.

Hippomenes (*hi POM muh neez*)—Mortal who raced against Atalanta to win her hand in marriage. Aphrodite gave him three golden apples, which he used during the race to distract Atalanta. The plan worked, but Hippomenes forgot to thank Aphrodite, so the goddess turned the couple into lions.

Hydra (*HIE druh*)—One of the beasts born to Echidna and Typhon, the Hydra was a huge water snake with nine heads. The hero Heracles managed to kill it and dipped his arrows in its poisonous blood. Ironically, it was this blood that led to Heracles' own death.

Hypnos (*HIP nos*)—Greek god of sleep whose Roman name was Somnus.

Icarus (*IK ur us*)—Son of the inventor Daedalus. When the two of them tried to escape a prison using man-made wings, Icarus was so excited to fly that he ignored his father's advice and soared too high. The heat of the sun melted the wax that held his feathered wings together, and he drowned in what is now called the Icarian Sea.

Io (*EYE oh*)—Mortal maiden loved by Zeus, who turned her into a cow to hide her from Hera. Although Io escaped, Hera sent a gadfly to torture her. When Io was returned to human form, she became a queen in Egypt.

Iphigenia (*if i juh NEE uh*)—Daughter of Agamemnon and Clytemnestra whom Agamemnon used as a sacrifice to procure favorable winds so he and his fleet could sail to Troy. Artemis was said to have spared the innocent girl, and Iphigenia became one of the goddess' attendants.

Iris (*EYE rus*)—Goddess of the rainbow and one of Hera's messengers. Mortals believed she traveled to and from Mount Olympus on her rainbow, so her name is now associated with bright colors.

Janus (*JAN us*)—Highly revered Roman god who was the guardian of doorways and beginnings. He was shown with two faces, one looking forward and one looking backward.

Jason (*JAY sun*)—Greek hero who led the Argonauts on their quest for the Golden Fleece. He was able to capture the fleece with help from the sorceress Medea, whom he later married. When Jason tried to leave Medea, she killed their children along with Jason's new lover. Jason died when a plank from his ship, the *Argo*, fell on him.

Jocasta (*joh KAS tuh*)—Queen of Thebes and husband to King Laius. The royal couple gave up their child at birth because of a frightening prophecy, but the son, Oedipus, later returned. After Oedipus unknowingly killed his own father, Jocasta unknowingly married him. When the truth was revealed years later, she killed herself in shame.

I

J

Jove (*JOHV*)—Another Roman name for Jupiter, the king of the Olympians.

Juno (*JOO noh*)—Roman name for Hera, queen of the Olympians. See **Hera**. In Virgil's *Aeneid*, Juno thwarts all of Aeneas' plans because of her hatred for the Trojans. A juno was the name Romans gave to a woman's protectorate; just as every man had a genius, every woman had a juno, a spirit they considered to be a guardian angel.

Jupiter (*JOO pi tur*)—Roman name for Zeus, god of the heavens. See **Zeus**.

Justitia (*joo STISH ee uh*)—Roman goddess of morality, also known as Justice, who was associated with the Greek goddess Themis. Statues and paintings of her are still common in courthouses, and she is often featured wearing a blindfold, holding a sword in one hand and a scale in the other.

L

Lachesis (*LAK e siss*)—See **Fates**.

Laestrygonians (*lee strie GOH nee unz*)—Race of giants that hated men. In Homer's *Odyssey*, eleven ships full of men were attacked by these ruthless monsters.

Laius (*LAY us*)—King of Thebes and wife of Queen Jocasta who gave up their child at birth because of a prophecy. The boy, Oedipus, later killed Laius, not realizing they were related. Oedipus then unknowingly married his own mother, Jocasta.

Laocoon (*lay OH koh on*)—A Trojan priest and son of King Priam and Queen Hecuba. He tried to warn the Trojans about the wooden horse left by the Greeks, but Athena sent serpents that killed him and his two sons.

Latinus (*la TIE nus*)—King of Latium and husband of Amata in Virgil's *Aeneid*. Latinus welcomed Aeneas to Italy and believed he should marry his daughter, Lavinia, but Amata wanted Lavinia to marry Turnus.

Lavinia (*luh VIN ee uh*)—Only surviving child of King Latinus and Queen Amata in Virgil's *Aeneid*. Her mother wanted her to marry Turnus, but her father believed her destiny was to marry Aeneas. She became Aeneas' second wife.

Leda (*LEE duh*)—Queen of Sparta who was seduced by Zeus after he took the form of a swan. She bore quadruplets, including Zeus' daughter Helen, who was taken by Prince Paris of Troy.

Leto (*LEE toh*)—When Leto became pregnant with twins by Zeus, the jealous Hera ordered all lands to refuse her. She roamed helplessly until being welcomed onto the floating island of Delos. Leto's twins, the Olympians Apollo and Artemis, later defended Leto when Niobe bragged that she was a better mother because she had more children.

Luna (*LOO nuh*)—Roman name for Selene, goddess of the moon. See **Selene**.

M

Maia (*MY uh*)—Roman goddess of the spring and a daughter of Faunus. The month of May was named for her.

Mars (*MARZ*)—Roman name for Ares, god of war. See **Ares**.

Medea (*me DEE uh*)—Sorceress who helped Jason get the Golden Fleece from her own father and then used trickery to get him the throne of Iolcus. When Jason left her to marry another woman, Medea killed the woman along with her own children by Jason. Medea fled to Athens where she married King Aegeus, but she was exiled after trying to kill Aegeus' son, Theseus.

Medusa (*me DOO suh*)—Mortal woman punished for her vanity by Athena. Her hair became a writhing mass of snakes, and her face was so hideous that she and her Gorgon sisters turned people into stone. The hero Perseus killed Medusa and presented her head to Athena; Medusa's head often appears on Athena's breast plate or her aegis.

Megaera (*me JEE ruh*)—See **Furies**.

Megara (*MEG uh ruh*)—Heracles' first wife. When Hera made Heracles insane, he killed Megara and their children. To repent, he performed twelve labors for his cousin Eurystheus.

Melpomene (*mel POM i nee*)—See **Muses**.

Menelaus (*men uh LAY us*)—King of Sparta and younger brother of Agamemnon. Menelaus' wife, Helen, was taken to Troy by the Trojan Paris, and Menelaus and Agamemnon led one thousand ships to Troy to get her back, thus starting the Trojan War.

Mentor (*MEN tor*)—Loyal advisor to Odysseus who taught Telemachus while Odysseus was away for twenty years.

Mercury (*MUR kyur ee*)—Roman name for Hermes, a messenger god. See **Hermes**.

Merope (*MUR oh pee*)—Queen of Corinth who, along with her husband, Polybus, adopted an infant they named Oedipus. They raised him to believe he was their biological son, but he was actually born to King Laius and Queen Jocasta.

Metis (*MEE tiss*)—Athena's mother, who was swallowed alive by Zeus. Athena later sprang fully grown from Zeus, and Metis continued to advise Zeus from inside his head.

Midas (*MIE diss*)—Greedy king who, when given one wish by Dionysus, asked that everything he touched would turn to gold. When he realized he would die because he could never touch food, Midas begged to have the "gift" taken away. Later, Apollo cursed him with the ears of an ass when Midas chose Pan rather than Apollo in a music contest.

Minerva (*mi NUR vuh*)—Roman name for Athena, goddess of war and wisdom. See **Athena**.

Minos (*MIE nos*)—King of Crete and husband of Queen Pasiphae, he demanded that fourteen Athenian youths be sacrificed every nine years to feed the Minotaur. Minos' daughter Ariadne helped the hero Theseus slay the beast.

Minotaur (*MIN uh tar*)—Creature with the body of a man and the head of a bull. He was the offspring of King Minos' wife, Pasiphae, and a bull. Minos imprisoned the beast in the Labyrinth, a maze built by the inventor Daedalus, but the hero Theseus later killed the beast.

Mnemosyne (*nee MOZ i nee*)—Titan goddess of memory and mother of the nine Muses by Zeus.

Moirai (*MOY rie*)—Another name for the three Fates. See **Fates**.

Morpheus (*MOR fee us*)—God of dreams and the brother or son of Hypnos. Morpheus could assume the shape of any human and appear to mortals as they slept.

Muses (*MYOO zez*)—Nine daughters of Mnemosyne and Zeus who provided inspiration for artists. The are Calliope (eloquence and epic poetry), Clio (history), Erato (love poetry), Euterpe (music and lyric poetry), Melpomene (tragedy), Polyhymnia (sacred music), Terpsichore (dance), Thalia (comedy), and Urania (astronomy).

Myrmidons (*MEER mi dons*)—Troop led by Achilles during the war against the Trojans. Some stories say they were originally worker ants, transformed by Zeus into strong, loyal humans.

N

Narcissus (*nar SISS us*)—Arrogant mortal who loved only himself. After Narcissus destroyed Echo by shunning her affection, Nemesis punished him by making him fall in love with his own reflection. He wasted away and became the narcissus flower.

Nausicaa (*noh SIK ay uh*)—Daughter of King Alcinous who found the weary Odysseus on the shores of Phaeacia and helped him back to her father's palace.

Nemean Lion (*ne MEE un LIE un*)—One of the beasts born to Echidna and Typhon, the Nemean Lion had impenetrable skin. When Heracles was sent to kill it, he squeezed it to death and then used its own claws to skin it. Heracles is often pictured wearing the Nemean Lion's skin on his back.

Nemesis (*NEM uh siss*)—Goddess of punishment and a daughter of Erebus and Nyx.

Neoptolemus (*nee op TOL e mus*)—Son of Achilles who went to Troy after his father was killed by Paris. He was the first to enter the belly of the wooden horse and later killed King Priam.

Neptune (*NEP toon*)—Roman name for Poseidon, god of the sea. See **Poseidon**.

Nessus (*NESS us*)—Centaur who tried to attack Heracles' wife, Deianira. Heracles shot him with a poisoned arrow, but as Nessus was dying, he gave Deianira a vial of his blood and told her it would someday revive Heracles' love. The poisonous blood burned Heracles instead.

Nike (*NIE kee*)—The Greek winged goddess of victory.

Niobe (*NIE oh bee*)—Vain daughter of Tantalus and granddaughter of both Zeus and Atlas. As Queen of Thebes, she was infuriated that women honored Leto, the mother of only two children, while she herself had fourteen. Leto sent her son, Apollo, to kill Niobe's seven sons and then sent her daughter, Artemis, to kill the seven daughters. The proud Niobe turned to stone and was placed on a mountainside in Phrygia, where streams of water flow constantly from her eyes.

Nymphs (*NIMFS*)—Minor female divinities associated with nature. Nymphs often attended to the gods and goddesses.

Nyx (*NIKS*)—Personification of night who was born from Chaos. Mother of Aether, Hemera, Thanatos, Hypnos, Nemesis, Eris, and the Fates.

O

Oceanids (*oh see AN ids*)—Three thousand sea nymphs born to the Titans Oceanus and Tethys.

Odysseus (*oh DISS ee us*)—Mortal man who was the best strategist for the Achaeans during their battle against the Trojans. He devised the plan for the Trojan horse, and Homer's epic the *Odyssey* details the ten years Odysseus spent trying to get back to his wife, Penelope, in Ithaca. The Romans referred to Odysseus as "Ulysses."

Oedipus (*ED i pus*)—Son of King Laius and Queen Jocasta of Thebes. After hearing a disturbing prophecy, his parents ordered servants to hang their baby. Oedipus was adopted instead, and as a young man returned to Thebes where he unknowingly fulfilled the prophecy of killing his father and marrying his own mother. When the truth was revealed, he blinded himself in shame.

Olympians (*oh LIMP ee enz*)—The twelve gods and goddesses who presided over Greece from Mount Olympus. The first generation included Zeus, Hera, Poseidon, Demeter, Hades, and Hestia, and the second generation included Athena, Hephaestus, Aphrodite, Hermes, Apollo, Ares, and Artemis. However, Hades spent so much time in the Underworld that he is not considered an Olympian, and Hestia was eventually replaced by Dionysus.

Orpheus (*OR fee yus*)—Son of Apollo and Calliope whose mortal wife, Eurydice, died. Orpheus played his lyre so beautifully that Hades allowed Eurydice to return to earth, but only if Orpheus did not look back at her as they ascended. At the last second Orpheus turned, and Eurydice slipped back down to the Underworld forever.

Orthos (*OR thohs*)—Two-headed dog who was an offspring of Echidna and Typhon. He guarded the red cattle of Geryon, but Heracles killed him when he captured the cattle.

Pallas (*PAL us*)—Son of King Evander of Pallenteum who befriended Aeneas and joined him in his fight against the Italians. Pallas died while fighting Turnus, and Aeneas felt responsible for his death. When Aeneas later met Turnus in battle, he showed the Italian no mercy.

Pan (*PAN*)—Minor deity who was half goat and half man. He ran through the forests at night causing panic and is usually pictured carrying the panpipes. The Romans called him Faunus.

Pandora (*pan DOOR uh*)—First mortal woman. She was created by the gods and sent to earth as a punishment for Prometheus, who had stolen fire for mankind. The curious Pandora opened a sealed box that contained all the ills and evils that now plague the world.

Paris (*PAIR us*)—Mortal who chose Aphrodite as the most beautiful goddess in a contest. As his reward, Aphrodite helped him take the lovely Helen away from her husband, the Greek king Menelaus. Paris' actions led to the bloody Trojan War, and Paris proved to be cowardly in battle but eventually killed the great Greek warrior Achilles.

Pasiphae (*pa SIF ay ee*)—Queen of Crete, wife of Minos, and mother of Ariadne. She was tricked into mating with a bull and produced the hideous Minotaur. This half-man, half-bull was imprisoned in the Labyrinth and later killed by the hero Theseus.

Patroclus (*pa TROH klus*)—Closest friend of Achilles. When Achilles refused to fight against the Trojans, Patroclus entered the battle wearing Achilles' famous armor, tricking the Trojans into thinking Achilles had returned. But the Trojan Hector killed Patroclus and Achilles re-entered the battle, vowing revenge.

Pegasus (*PEG uh sus*)—Winged horse that was an offspring of Medusa and Poseidon. Pegasus lived on Mount Olympus and fetched Zeus' lighting bolts.

Peleus (*PEE lee us*)—Father, by Thetis, to Achilles. Peleus was the only mortal man to actually marry a goddess; no immortal wanted to marry Thetis because it was foretold that any son born to her would become stronger than his father.

Pelias (*PEE lee us*)—King who took the throne from his brother, Aeson, with the understanding that Aeson's son Jason would eventually get the throne. Instead, Pelias tried to kill Jason by sending him on a dangerous mission to get the famed Golden Fleece. Pelias was later killed by Medea.

Pelops (*PEE lops*)—Boy whose father, Tantalus, killed him and tried to serve him to the gods as a trick. Pelops was restored to life by the deities.

Penelope (*pe NEL oh pee*)—Odysseus' wise and faithful wife who, always hopeful that her husband would return from the Trojan War, spent years fending off suitors. At the end of Homer's *Odyssey*, she was reunited with her husband.

Peneus (*pe NEE us*)—River god and the father of Daphne. He changed his daughter into a laurel tree when she was being pursued by Apollo.

Persephone (*pur SEF uh nee*)—Only child of Demeter by Zeus. She was abducted by Hades and, because she ate the food he offered, had to remain in the Underworld for part of the year. For the rest of the year she returned to her mother, who celebrated her arrival with the season of spring. Persephone was also sometimes called Kore, and the Romans called her Proserpine.

Perses (*PER seez*)—Son of Perseus and Andromeda. He was raised by his grandparents and inherited the throne from Cepheus. His own descendants founded Persia in his honor.

Perseus (*PER see us*)—Son of Zeus and Danae who was sent by the evil King Polydectes to kill the gorgon Medusa. The hero completed the task and used Medusa's head to turn Polydectes into stone. He also rescued and married Andromeda and remained loyal to her.

Phaedra (*FEE druh*)—Wife of the hero Theseus. When her stepson Hippolytus refused her advances, she accused him of rape in her suicide note. Theseus then exiled his innocent son, who soon died.

Phaethon (*FAY i thon*)—Son of Helios, the sun god, and the mortal Clymene. He asked to ride his father's chariot, but he lost control and nearly destroyed the world. Phaethon died as a result.

Philemon (*fih LEE mon*)—Old man who, along with his wife, Baucis, provided hospitality to the disguised Zeus and Hermes. As a reward, their tiny home was turned into a temple, and they were granted the wish of dying at the same time. Zeus transformed them into intertwining trees.

Philoctetes (*fill ok TEE teez*)—Man who lit Heracles' funeral pyre and was given his bow and arrows that had been dipped in the poisonous blood of the Hydra. He used one of these arrows to kill the Trojan Paris in the Trojan War.

Phineus (*FIN ee us*)—Blind prophet punished by Zeus for revealing too much about the future. After being attacked repeatedly by the Harpies, Phineus was saved by crew members of the *Argo* and told the Argonauts how they could pass through the Clashing Rocks.

Phobos (*FOH bus*)—The personification of fear. The son of Ares and brother to Deimos.

Pluto (*PLOO toh*)—Roman name for Hades, god of the Underworld. See **Hades**.

Polybus (*POL i bus*)—King of Corinth who, along with his wife, Merope, adopted an infant they named Oedipus. They raised him to believe he was their biological son, but he was actually born to King Laius and Queen Jocasta.

Polydectes (*pol i DEK teez*)—Evil brother of Dictys. Polydectes wanted to marry Danae so he tried to get rid of her son, Perseus, by sending him on a mission to kill Medusa. In the end, the heroic Perseus turned Polydectes to stone by showing him Medusa's head, and Dictys became king.

Polyhymnia (*pol ee HIM nee uh*)—See **Muses**.

Poseidon (*poh SIE dun*)—Greek god of the sea whose Roman name was Neptune. Fathered many children, including Pegasus and the Cyclops Polyphemus. Poseidon was enraged when Odysseus blinded Polyphemus, so the god tormented Odysseus for years while the hero tried to get back to his homeland of Ithaca.

Priam (*PREE um*)—King of Troy and husband of Hecuba. Father of numerous children, including Hector, Paris, and Cassandra. After Achilles killed Hector, Priam entered the Greek camp and begged Achilles to return Hector's body to him. Priam was later killed by Achilles' son, Neoptolemus.

Procrustes (*proh CRUST eez*)—Devious villain who offered travelers a place to sleep. If they were too tall to fit his bed, he would cut off their heads; if they were too short, he would stretch them to fit. Theseus finally got rid of Procrustes by chopping him down to fit the bed.

Prometheus (*proh MEE thee us*)—Titan who created and protected men. When he stole fire to give to mankind, Zeus punished him by chaining him to a rock, where his liver was pecked out day after day. Prometheus was finally rescued by Heracles.

Proserpine (*pro SUR pi nuh*)—Roman name for Persephone. See **Persephone**.

Psyche (*SIE kee*)—Beautiful mortal who made Aphrodite jealous. Venus ordered her son Eros to punish Psyche, but he fell in love with her instead. He secretly married Psyche on the condition that he only visit her in the darkness. The curious Psyche found out his identity, however, and was punished by Aphrodite. Psyche was eventually forgiven and welcomed on Mount Olympus.

Pygmalion (*pig MAY lee on*)—Sculptor who fell in love with one of the statues he created. Venus helped Pygmalion by turning the statue into a real woman.

Pyramus (*PEER uh mus*)—Young man forbidden to be with the girl who lived next door to him. The two ran away together and, because of a tragic misunderstanding, ended up killing themselves.

Pyrrha (*PEER uh*)—Pyrrha and her husband, Deucalion, were spared from a great flood caused by Zeus, and they repopulated the world by throwing stones that became new men and women.

Pythias (*PITH ee us*)—Young man who was wrongly accused by King Dionysius and sentenced to death. His best friend, Damon, willingly took his place in prison so Pythias could settle his affairs. The men's friendship so impressed the cold-hearted king that he set them both free.

Remus (*REE mus*)—Twin of Romulus. See **Romulus**.

Rhea (*REE uh*)—Daughter of Gaea and Uranus. Rhea bore five children, but her husband, Cronus, swallowed them. She hid her sixth child, Zeus, who later saved his siblings and overthrew his father and the other Titans in a massive battle.

Romulus (*ROM yoo lus*)—Son of Mars and twin of Remus. The infants were almost killed in the Tiber River, but they were saved and reared by a wolf. Later, a shepherd adopted them. In an argument about the founding of a new city, Romulus killed Remus, and he named the new city after himself: Rome.

Ruin (*ROO in*)—Daughter of Zeus and Eris, also known as Ate. Agamemnon blamed Ruin for making him take Achilles' slave girl away and causing strife within the Achaean ranks during the Trojan War.

Rumor (*ROO mor*)—Swift-footed daughter of Gaea who loved to spread vicious news. In Homer's *Odyssey*, she told everyone about the slaying of the suitors, and in Virgil's *Aeneid*, she spread the word about Dido and Aeneas' affair and told Dido that Aeneas was leaving.

R

Saturn (*SAT urn*)—Roman name for Cronus, king of the Titans. See **Cronus**.

Scylla (*SIL uh*)—Six-headed beast who lived in a cave. Across the channel from her was the whirlpool Charybdis. Odysseus lost six of his men to Scylla when his ship tried to pass between the two.

Selene (*se LEE nee*)—Goddess of the moon, whose Roman name was Luna.

Semele (*SEM e lee*)—Mortal woman tricked by the jealous Hera into asking to see Zeus in full armor. The sight burned Semele, but Zeus rescued their unborn child, Dionysus, from Semele's womb and later gave birth to him.

Silenus (*sie LEE nus*)—Faithful companion to Dionysus. After King Midas took care of Silenus, Dionysus rewarded the king by granting his wish to have the golden touch.

Sinis (*SEE niss*)—Villain known as the "Pine Bender." He tied his victims' heads to one bent tree and their ankles to another and then let the trees go. Sinis was finally killed by Theseus.

Sinon (*SEE non*)—Greek soldier and Sisyphus' son. Sinon convinced the Trojans to take a huge wooden horse inside their walled city, but it actually held Greek soldiers who then led the charge against Troy.

Sirens (*SIE renz*)—Beautiful women who lured men onto their island with their songs. When the men came ashore, however, the Sirens turned into ugly birds and killed the men. Odysseus was warned about their powers, so he had his men put wax in their own ears and tie him to the mast so he could hear their song. Sometimes the Sirens are depicted as mermaids.

Sisyphus (*SIS i fus*)—Mortal who tattled on Zeus and outwitted death twice before being sent to Tartarus. There he was made to push a boulder up a hill just to have it roll back down to the bottom again. Sisyphus' son was Sinon.

Sol (*SOL*)—Roman name for Helios, god of the sun. See **Helios**.

Somnus (*SOM noos*)—Roman name for Hypnos, the Greek god of sleep.

Sphinx (*SFINKS*)—Creature with the head of a woman, the body of a lion, the wings of an eagle, and the tail of a dragon. In the myth of Oedipus, the Sphinx asked a riddle and killed anyone who did not know the answer. When Oedipus answered it correctly, the Sphinx died of shame.

Tantalus (*TAN tuh lus*)—An ungrateful son of Zeus who always wanted more than he had. He served the gods his own son, Pelops, and was punished by being surrounded by food and water but not being allowed to eat or drink. Tantalus was the great-grandfather of Menelaus and Agamemnon.

Telemachus (*tuh LEM e kiss*)—Odysseus' only son, an infant when Odysseus left for Troy and twenty years old when his father returned. Telemachus helped his mother, Penelope, keep suitors away and then worked with Odysseus to slay them all.

Terpsichore (*turp SIK ur ee*)—See **Muses**.

Thalia (*THA lee uh*)—See **Muses**. Thalia is also the name of one of the Graces. See **Graces**.

Thanatos (*THAN uh tos*)—Personification of death; son of Nyx.

Themis (*THEM iss*)—One of the daughters of Gaea and Uranus, she represented justice and law. The Romans called her Justitia, and courthouses often have statues of this goddess wearing a blindfold and holding up a scale to symbolize that justice should be impartial.

Theseus (*THEE see us*)—Heroic king of Athens. As a youth, Theseus went to Athens to meet his father, King Aegeus, and killed Procrustes and Sinis along the way. He also volunteered to be sacrificed to the Minotaur and killed it instead. Theseus was known for bringing democracy to Athens, but unfortunately, he caused his own father's death and later exiled his innocent son.

Thetis (*THEE tiss*)—Mother of Achilles and wife to the mortal Peleus. Thetis was forced to marry a mortal because a prophet said any son born to her would be far stronger than his father. Thetis tried to immortalize Achilles by dipping him into the River Styx, and she also tried to hide him so he would not go fight at Troy.

Thisbe (*THIZ bee*)—Young woman who was forbidden to be with the boy who lived next door to her. The two ran away together and, because of a tragic misunderstanding, ended up killing themselves.

Tiresias (*tie REE see us*)—Prophet who told Oedipus that the plague in Thebes would only end when the true killer of King Laius was found. Tiresias also gave advice to Odysseus when the hero traveled to the Underworld.

Tisiphone (*ti SIF oh nee*)—See **Furies.**

Titans (*TIE tenz*)—Children of Gaea and Uranus. Two of the Titans, Rhea and Cronus, parented the six Olympians, who eventually overthrew the Titans.

Turnus (*TUR nus*)—Italian king who was told he would marry Lavinia. After Aeneas arrived in Italy, however, Lavinia's father wanted her to marry Aeneas. Turnus became Aeneas' nemesis, but later lost his life to Virgil's hero.

Typhon (*TIE fon*)—Hideous monster with one hundred heads. He tried to destroy Zeus but was instead pinned under Mount Etna. Some say he became the source of all violent winds.

Ulysses (*yoo LIS eez*)—Roman name for Odysseus. See **Odysseus.**

Urania (*yoo RAY nee uh*)—See **Muses.**

Uranus (*yoo RAY nus*)—Son and husband of Gaea. Father of numerous children, including the Titan Cronus, who castrated Uranus and overthrew him.

Venus (*VEE nus*)—Roman name for Aphrodite, goddess of love and beauty. See **Aphrodite.** In Virgil's epic the *Aeneid*, Venus is the protective mother of the hero Aeneas.

Vesta (*VEST uh*)—Roman name for Hestia, goddess of the hearth. See **Hestia.**

Vulcan (*VUL ken*)—Roman name for Hephaestus, god of the fire. See **Hephaestus.**

Zephyrus (*ZEF i rus*)—The West Wind.

Zeus (*ZOOS*)—The most powerful Olympian and god of thunder. Zeus overthrew his father, Cronus, and led the other five Olympians in battle against the Titans. Zeus married his own sister, Hera, although he fathered children with numerous other women. Some of his most well-known children were Athena, Ares, Apollo, Artemis, Hermes, Dionysus, Perseus, and Heracles.

INDEX

H

What reviewers have said about
Panorama: An Introduction to Classical Mythology

Just as the golden thread of Ariadne guided a young hero through the dark and twisting Labyrinth, so too do the words of Carrie Kennedy guide the reader through the sometimes confusing world of classical mythology. In a relaxed and conversational style, Kennedy skillfully weaves myth, legend, and language into a wonderful presentation that will be enjoyed by readers of all ages. *Panorama* is the ideal source for anyone looking to fully engage the mythic experience."

JAY D'AMBROSIO
Ancient history teacher and author of *Rethinking Adolescence: Using Story to Navigate Life's Uncharted Years*

"I enjoyed this book tremendously. The concept of organizing myths by theme is inspired and is a great strategy for dealing with a lot of material in a thought-provoking way. The teacher's guide will be of considerable help to English, Latin, or history teachers, providing a wonderful variety of ways to make classical mythology relevant to today's students. Kudos to Ms. Kennedy for her creativity."

PENNY CIPOLONE
Latin teacher and member of the Medusa Exam committee

"*Panorama* is a must-have for a homeschooling family. Children of all ages will enjoy the read-aloud myths and the beautiful images, and the book allows a family to bring mythology into the home with confidence and enthusiasm. Enjoy!"

ANNIE MCKENNA
Homeschooling mother of five children

"Through its stylish design, engaging prose, and remarkable clarity, *Panorama* makes an enormous contribution toward the heightening of our cultural literacy. With so much of our music, art, drama, and literature being informed and inspired by classical mythology, we can't help but profit from a deeper understanding of its treasure trove of tales. *Panorama* is an indispensable tool for mining those rich depths."

STEPHEN CATANZARITE
Managing Director, Lincoln Park Performing Arts Center, and author of *Achtung Baby: Meditations on Love in the Shadow of the Fall*

"Easy to read and heaven to use as a textbook, *Panorama* is the perfect source for teaching literature and mythology. Carrie Kennedy shows us that Ariadne's thread leads us back to our own beginnings."

NORMA GOLDMAN
Author of several acclaimed Latin textbooks and an expert on Roman costume

"I found *Panorama* so engrossing that I read it right through. The organization and style are superb, I was constantly pleased by the text I found in the sidebars, and while the information is never oversimplified, the whole book remains very accessible."

DAVID SANSONE, PH.D.
Classics Department Head, University of Illinois at Urbana-Champaign, and author of *Ancient Greek Civilization*

For orders and information, please visit www.clewpublishing.com